# CONSTANCE
# ROURKE
## AND AMERICAN CULTURE

# CONSTANCE ROURKE

## AND AMERICAN CULTURE

### BY JOAN SHELLEY RUBIN

THE UNIVERSITY OF NORTH CAROLINA PRESS

CHAPEL HILL

Library of Congress Cataloging in Publication Data
Rubin, Joan Shelley, 1947–
Constance Rourke and American culture.
Bibliography: p.
Includes index.
1. Rourke, Constance Mayfield, 1885–1941.
2. United States—Civilization. 3. Americanists—
United States—Biography. I. Title.
E175.5.R8R9    973.91    79-9272
ISBN 0-8078-1402-4

Frontispiece:
CONSTANCE ROURKE IN 1928
*(Courtesy of Mrs. William J. Butler)*

TO MY PARENTS

# C O N T E N T S

# ACKNOWLEDGMENTS

My greatest debt is to David Brion Davis, whose unfailing generosity and encouragement have sustained me since I first began an earlier version of this study under his direction. He has shown me, by precept and example, what Constance Rourke might have called "the highest possibilities" of intellectual history. David D. Hall's scholarship and friendship have meant a great deal to me. He shaped my interests at the outset, perceptively commented on the manuscript at several stages, and influenced the final draft at crucial points. I am also thankful to Alan Trachtenberg, who went out of his way to offer countless helpful suggestions over the years. Early in my work, Warren Susman shared with me his imaginative interpretation of materials related to my subject, to my incalculable benefit. Elsa J. Dixler has been a skillful editor, a valiant companion on a strenuous research trip, and, most important, a willing listener. Jean Matthews, Jane Abray, and my other colleagues at the University of Western Ontario eased the process of revision with good advice and good cheer. I have profited as well from the insights of many others: Daniel Aaron, John Morton Blum, Manuel Brontman, Richard Dorson, Neil Harris, James Hoopes, Bernice Kaczynski, Bruce Kuklick, Howard Lamar, Donald Meyer, Richard H. Pells, Cynthia Rubin, Linda Rubin, George W. Shaw, Donald Sklar, and William Stott. I have been fortunate that Malcolm Call and Sandra Eisdorfer of The University of North Carolina Press guided the manuscript into print, for they improved it immeasurably along the way.

I am grateful to Carl E. Shoaff, Jr., of Carbondale, Illinois,

## Acknowledgments

Constance Rourke's heir, for his kind permission to quote from Rourke's unpublished papers. The late Margaret Marshall, writer, editor, and close friend of Rourke's, granted me the privilege of several interviews. I am obliged to Marshall's executor, Fred Fleck, and to her granddaughter Anne Fleck, for permitting me to examine and to quote from the Papers of Margaret Marshall, on deposit at the Beinecke Rare Book and Manuscript Library, Yale University. Two other friends of Rourke, Linda Butler and Nelle Curry, warmly offered their reminiscences. I have used their thoughtful unpublished essays with their consent. I am indebted to Mrs. Butler as well for her unflagging enthusiasm about my project and for permission to include her priceless photographs of the Rourkes. William Goodman, formerly of Harcourt Brace Jovanovich, supplied useful information and arranged access to correspondence between Rourke and her editors. Quotations from the letters of Elizabeth Bevier Hamilton and Donald Brace appear by permission of Harcourt Brace Jovanovich. Lewis Mumford graciously answered my questions and sent me his correspondence with Rourke, from which I have quoted with his permission. I should also like to thank Mrs. Bernard DeVoto for allowing me to publish excerpts from the letters of Bernard DeVoto.

A fellowship from the American Council of Learned Societies provided funds for research in 1976-77. A portion of this study has appeared in somewhat different form in *American Quarterly* (Winter 1976) and was reprinted in *Recycling the Past*, edited by Leila Zenderland (University of Pennsylvania Press, 1978).

My husband, Tai C. Kwong, has lived with Constance Rourke as long as he has lived with me, patiently enduring the times when it must have seemed that there was not enough room for the three of us. He has enabled me to work in the best sort of context—one of support and understanding.

# INTRODUCTION

In 1926, Lewis Mumford, like so many others of his generation, issued a sweeping condemnation of life in the United States. Writing in *The Golden Day*, primarily a study of nineteenth-century American literature, Mumford asked, "Beneath the organized vivacity of our American communities, who is not aware of a blankness, a sterility, a boredom, a despair?"[1] Mumford located the source of a "raw and rude" national temper in the deterioration of European culture during the years of American settlement. Lacking "all those memorials of a great past that floated over the surface of Europe," the American was, as Mumford depicted him, "a stripped European." "It was to America that the outcast Europeans turned," Mumford continued, "without a Moses to guide them, to wander in the wilderness; and here they have remained in exile, not without an occasional glimpse, perhaps, of the promised land."[2] As bleak as the prospects seemed, however, Mumford looked forward to the possibility that Americans could still create a "full culture," that they could escape their state of exile in the wilderness and settle in a "new world." At the close of *The Golden Day*, he exhorted his readers to help "conceive" that world, to participate in a "criticism of the past" in order to "bring into the foreground those things that have been left out of the current scheme of life and thought."[3] Throughout the 1930s, many writers answered Mumford's call, embarking on an effort to identify native contributions to the arts. But the work of one reader of Mumford—Constance Rourke—seemed especially reassuring to the intellectual in search of a cultural heritage. Praising Rourke's *Charles Sheeler:*

## Introduction

*Artist in the American Tradition* (1938), William Carlos Williams wrote Sheeler, "It is something for us all that Rourke has grasped so much of what we have been thinking and saying for the past twenty years and objectively summarized it in you. She seems on the way to becoming our Moses."[4]

Between 1915 and her death in 1941, Constance Rourke produced six books: *Trumpets of Jubilee* (1927), *Troupers of the Gold Coast* (1928), *American Humor* (1931), *Davy Crockett* (1934), *Audubon* (1936), and the Sheeler biography. A seventh, based on a massive, fragmentary manuscript, appeared posthumously as *The Roots of American Culture* (1942). In addition, she was the author of over one hundred articles and reviews for such periodicals as the *New Republic* and the *Nation*. Everything Rourke wrote documented America's artistic resources. Yet the recognition of her efforts has faded since the day her colleagues looked to her for guidance to a cultural "promised land." Her best-known work, *American Humor*, continues to draw attention, but often only for its value as a repository of frontier tales or for its perceptive comparisons between popular humor and literature. Rourke's contributions to folklore and to literary scholarship are noteworthy. Nevertheless, it is the central argument of this study that her true significance lies elsewhere. Rourke was most important not for her preservation of folk materials or for any of her particular critical judgments, but rather, as Williams's remark suggests, for the way she came to terms with issues confronting the intellectual in modern America.

The most compelling of those issues, the critique of America as culturally barren, materialistic, and provincial, was of course an old story. In the colonial period, Benjamin West, and many younger painters, had retreated to Europe for the professional climate unavailable at home; one hundred years later Henry James followed them, enumerating the "items of high civilization" he thought America lacked. But the complaint took on new dimensions in the first decades of the twentieth century.

[xii]

For Rourke, starting out to write just before World War I, the most influential critic of American materialism was Van Wyck Brooks. As early as 1908, Brooks had begun his analysis of America's deficiencies, which Mumford and others later reiterated or refined. Was it true, as Brooks declared, that the expansion of commerce had overshadowed and diminished the arts in America? Or had Americans managed to create ample, if undiscovered, traditions which guaranteed the nation's artistic future? Rourke's preoccupation with the questions Brooks raised makes her career the richest example of the search for what he called a "usable past."

To formulate her response to Brooks's critique, Rourke had to deal with another set of problems: the nature of culture and myth. What was the meaning of the term "culture"? What process of growth did it imply? Nineteenth-century scholars, especially anthropologists, had regarded culture in a way that devalued America's accomplishments. Modern investigators, however, introduced alternative standards for measuring cultural development. Rourke adapted those new standards to a reappraisal of the American past. In particular, she profited from the attention intellectuals in her time paid to ancient culture and to the primitive activity of mythmaking. No concept was more important in Rourke's work than the concept of myth; no idea served as many functions, or bore as many burdens, as the idea that Americans were mythmakers. Rourke played no original part in the theoretical discussions of culture and myth among her contemporaries, but she was unique in applying the conclusions of those debates to American materials. In the years following her death, the American Studies movement would extend Rourke's interpretations even further until, for a time, descriptions of national mythmaking dominated the field of American cultural history.

Other dilemmas faced Rourke as a result of her position as commentator on American life. Her role as critic placed her at a distance from the common man. Nineteenth-century writers had often applauded that distance, stressing the need for leaders to elevate the masses. But detachment could easily turn to isolation, especially in business-oriented America. At the time Rourke was growing up, around 1900, Progressive reformers had started to point out the dangers of too much detachment, warning educated men and women against cutting themselves off from the "real world." Intellectuals, many Progressives argued, must be engaged with society, and culture, they thought, should have social uses. Early in her career, Rourke satisfied some of the insistence on involvement by choosing to write for a popular, rather than an academic, audience. But when the Marxists of the 1930s intensified Progressive demands by assigning art an explicit political function, Rourke had to reassess her own sense of the critic's responsibilities.

Each of the issues that Rourke addressed—the adequacy of American traditions, the definition of culture, the character of myth, the effects of popular prose style, and the connection between politics and criticism—forms the basis of a chapter in this book. This thematic structure, rather than a biographical approach, reflects the view that Rourke's contributions should be regarded as a whole, that she did not change very much once she began writing about American subjects. Though her work entails some shifts in emphasis and scope, especially in her last years, she arrived at her basic position early on. In a variety of ways, and with imagination and eloquence, she said the same things again and again. But if the outlines of Rourke's ideas are readily apparent, the assumptions underlying them require excavation. This study establishes the context for Rourke's defense of American culture—the controversies that engaged her, the books that influenced her thinking, the premises that lay beneath her vocabulary. The opening chapter, on Rourke's life, adds personal history to the range of sources she drew upon. Rourke was involved in an extremely close relationship with her mother and had strong ties to the campaign for progressive education. Both facts had implications for the tone and substance of her writing.

The contradictions, the uncertainties, the straining that sometimes undermined Rourke's affirmative stance are also the subject of this study. The issues that animated Rourke's career are enduring ones for anyone concerned with American culture, and the limitations of her defense have as much to teach us as her considerable achievements.

# CONSTANCE ROURKE
# AND AMERICAN CULTURE

# 1

## L I F E

"Everyone who begins talking about C.," one of Rourke's acquaintances wrote in 1945, "soon shifts to her mother."[1] As dominant in life as she was in memory, Elizabeth Davis Rourke was an accomplished, powerful, and demanding woman whose own history is essential background to that of her daughter. She was born in 1852 in southern Illinois to Phoebe Mayfield and Joseph Bonaparte Davis, a farmer and lay minister who conducted revivals. Though accounts of her early years differ, she probably attended a private academy for girls in St. Louis and spent some time at college in the area. But her family believed in only limited education for women, and she defied parental authority by deciding to become a teacher. She was also married, though exactly when, where, and to whom is not known. Again contravening traditional expectations, she soon obtained a divorce. By 1878, the year of her mother's death, she had rebelled strongly against her revivalistic heritage but had carried the evangelical spirit to another quarter: education. In St. Louis she had almost certainly first encountered progressive ideas about training the young, possibly from Susan Blow, the pioneer in kindergarten education. Around 1878, she set out for Chicago to enroll in the Cook County Normal School, where she studied kindergarten methods. In 1881, she was teaching in what her obituary described as the "First Mission kindergarten in the slum district of Chicago."[2] At this time—as a symbol of independence or a desire to leave her past behind—she changed her name to Constance.

She returned as a kindergarten teacher to St. Louis, probably in 1882, where she met and married Henry Button Rourke. A "designer of hardware specialties" by trade,[3] Henry Rourke was an Irish immigrant who had come to America alone and who had broken his ties to the Catholic church. According to Mrs. Rourke, the two rebels were well matched, happily moving to one or another midwestern or eastern city where Henry Rourke's business took them, living in hotels or boardinghouses. Though she seems to have given up teaching after her marriage, Mrs. Rourke took a number of art lessons, including instruction in metal work. On November 14, 1885, a daughter—named Constance Mayfield in honor of her mother and mother's mother—was born in Cleveland.

Almost immediately the Rourke family took the shape it was to retain for the next fifty-five years. Henry Rourke had contracted tuberculosis, and by the time the baby was a year old, he was in a sanitarium in Colorado. On his wife, now thirty-four, fell the sole responsibility of child rearing. In an apparent effort to provide a secure future for herself and her daughter, Mrs. Rourke made two "business visits" to Grand Rapids, Michigan, in the late 1800s, though whether she intended to take over her husband's trade and why she chose Grand Rapids remain unclear. (It is not the case, as one writer has asserted, that her father lived there; he had died years earlier.)[4] In 1887 or 1888, Henry Rourke died. During the winter of 1888, Mrs. Rourke and Constance arrived in Grand Rapids. With her baby in her arms, the young widow went from door to door to obtain students in drawing, painting, and copper work. Eventually she resumed formal teaching, returning to St. Louis in the summer of 1890 for additional study of kindergarten education. The following year she began what one acquaintance called "something of a crusade" for kindergartens in Grand Rapids, converting thirteen other women to her cause and instructing them in the techniques she had learned.[5] By 1892, she had become a principal, and in 1904, after holding several other posts, she assumed charge of the school she headed for twenty years. She also conducted an evening "Americanization" program for immigrants. Throughout her career, she continued to investigate progressive educational techniques, spending many summers at universities. In the fragmentary records of her life, two names stand out among the figures with whom she studied: John Dewey and, according to one source, Colonel Francis Wayland Parker, who, with Dewey, made Chicago in the 1890s a center of classroom innovation.[6]

The psychological, not to say the physical and financial, burdens of being both professional woman and single parent may account for some descriptions of Constance Davis Rourke's personality. Some observers thought her abnormally secretive. One family friend, Helen Balph, recalled the "grim satisfaction" with which Mrs. Rourke announced, "I have never been one to wear my heart on my sleeve." In language which calls to mind Charlotte Perkins Gilman's description of her mother, Balph characterized the elder Constance Rourke as "rather chary of expressed affection, even for C."[7] Competent and authoritative, to some Mrs. Rourke was also impossibly authoritarian. A history of Grand Rapids reports that she was "for many years a principal in Grand Rapids public schools and seemingly with little or no effort won the title of 'tyrant.' "[8] One acquaintance, collecting biographical material on the Rourkes, gathered numerous stories of the principal's rigid domination over teachers working under her—stories emphasizing willful malice, unjust and arbitrary behavior. So many anecdotes testify to Mrs. Rourke's unpleasant temperament that it is hard not to believe them, though one can charitably ascribe her autocratic behavior to the need to survive under difficult circumstances.

Mrs. Rourke's encounter with Dewey and probably with Blow and Parker, as well as her "Americanization" activities, link her—and her daughter—to that movement for humanitarian reform that many historians have described as an aspect of American Progressivism. Progressive education encompassed the belief that children learned when they were free to express their own impulses and when the subject matter they explored was the outgrowth of their own interests and experiences. But the object of cultivating each child's capacity for self-expression was to increase his ability to participate in society, and so to strengthen democracy. That aim for instruction, in Lawrence Cremin's words, cast the school "as a lever of social change."[9] Cremin has argued that the progressive educator's assumptions connected him to "Progressives" generally. Figures like Jane Addams or Herbert Croly, for example, shared a commitment to self-expression and placed their hopes for the regeneration of society in the use of democratic institutions to realize human potential. Progressive teachers, settlement workers, and journalists, Cremin has noted, all operated from the premise that "culture could be democratized without being vulgarized";[10] they held a common faith, as Henry May has also maintained, in the reformer's own sense of moral responsibility and in his ability to awaken the consciences of others. Though other historians, Christopher Lasch among them, have reserved the term "Progressive" for those interested in strictly political measures like the initiative and referendum,[11] or abandoned the designation altogether, one can at least assert that progressive education was a variety of a broad interest in social welfare that coincided with the Progressive era in politics.

By 1896, Constance Rourke was a model child of the Progressive era. Her mother not only stressed the place of the arts in the elementary school curriculum; she trained her daughter to use music, drawing, metal, and painting as vehicles of "free expression." (Religion, on the other hand, formed no part of

Rourke's upbringing.) Paradoxically, young Constance's creative efforts were a reflection not so much of her inner self as of
her mother's values, confirming Mrs. Rourke's pedagogical convictions. Nevertheless, Rourke's early exposure to the arts gave
her an attitude and a vocabulary upon which she could build
when she later turned to criticism.

Outwardly, at least, Rourke seems to have responded with exclusive devotion to the mixture of detachment and ambition her
mother conveyed. A review of certain features of Mrs. Rourke's
life suggests why. Her unconventional career and divorce, the
absence of her husband from the household within a year of Constance's birth, her solitary move to Grand Rapids all conspired
to drive Mrs. Rourke in upon her own resources. Given the reports of her tyrannical behavior, it is easy to imagine her spin-
ning a web of possessiveness around her daughter, using her to
bolster her own strength and self-sufficiency. "I have always
considered her," Helen Balph reminisced about Mrs. Rourke,
"for subtlety and driving, inflexible will, the most formidable
person I have ever known."[12] Mrs. Rourke had gone a long way
toward achieving fame and professional stature, but her daughter, she might well have resolved, would go even further.
Though she taught her to respect Henry Rourke's memory, Constance was hers alone, hers to love and be loved by, hers also to
control and to live through. Accepting that hypothesis, it is not
surprising to learn that as a child Rourke reportedly announced
her intention to "marry, have a baby, and get a divorce at
thirty-five,"[13] thereby duplicating as best she could the pattern
of her mother's life. Nor is it any wonder that one of the few
surviving documents from Constance's youth, a letter dated
1896 and presumably sent to Mrs. Rourke in Chicago, reflects
the influence of her mother's professional interests: "I wish you
would visit Cook County Normal while you are there so when
you come home you can tell me about it."[14] Both statements
support the view that Mrs. Rourke made her daughter an exten-

sion of herself, and that Constance knew at an early age that the route to maternal affection lay in acting solely as her mother's agent.

In consequence, as a high school student Rourke was reportedly an aloof, bookish, unfashionably dressed girl without any "real friends."[15] Some thought her a snob, though her fellow students may have ostracized her for being an intellectual as much as she snubbed them. She belonged neither to the sorority crowd nor to the "Independents," participating only in the Library Society and a large basketball club. Restrained with her peers, she invested all her emotion in her mother, to the extent that, according to some acquaintances, her conversation even took on Mrs. Rourke's self-righteous tone.

As close as they were, the Rourkes in 1903 willingly submitted to a separation—the first of many endured for Constance's benefit. Whether at her mother's or her own instigation, in the fall Rourke set out for Poughkeepsie to enroll in Vassar College. Vassar promised young women solid training in independent thinking, offering an education backed by traditions of social responsibility as well as social grace. It was a logical choice for a woman determined to provide the best for her daughter, and perhaps to see her attain the intellectual and social benefits of the eastern education she herself had never had. An exceptionally good English teacher with whom Rourke studied during a year of postgraduate work following high school, probably in anticipation of entrance examinations, may have corroborated the importance of a Vassar education.[16] Having maintained her intention to follow her mother's example and become a teacher, Constance herself may have suggested the plan.

Nevertheless, despite Vassar's attractions, the transition to life in Poughkeepsie must have been an extremely difficult one for Rourke. None of the correspondence between Rourke and her mother for her undergraduate years remains, a fact that suggests, in light of the large number of letters preserved from later years, that the documents testified to a time of emotional pain both Rourkes wanted expunged from the historical record and from their own memories.[17] Certainly Constance's letters home in the immediate post-Vassar period, written in 1910 following a year of travel with her mother, reveal a distress at separation that could only have been deeper in Rourke's college days. For example, disturbed that her mother might disrupt their vacation together by conducting a summer school, Rourke declared, "I nearly cried when I read that part of your letter and it has made me fairly sick all day. You have no idea how it made me feel when the one thing that I have counted upon most is a quiet summer together, no matter where. . . . It is not very easy for me to be here alone, any more than it is pleasant for you to be in Grand Rapids without me and we must arrange so as to have at least our summers free and together."[18]

To some extent, Rourke seems to have handled the separation by adhering to the pattern she had followed in high school: withdrawal from her peers and affirmation of her dependence on her mother. She decided to study English and submerged herself in her work. Few of her classmates were close friends. Despite the numerous clubs and societies on campus, Rourke shared only slightly in the organized aspects of college social life, participating in *Der Deutsche Verein* and, briefly and peripherally, in dramatics and debate. But there was another aspect of turn-of-the-century Vassar that engaged Rourke, one that could alleviate pangs of homesickness. Although the college in Rourke's days was the setting for "sister classes" singing to each other in white dresses, elaborate celebrations of seniors' birthdays, and festive dinners for "Prexy,"[19] it was also the Vassar of the Progressive era. The comfortable, almost closed world of the campus, strictly supervised by the Lady Principal and bounded by rituals and regulations, undoubtedly bred in Vassar students the idea that they inhabited a privileged, special community. But in the early 1900s, professors like Lucy Maynard Salmon, Laura J. Wylie, and Gertrude Buck were reminding their charges that privilege conferred responsibility, that educated women were obligated to undertake social service. In response, students founded a settlement association (Rourke joined it in her first year), a committee to improve the welfare of the college maids, and clubs concerned with economics and politics. As Professor Herbert E. Mills recalled, "with increasing vigor and momentum in the first decade of the twentieth [century], students were displaying that awakened social compunction and were filled with that intense sense of social obligation which characterized so many of the finer men and women of that period. . . . Seniors asked: 'What can I do?' 'Where can I be useful after leaving college?' "[20] Those questions, though demanding, were familiar ones for Rourke, and made it easier, one imagines, for her to tolerate living on her own. The atmosphere of social action at Vassar reinforced the doctrine with which Rourke had grown up: that each individual was morally required to work for reform. Surrounded by friends and teachers who espoused the attitudes implicit in her mother's kindergarten activities, Rourke must have felt more "at home." The sense that she was dutifully implementing Mrs. Rourke's values would also have shortened the distance between Grand Rapids and Poughkeepsie. In addition, the spirit of Progressive reform at Vassar could offset the difficulties of separation by giving meaning to Rourke's sacrifice: she was engaged in vital undertakings that had to assume precedence over selfish concerns.

Whatever its emotional benefits, the emphasis on social responsibility that colored Rourke's college experience had a lasting impact on her convictions and on the direction of her professional life. Within Vassar's classrooms, Rourke learned that service could take unexpected forms. In 1916, Gertrude Buck published *The Social Criticism of Literature*, an essay summarizing the outlook that "animated" "every course in English in Vassar College"—courses that Rourke took and later taught. After cataloging rival definitions of the critic's task, Buck argued the case for "social criticism," for the study of literature in terms of its value for a given individual. In contrast to nine-teenth-century critics who let conventional morality and sup-posedly timeless standards determine their judgments, "social criticism" dictated that the test of great writing was whether it enriched the life of the reader. Significantly, Buck's acknowl-edgments thanked the man so important to Mrs. Rourke's orien-tation: Professor John Dewey. "Social criticism" was a species of pragmatism: a book was "good" if it "worked." One's assess-ments were only the results of a given "experiment" with a piece of writing, having, in Buck's words, no more than "a present validity and a relative truth." As Buck noted, a critic's "childish estimate of *The Swiss Family Robinson* probably differs widely from his grown-up verdict upon it. But his second judgment is not necessarily a truer judgment than the first, nor the first than the second. Each opinion, if indeed it is not a mere parroting of other people's ideas, but honestly his own, is as 'true' as the other—and no truer; since each precisely records the value of the book to him at a given stage in his development."[21] "The real, that is, the social, value of literature," Buck concluded, "depends primarily not on what is read, but on how it is read." Buck also acknowledged the influence of her colleague Laura Wylie, whose "leadership" had installed "social criticism" at Vassar. Wylie's concern with the connections between literature and society extended to the origins, as well as the consequences, of an author's work. As Rourke herself recalled, Wylie persis-tently guided her students in a search for the "social forces be-neath rhyme and rhythm and metaphor."[22]

Rourke could not have escaped certain implications of her professors' approach. First, if the measure of literature was only the benefit it offered to the reader, then a current bestseller might serve as well as *Paradise Lost*. In other words, popular writing could be as valuable as the classics—to the individual, to society, and, the young Constance Rourke might have rea-soned, to the student of a culture. "Social criticism" opened the way to relativism. It also legitimized the examination of such forms of popular expression as folktales or frontier theatricals—materials to which Rourke would eventually turn. Second, "social criticism" was democratic criticism, removing literature from what Buck called an "aristocratic preserve." Prospective authors might take note that it was acceptable—not to say desirable—to cast their writing in language that would appeal to a wide audience. A writing style accessible to the average reader could help to produce the "continuous personal reaction upon literature" that was the goal of "social criticism." Additionally, Buck's and Wylie's views contained a political message. For "social criticism" was so named because its practitioners viewed the process by which an individual profited from a work of art as a social activity. As Buck explained, the poet transmitted to his reader his "intensified consciousness." That consciousness or heightened awareness opened him to a fuller life, and so elevated him to the level of the poet. The transfer of ideas from writer to audience meant that the writer's "individual gain in perception" no longer remained within him but was instead "socialized."[23] Repetitions of this cooperative endeavor, according to Buck, would insure the continual "leveling up" of society, because the poet would always stay a step ahead of his consciousness-hungry audience. Literature thus became "a primary means by which the race advances."[24]

It was a means, moreover, that closely resembled progressive education. Buck's acknowledgment of Dewey was no frivolous compliment but rather the key to her (and Rourke's) political perspective. Dewey insisted, in Lawrence Cremin's words, that the " 'embryonic community' " of the school should "*reflect* the life of a larger society. . . . But even more important, [it] was to *improve* the larger society by making it more 'worthy, lovely and harmonious.' " In a democracy, for Dewey, as for progressive educators generally, the ultimate goal of education was, as Cremin has put it, "to make human beings who will live life to the fullest" by continuously enlarging their participation in society.[25] One has only to substitute the word "literature" for

Dewey's use of "school" or "education" to see the affinity between Buck's theory and Progressive ideals; for example, she argued that "literature is not only a creature but a creator of the society it serves."[26] Hence criticism was more than simply compatible with politics: it was politics. Rourke's description of Wylie's classes reveals the amalgamation at work. As she taught her students to regard literature in social terms, she argued, in Rourke's words, that "poetry itself" was possibly "revolutionary."[27] Writing not only derived from social conditions; it could alter them. Given her professors' assumptions, Rourke's withdrawal from the college settlement association after her freshman year did not mean that she was wavering in her commitment to social service. The reading of poetry, after all, could be as "revolutionary" as the instruction of immigrants, and literary interpretation as much a fulfillment of one's obligation to society as settlement work.

The dominance of Buck's and Wylie's ideas at Vassar does not mean that Rourke adhered religiously to every tenet of "social criticism." Nor did she ever acknowledge Dewey's direct influence, though she did mention approvingly his educational proposals.[28] Nevertheless, Rourke admitted in a eulogy of Wylie that the result of her Vassar experience was a "method" and "a greatly heightened sense of social values in literature."[29] Rourke's admiring references to the two professors, her eventual position as Buck's assistant on the Vassar faculty, and her close personal relationships with both women leave no doubt that "social criticism" was the basis for Rourke's own critical theory. Here were lessons that would shape everything Constance Rourke wrote.

When she graduated from Vassar in 1907, one of her gifts was a copy of Jane Addams's *Twenty Years at Hull House*.[30] Rourke's immediate plans were to carry out her social responsibilities by giving lessons of her own. Her classmates had voted her the first recipient of the William Borden Fund, a stipend for travel in Europe, but Rourke deferred the award and re-

[13]

turned to Grand Rapids for a year of primary school teaching. In the early twentieth century, an educated woman still incurred the charge that college had "unsexed" her; if she drifted further from prescribed female roles by working, she had to bear even greater opprobrium. But the same factors that eased Rourke's stay at Vassar must have helped her to overcome prejudices against career women. Again, the sense that she, her classmates, her instructors, and her mother were all part of a nationwide reform effort—in the company of those who not only approved of but insisted on women's participation—would have allowed her to challenge conventional expectations successfully. In contrast to the situation of the college girl of Addams's generation who felt forced to come home and do nothing, for Rourke the "family claim"[31] entailed following her mother's example of social service. Teaching, moreover, was a career that minimized social disapproval: it had become "woman's work." Eight out of ten schoolteachers in Rourke's day were women; two-thirds of all professional women in 1910 were teachers. (The percentage is somewhat lower for Vassar alumnae; of those working women who graduated before 1912, almost half were employed as teachers.) In the face of discrimination in other fields, teaching offered, along with nursing, a "course of least resistance."[32] To note the factors which facilitated Rourke's pursuit of a profession is neither to detract from her strength and independence nor to deny the difficulties facing any career woman of her generation. As Peter Filene has pointed out, those who undertook such "woman's work" as teaching paid the price of inequality with men. But the fact that initially Rourke could assume a professional role with relative ease helps to explain how, later on, she managed to overcome the odds against a woman who aspired to be a critic.

In her 1909 report to the Borden Fund Committee, Rourke indicated that she had "planned" to teach, though she found herself "rather unexpectedly" in the "early primary grades." In part, she may have undertaken the teaching stint to pass the time until her mother could accompany her to Europe. Rourke does not seem to have thought of traveling unchaperoned, and postponing her Borden fellowship until 1908 had the advantage of accommodating her mother's desire to attend the Third International Art Congress in London that year. No doubt financial factors also influenced her decision to delay her trip. Regardless of such considerations of expedience, however, she discovered that the teaching experience "served not only to contribute toward a practical educational equipment, but to color and direct [her] general purpose." She told the Borden Fund Committee, "I enjoyed the work thoroughly and as the months progressed I became convinced of its wide and interesting possibilities." In her own classroom, she pursued educational innovation. "Freedom to experiment, within certain bounds, was allowed," she reported, "and I found the beginnings of a plan whose purpose was to secure greater economy of time and energy for the student and for the teacher by partial rearrangement of the curriculum and daily program, and by some change of method." [33] The fact that previously published sketches of Rourke's life have overlooked her period of teaching may seem unimportant in light of her subsequent achievements. The missing year is significant, though, because her concern with experimentation, efficiency, and, most important, social change through education, stamps her with the mark of the reformer in the Progressive era, a characteristic she retained as a writer. Rourke was partly a reform-minded schoolteacher at heart.

When she and her mother set out for Europe, she carried her interest in reform with her. The Borden Fund provided $1,500 "to enable some member of the senior class to enjoy a year of leisure and study in Europe with the general purpose of a larger and broader view of life and the intensifying of life toward social service." (The following year the description of the Fund stipulated that the holder have taken two years of English and economics, in order to travel and study "with a view to some form of social usefulness.")[34] With those ends in mind, Rourke proposed to "extend [her] foundation" for teaching through "three types of activity" abroad: "investigation of foreign educational method and curricula, travel, and an intensive study in literary criticism, which though not limited to an educational aspect, should tend to amplify suggestions for teaching."[35] To promote her objectives, she visited a variety of schools in England, focusing on those conducting educational experiments. She also tried to learn as much as she could about what she called "current social movements" in Britain, and attended lectures by J. A. Hobson and Sidney Webb on unemployment.[36] She was a moderately sympathetic observer of suffragist meetings, favoring women's right to vote but deploring the tactics by which Mrs. Pankhurst and other radicals attacked the liberals.[37] Her goal of travel took her to northern France and England for the summer of 1908, to Paris for the winter, and to Italy, Switzerland, Germany, and Austria the following summer.

As for her literary interests, Rourke turned to a subject for which the Vassar English department had prepared her well: the "psychology of narration." In Gertrude Buck's course on descriptive writing she had studied the "theory of the narrative"; the summer reading list Buck proposed for interested alumnae contained a section entitled "The Theory of Narrative Writing and of Writing in General." However perplexing such terms may now appear, "the narrative" was an important critical category in Rourke's day. "Psychology," moreover, represented a modern approach. Rourke investigated the narrative in large part because, as she put it, "narrative writing and narrative literature play so important a part in the elementary curriculum: the theme seemed to combine the value and interest of literary study with a very profitable range of suggestion for practical work."[38] In addition, her research into the narrative form almost certainly led her to folktales and ballads, to the popular French verses called *fabliaux*, thereby furnishing the basic interest for what was to become *American Humor*.

Europe sparked more than Rourke's intellectual preoccupations. Her winter in Paris wrought important changes in her view of the world. Referring indirectly to her own experience in her book on Charles Sheeler, she observed, "it was a good time to be in Paris, around 1909. . . . [Sheeler] discovered, as did others who approached this [modern] art in these years, that when he had left it he looked at both art and nature with new eyes." [39] One imagines her setting out from Montparnasse, where she and her mother lived, to absorb all she could of the paintings of Cézanne, Picasso, and Braque, receptive to new ideas, caught up in discussions about controversial artists. She found modern music equally "stimulating," frequently attending concerts with a group of Vassar friends who were also abroad. Toward the end of her stay, her mother returned to Grand Rapids, and she went alone to London, where she explored the Tate and National galleries with an artist friend (perhaps a suitor?) who engaged her in "a most extremely interesting and stimulating talk about painting, writing, art, and the art life." [40] Just before leaving for home, Rourke admitted to her mother what she had been thinking about for several months: "I am very genuinely interested in education, but I also feel the necessity of doing continuously a certain amount of creative work. This as far as I can see is incompatible with a 'career' as a teacher. . . ." [41] Something—the exposure to modern art, the excitement of travel, even, possibly, a romantic episode —had intervened to disrupt Rourke's single-minded dedication to teaching. The emphasis on creativity with which Mrs. Rourke had raised her daughter now threatened to undo the carefully laid plans for her future.

Rourke's change of heart hardly constituted full-fledged rebellion. All she proposed was that she "continue to study education and put the fruits into the form of essays and lectures." In addition, the plan of becoming a sort of free-lance education writer would permit her to pursue two other activities: the writing of fiction and poetry, and the study of American culture.

Rourke had tried her hand at creative writing off and on since childhood. Now she looked forward to free-lancing so that her "arrangement of time would be elastic and [she] could yield to the desire for other forms of expression" when she pleased. The wish she voiced in the same letter "to know more of fundamental movements in America" represented a new concern that one can only guess was the outgrowth of her stay in Europe. No one knows when and why Rourke turned to American subjects, but it is probable that, like other expatriates, she saw America more clearly from afar, and that her examination of European folktales prompted her to look for similar materials at home. She was still anxious to satisfy the "requirements of social service and the expectations of my college friends,"[42] but, significantly, she thought she could do so primarily through writing. The common aims of progressive education and "social criticism" meant that she could move from one to the other without forsaking her commitment to reform.

Her wider horizons notwithstanding, Rourke's experience in Europe did not diminish the intellectual seriousness and detachment that had characterized her as an undergraduate, though it did increase her self-assurance and poise. She maintained her devotion to Mrs. Rourke, working alone hour after hour in the British Museum or the Bibliothèque Nationale. As she examined her desire to teach, she also seems to have settled on an objective that she would pursue for the rest of her life: the goal of living at home with her mother. In December of 1909 she had written, "Our very first Christmas apart, and the last one."[43] "The beautiful part" of her free-lancing plan, she stressed, was "that in this way we needn't be separated at all." Instead, she hoped she could become successful enough to free her mother from teaching so that the two might move to Chicago. In a statement that underscores her mother's premium on self-sufficiency, Rourke expressed her expectations for free-lance writing: "It seems to me that there is more opportunity for future happy independent life together in this way than the other, I mean the plan of beginning at once to teach. . . ."[44]

Before Rourke could realize these hopes, she learned of an opportunity that caused her to modify her intentions temporarily. A family in Poughkeepsie offered her a position as tutor for their young son. Though she acknowledged her preference for returning to Grand Rapids, she saw the job as a chance to develop a course of study for a child—thus continuing her educational work—while affording her time for "leisurely creation."[45] Some day she wished to publish the course of study. Meanwhile, the tutoring would satisfy the expectations of her Vassar instructors that she resume teaching, and would also, she hoped, mean "a strengthening of certain relations with the college and perhaps variously new suggestions in New York."[46] Her acceptance of the tutoring position firmly established the practice she had begun by attending Vassar and staying on alone in Europe —the exchange of the emotional comforts of home for the gratifications of a successful career.

The Rourkes' habit of writing almost daily letters to each other, especially between 1909 and 1915, meant that Constance could take at least some of those comforts with her. Rourke's correspondence—addressed most often "Dearest Mama" and signed with some variation of "Always your own babe"— evinces a preoccupation with reporting details of daily dress, food, and activities, as if to supply a picture of her life so complete that it would nullify her absence. The discussions of books and ideas, of plays and exhibits, and of plans for work that fill these letters reflect Rourke's certainty that she and her mother shared common intellectual interests. That certainty, coupled with the conviction that her mother was at least spiritually with her, undoubtedly lessened the difficulties of living apart.

Nevertheless, Rourke's letters home in this period make one wonder to what degree she won her mother's support at the price of her own identity. She seems to have been inordinately concerned with form, as if she needed to comply with Mrs. Rourke's standards of proper correspondence. "I am putting one statement after another in ridiculous fashion," Rourke apologized in one letter, "but I wished to speak of immediate things." The next day she added, "I was ashamed of the hasty and badly written note which I was obliged to send you yesterday."[47] In their consciousness of propriety the Rourkes may only have been observing conventions of "good breeding." But the word "ashamed" is a charged one, suggesting that Mrs. Rourke communicated to her daughter the sense that errors of form were personal affronts. Rourke's abstract style and controlled tone also tend to confirm the speculation that Mrs. Rourke exacted total deference from her daughter: Rourke's steady account of events and decisions in almost emotionless language, with scarcely any disagreement or unpleasantness, is a possible sign that she could not risk angering her mother by asserting her own wishes.

Certainly Rourke was willing to defer to her mother's judgment in matters affecting her career. In the spring of 1910, when Laura Wylie offered Rourke a Vassar instructorship in English, her initial happiness gave way to anxiety about her mother's approval. "I am not very sure from your letter of this afternoon," Rourke wrote, "whether you thought that I had better accept or not." She continued: "I thought that when I was at home we decided this was the best move that I could make, and it truly seems so to me now. . . . Now if you have the least reason against this please tell me, for I would follow your wishes absolutely in the matter. I was so under the impression that you actually wished this most. . . . It really is something of an achievement, I think, and will mean a great deal in the way of prestige now, for writing, and further teaching. More than that I couldn't have better training professionally. But please do write frankly dearest mama, exactly what you think."[48] In her extreme solicitude for her mother's feelings, Rourke was virtually functioning as an adjunct to the older woman, trading for emotional support the right to control her own life.

Because Mrs. Rourke agreed that the Vassar "move" promised "prestige" and "good training," Constance accepted the position, planning to stay no more than two years. She remained until 1915, teaching courses in expository writing to both beginning and advanced students. "Social criticism" was in full force in the English department. Some terms Rourke shared duties with other instructors, notably Gertrude Buck, but other courses, including one in "argumentation," were hers alone. In between classroom responsibilities, she worked on her "Psychology of Narration" paper. It is important to recognize that Rourke's decision to teach at Vassar was entirely consistent with her earlier commitment to education. Like her colleagues who joined her in a club of college and town English teachers, she thought of herself as primarily an educator rather than a literary scholar. (For example, she considered attending the National Education Association meetings with her mother in 1911.)[49] Identification with teachers at any grade level was common at this time even among published critics like Laura Wylie, who wrote Rourke in 1918 to ask whether she would consider coming back to "education."[50]

Rourke's Vassar years were relatively tranquil ones. She suffered from a beginning teacher's usual lack of confidence, but to her mother reported only satisfaction with her work. Her letters home read as if every day were a kind of test—with Mrs. Rourke as the examiner: "I feel that I have accomplished a good deal, and the day has been more than pleasant."[51] She took equal care to report the financial "economies" of which she knew her mother approved. Amy Reed, one of Rourke's colleagues in the English Department, later commented revealingly that "to many of us her mind seemed analytic rather than creative and in personal relations she was cool and detached, sometimes arousing antagonism by a certain ruthlessness in carrying out her purposes."[52] Reed's remark documents the persistence of traits that had characterized Rourke at least since high school. Nevertheless, many of her long-term friendships, several involving students, date from this period, perhaps because her status as a faculty member protected her against getting too close. In her free time, she continued the study of the piano she had begun as a child, took painting lessons, and even seems to have taught a little painting herself. On one of her periodic excursions to New York, she saw the Armory Show, to which she responded with the receptivity to modernism her European trip had nurtured: "For new, wide, independent experiment and expression the whole exhibition is a marvel. Of course there are the extremists, but even they are stimulating, and I found myself enjoying some of the most bizarre."[53]

By 1915, for reasons that are not entirely clear, Rourke's "purposes" no longer included teaching. As early as 1912, she seems to have investigated other job possibilities—though still in the teaching field.[54] In 1913, she indicated to her mother that she was considering some type of newspaper work.[55] The summer of 1914, part of which she spent studying Gaelic literature at the University of Chicago, seems to have been decisive, perhaps because her research triggered ideas for free-lance writing. When she returned to Vassar in the fall, she had decided to resign. As in 1910, she planned to continue writing about education, this time declaring her intention to publish a textbook on which she had been working. "The Rationale of Punctuation," which Rourke published in the *Educational Review* in 1915, may have been a section from this proposed text. She also anticipated giving a series of lectures for teachers and thought about attending some educational meetings. But she no longer wished to conduct classes.

Undoubtedly Rourke resigned her Vassar post in part because she did not enjoy teaching. Other factors, though, weighed heavily in her decision. One was the continuing desire to live with her mother. Another was her original scheme of writing, which she must have felt her years of teaching now justified her in implementing. Most significant—though least demonstrable —were difficulties of health. The first biographical sketch of Rourke, written by her friend Nelle Curry, noted that she left Vassar because of tuberculosis. Later, Curry learned that Rourke suffered only from the "threat" of the disease, an expression that suggests many possibilities. According to Curry, it was Mrs. Rourke who warned Constance of the "threat," fearful that her daughter would die the same way her husband had. It is not hard to imagine a woman of Mrs. Rourke's will imposing that idea on Constance in order, subconsciously at least, to bring her home once and for all. It is equally easy, moreover, to envision Rourke's compliance in the fiction, because illness would provide both a respectable escape route from teaching and a good reason for returning to her mother's care. Margaret Marshall, the literary critic who was Rourke's friend and the most astute commentator on her life, went so far as to suggest, albeit tentatively, that Rourke underwent some "mild" type of nervous collapse. Such a conclusion would be consistent with the histories of many educated American women who found themselves unable to pursue satisfying work (one thinks immediately of Addams and Gilman). On the other hand, another person close to Rourke, Linda Butler, has asserted that Rourke was suffering from "heart trouble," and that the tuberculosis diagnosis resulted from a mix-up in X-rays, about which Rourke knew. Because the Rourkes destroyed letters concerned with illness,[56] only friends' reminiscences and newspaper accounts remain to tell us that Rourke did experience a variety of symptoms—including stomach discomfort, heart palpitations, and insomnia—that made her a "partial invalid" at this time.[57]

Rourke's actions in the fall of 1915 tend to undermine the hypothesis that she suffered even a "mild" breakdown (without however ruling out emotional difficulties). Though she had left the faculty, she returned to Poughkeepsie to help plan Vassar's fiftieth anniversary celebration and to edit a book recording the festivities. As in the past, her drive for success and her rigid self-discipline held her homesickness in check. She had thought the summer in Grand Rapids "the happiest I have ever spent" and acknowledged that it was "a great wrench" for her to leave. But she was determined to complete the anniversary project because, apart from monetary considerations, it promised to further her career as a writer, and, in consequence, afford her more time at home. Her "deepest reason" for taking the editing work, Rourke told her mother on her way East, "had to do with my writing, and all that it will mean to both of us. It's hard for me to go, and I know it's hard for you. . . . But I do believe that for the future, in the very immediate future, this particular adventure will make for the happiness of us both. . . . We must both try to think of all the pleasant and happy things that we can do together when this ordeal is over."[58]

Rourke approached the prospect of a writing career with the knowledge that her course would not be easy. "From all I can hear and see," she announced to her mother, "success is difficult, especially if one aspires to belong to the very first rank as I do."[59] Her attitude was realistic, particularly because she was a woman. Generations of critics as different in viewpoint as Charles Eliot Norton, Barrett Wendell, John Macy, and Van Wyck Brooks had together shaped a vocation for the man of literary talents imbued with a sense of social responsibility: that of the American "man of letters." The phrase was an accurate one. In 1915, as in the nineteenth century, a man could set out, after a broad education, to secure a position on a magazine or at a university, where, in time, he might count on an audience for his ideas. Of course, not every would-be critic met with success, but it is reasonable to suppose that even the failures did not have to overcome the obstacle that would have confronted any female contender: the difficulty of being taken seriously at the outset. Gender disqualified a woman from assuming that eclectic role of part scholar, part popular authority that in our specialized society is now closed even to men. Instead, the literary woman's

vocation lay elsewhere: in scribbling "women's books," in editing ladies' magazines, in teaching at women's colleges. Like her
sisters who became teachers, she was relegated to the sphere of
"woman's work."

The Vassar anniversary record was itself a species of "woman's work," as remote from a history of Harvard as the *Ladies'
Home Journal* was from the *Atlantic Monthly*. Nevertheless,
that fact, though it severely limited Rourke's audience, may
have had its positive side, because it enabled her to establish her
identity as a writer before venturing into competition with
"men of letters." The same factors that had forged her commitment to education helped to strengthen her determination to
write: her awareness of Progressive women and the support of
her mother. Her tasks at Vassar bound her once more to the college's ideal of social service. She arranged for Lillian Wald,
Julia Lathrop, and Emily James Putnam (whose topic was
"Women and Democracy") to speak at the Jubilee, and organized a coeducational conference for students on the function of
extracurricular activities. The importance of the project to Vassar and to the cause of women's education meant that Rourke's
literary ambitions were consonant with her intention to do useful work. In addition, her mother's understanding sustained her
as she prepared to cut herself adrift from institutional affilia-
tions. As she concluded her letter reviewing her goals, "We
both have a real capacity for happiness, and sympathy, and
understanding of each other—of the finest and deepest sort—
and that's the great thing. My thoughts will be with you certainly—as yours will be with me—and we know that we love
each other more than anyone or anything in the world."[60]

Throughout her stay in Poughkeepsie, Rourke diligently carried out her responsibilities, operating with what Amy Reed
called "unrelenting thoroughness." Again one feels the emotional presence of Mrs. Rourke. It is almost as if Rourke were a
child reciting to her mother the maxims she had learned: "All
these things have to be exact. Indeed I am anxious that it shall

be letter-perfect. I have undertaken the work and I must do it well."[61] In her spare time she pursued her own writing—the "psychology of narration" book, the textbook, and short stories.

In January of 1916 the celebration took place, and Rourke went home to Grand Rapids, finally executing the plan she had formulated in Europe five years earlier. But the period that followed was less than the idyllic one she had projected. Her health worsened. Her mother continued to teach, but without Constance's steady income their financial situation was rather desperate. (Money had never been plentiful for the Rourkes, though one story has it that Mrs. Rourke financed her daughter's Vassar education with a secret inheritance from her father, while allowing Constance to think she was making tremendous sacrifices.)[62] Because Rourke was at home, virtually no correspondence between mother and daughter exists for the years between 1915 and 1920, but a letter from Laura Wylie in 1918 refers to "all the trials you have been through."[63] Rourke's physical difficulties did not lessen her determination to write; in fact, illness may have given her the time and freedom to do so. Nevertheless in 1917 Rourke resumed teaching—this time in a Grand Rapids high school. She may have taken the position purely for the money, though her interest in education was sufficiently strong that she published an article on elementary school teachers in February of 1919. Eight months earlier her first book review had appeared in the *New Republic*, a fact that indicates how gradual her transition was from teaching to criticism.

In 1919, the *New Republic* printed Rourke's first full-length article, an essay on vaudeville. By the following year, when her letters to her mother resume, writing had become her primary interest. Again one finds her paradoxically leaving home in order to stay there. She spent about five months in the East, canvassing editors like William Rose Benét of the *New York Evening Post* for reviewing assignments that could sustain her through the winter in Grand Rapids. Her letters indicate that she toyed with the idea of finding a permanent position in New York, and considered having her mother join her, but she preferred a steady flow of books to review from her home.[64] Though she found her absence from Grand Rapids as trying as ever, she believed that personal contacts with editors and publishers were essential for her success. Her correspondence reveals some of the cool calculation Amy Reed had noticed; it repeatedly emphasizes the importance of "solidifying connections" and "getting the most out of all these possibilities."[65] In June of 1920, she made one of her most important contacts. A former student, Ruth Pickering (Mrs. Amos) Pinchot, gave her a letter of introduction to Van Wyck Brooks, the editor of the *Freeman*. He began to supply her with reviewing work and, a year later, suggested the study of American popular figures that eventually took shape as *Trumpets of Jubilee*.[66] But Rourke was full of plans for writing. In July of 1920 she published an essay on Paul Bunyon in the *New Republic*. Her intention to expand the article into a book—a proposal with which she approached Harcourt, Brace, and Howe—ran afoul when a Michigan forestry professor who had collected Bunyon stories decided against collaborating with her. Still, her "psychology of narration" project continued to draw her attention as late as the fall of 1920, when she discussed writing a book on the "narrative" with Howe. About the same time she submitted a shorter version of the "narration paper" to the *Yale Review*, which rejected it.

The years between 1920 and the publication in 1927 of her first book, *Trumpets of Jubilee*, were a watershed in Rourke's life. Her successes as a reviewer increased her confidence in her abilities. The sale of *Trumpets* and its serialization in the *Woman's Home Companion* yielded $10,000, which insured that she could continue to free-lance. As she found her direction as a writer, her interest in education receded, though as late as 1924, when her mother retired at the age of seventy-two, she considered moving their household to Poughkeepsie and resuming her Vassar appointment. Instead, the two settled into the modest white frame house they had purchased together, furnishing a study for Constance upstairs and filling all the rooms with the early American antiques both loved to collect. At the same time she was becoming stronger professionally, she began to bring her health under control. A medical checkup in Poughkeepsie convinced her that she suffered from a prolapsis of the stomach. Once outfitted with a special corset, she overcame the digestive problems and lassitude that had plagued her, and reported that the doctor had ascribed all of her ailments, including the earlier heart palpitations, to the stomach condition.[67] Her clear blue eyes took on a winning sparkle, and her long hair, snow-white by the time she was forty, gave her a striking appearance. To some she was an imposing figure—her head large in relation to her spare frame, her bearing regal—but observers also described her as delicate, with an air of grace and warmth, a rich, throaty laugh, and a sense of self-possession that deepened as her reputation grew.

In the 1920s, Rourke and her mother seem to have accepted, intellectually at least, the idea that she would be away for long periods. A letter Rourke wrote at the start of the decade refers to Mrs. Rourke's commitment to her daughter's independent career: "I know just how you feel about my freedom of movement and all, and I am conscious of this; but just the same it is always hard for me to be away from you, and I like to have things as comfortably arranged as possible."[68] On several occasions her mother stayed with Dr. William J. Butler and his talented wife Linda, who were among the Rourkes' closest acquaintants. Otherwise, she had friends move in with her or hired a housekeeper, though she always lived extremely frugally. Mrs. Rourke encouraged her daughter to take whatever time away from home she needed for her writing, sensing, one imagines, that she had more to gain by letting Constance achieve professional recognition than by curtailing her independence. A letter from 1926 indicates that she even suggested that Constance write to her less often.[69] Rourke remained very solicitous of the older woman's needs when she was out of town; with touching concern, and sometimes without her mother's knowledge, she planned rides from the railroad station, made sure the house was well-heated, insisted that she obtain help for errands and chores. Yet as her belief in the importance of her career developed, Rourke grew more and more willing to exercise the freedom her mother proffered. She began to truncate letters home with the phrase "Now I must turn to my work."[70] In 1922, the same year her mother underwent surgery for cancer of the breast, she traveled alone to Peterborough, New Hampshire, for her first stay at the MacDowell Colony. She was away from Grand Rapids for five consecutive months in 1924, postponing her return several times for the sake of "work" and "contacts."[71] For part of the summer she went back to Peterborough, where she wrote the bulk of *Trumpets of Jubilee,* and spent some time at the home of a Vassar friend in Sakonnet, Rhode Island. That same year she overrode her desire to be in Grand Rapids for her mother's birthday, because "it will be an enormous advantage for me to stay."[72] In 1926, she decided to remain in New York for Christmas in order to finish some research. By the late 1920s, Rourke often appeared the dominant personality: it was she who, reversing their earlier roles, complimented Mrs. Rourke on keeping her expenses "remarkably low"[73] and managed the stocks and checking account the two shared. Friends recalled that once when Rourke was at home she and her mother had a "showdown" over Mrs. Rourke's "insanely early" hours and that Constance continued to keep her own,[74] sometimes spiriting famous visitors in and out of the house after the older woman had gone to sleep.

But whatever the degree of independence she and her mother accommodated, Rourke herself drew the line at permanently residing on her own. "Even though I am having a wonderfully interesting time here," Rourke wrote from New York in 1924, "I shan't miss it at all when I come home. . . . I want most of all to be with you; and I shall be entirely happy with the quiet things we do together, and with my work."[75] Moreover, her independent travels did not significantly diminish the extent to which Rourke depended for her self-image on her mother. She thought of Mrs. Rourke as the source of her accomplishments, the force empowering her actions: "Certainly I know if the book comes to all that I hope it may, it will only be because your confidence and all your help are at the foundation of it."[76] Approaching her thirty-ninth birthday, she repeated a sentiment she had often declared: "I am tremendously and increasingly glad to be alive. I have had an exceedingly rich and ample life in all the ways that are best—and you have made these possible for me, as well as giving me the gift of life itself. . . ."[77] Though Rourke was generally unwilling to expose her work to scrutiny, her mother functioned as her best audience. "I'm most tremendously glad you had time to read the end of the Lyman Beecher this morning. . . ," Rourke wrote from an eastbound train in 1924. "I couldn't have borne it not to have you see it all before I left; and you don't know how encouraged and happy I feel that you liked it and found it interesting and 'dramatic.' "[78] Later, as if to underscore her role as her mother's agent, Rourke would come to regard her standing as a reputation the two shared, and her literary successes as joint victories. When she incurred some criticism from a reader of the *Woman's Home Companion*, she dismissed it with the remark, "we mustn't mind being called 'cynical.' "[79] Writing home on the day *Audubon* appeared, she asserted, "This will reach you on 'publication day' and it is a pretty good day for us."[80]

Rourke never expressed resentment toward her mother, nor did she comment directly on the closeness the two shared. The nearest she came to summarizing her view of the relationship appears in *Troupers of the Gold Coast* (1928), a biography of the actress Lotta Crabtree. In 1927, when Mrs. Rourke accompanied Constance to California for seven months of research, they deliberately duplicated the journey Crabtree and her mother had made up the Pacific coast. As Kenneth Lynn and

Linda Butler have astutely noticed, Rourke's perception of the similarity between the two mother-daughter pairs informed a passage ostensibly about Mrs. Crabtree: "So obscure, in the background for years, she had perhaps the richest talent of the two, and may have poured much of this into her child's life, shaping its mold, even providing the essential momentum for Lotta's comedy." Read with respect to the Rourkes, that statement repeats Constance's sentiments that her creative energy derived from her mother, that without her she was no one. Later on, discussing Crabtree, she made clear her belief in the benefits that relationship conferred:

> Her devotion—their common devotion—was unmistakable. The bond between Lotta and her mother was close—too close, too confining, even mysterious, some observers said—but there was no sign that it chafed. Perhaps Lotta had been swept into her career by Mrs. Crabtree's will; her life in consequence may have been narrowed or cramped. Yet this choice had given her in abundance possibilities which she had deeply enjoyed: there was no doubt of her special pleasure once she appeared before the footlights. Now they were both enjoying good fruits, less in their wealth than in the power to be themselves with extraordinary simplicity.[81]

Only one document in Rourke's papers—a letter written home from Poughkeepsie in 1921—suggests that the "bond" may have "chafed" more than Rourke could acknowledge. "I think even for you," Rourke wrote, "certain elements of my character must be difficult to understand, at least their intensity." She continued: "I am appealed to so strongly by the mystical, the inexpressible. There are times when I could have become a nun, I can understand that now. I could spend hours without speaking, days alone out of doors. I am a mystic. And added to that there is something wild in me. That is the reason

I shall never marry. Another, which is perhaps part of the same feeling, comes from the fact that I could never endure comment, interpretation general sort of life [sic], or anything of the kind." Again, there is a striking parallel between Rourke's description of herself and her characterization of Crabtree: she spoke of "wild orbits contained within" the actress, and attributed Crabtree's failure to marry to her "capacity to make sudden intense reversals."[82] Rourke's references to mysticism and "something wild" inside her allude to an inner world that her mother could not touch, a private realm of fantasy and feeling. Direct expression of emotions—in personal relationships or even creative activity—ran counter to all her upbringing had rewarded. If one accepts the idea that Mrs. Rourke dominated her daughter, at least in her early years, it is plausible to find Rourke retreating into an inviolate world of fantasy. Rourke's letter once more brings to mind the extreme case of Charlotte Perkins Gilman, who, when cut off from her mother's expressed affection, discovered that she could take refuge in a dream world of her own making.[83]

Mrs. Rourke did not force Constance to efface her individuality; mother-daughter relationships are never that simple. Rourke's insistence that her mother "understood perfectly" what she was trying to do[84] calls attention to the way Mrs. Rourke reinforced her daughter's sense of herself as a writer, strengthening her determination to continue her work. Rourke complied in her mother's dominance because the relationship proved emotionally rewarding; it made her happy. Marriage might have provided the same support, but Rourke had good reason to fear that it would hamper her career. Afraid that a husband would tame her "wildness," Rourke refused several proposals and actually broke one engagement.[85] In contrast, a strong maternal bond represented a type of freedom—it promised love and understanding without requiring the surrender of professional goals or the exposure of her intense, indefinable feelings.

But Rourke's description of "something wild" within her suggests that she may have exchanged one sort of domestication for another. In her letters, in her personal relationships, in her published works, she is a model of control. According to her acquaintances, she spurned psychoanalysis when it was most fashionable and even stopped using a "sleep-inducing exercise" because she was afraid of getting into "deep water."[86] Amy Reed, Rourke's colleague at Vassar, sensed in her a fear of confronting her emotions directly. In her tribute to Rourke, Reed recalled the time Constance had approached her for advice about improving her writing style. "Mindful of what seemed to me her tendency to abstraction and thinking also that she was a little too solemn about 'advice,' " Reed reminisced, "I answered, 'Put yourself through as much sensuous—and if possible sensual—experience as you can.' I was joking of course, but she said, 'thank you' very gravely."[87] If her inner life was a precious refuge from "comment" or "interpretation," her mother's strictures may have made her regard her feelings as potentially overwhelming and even somehow illicit.

The foregoing discussion might appear needlessly psychological, were it not for the striking facts that when Rourke came to write about the American character, she described it in terms of inner fantasy and emotion, and that she spent her career in an effort to establish a national identity. Such observations should not diminish our sense of Rourke's achievements; they merely suggest that personal experience partly determined her intellectual concerns. One also wonders what shape Rourke's life might have taken had she felt free to pursue true "self-expression." She might have continued her early efforts at poetry and fiction; at least she might have enlarged her capacity for spontaneity, for intimacy, for experiencing a range of emotions unburdened by the need to keep a part of herself hidden away.

Rourke's involvement in an active fantasy life discontinuous with her outward behavior would also explain why many of her friends agreed that no one knew her well. "To many people,

especially when she was young," wrote Nelle Curry, "she
seemed an enigma. . . . Often she was elliptical in utterance,
expecting people's minds to bridge the gap. . . . Many . . . felt
she was bafflingly complex, impossible ever to know completely."[88] Rourke's friendships with Linda Butler, Margaret Marshall, and Charles Sheeler were apparent exceptions to her usual
distance, though one wonders how much she held back even in
those relationships. Marshall, valuing her "ladylike" qualities
and her balanced temperament, still called her "essentially reserved."[89] Curry's remark supports rather than contradicts the
assertion that, as Marshall put it, Rourke had the ability to get
along with everyone, because she could cultivate a wide spec-
trum of acquaintances without making much investment of
emotion.

Rourke's enigmatic quality impressed the literary figures
whom she met with increasing frequency as her reputation
grew. One of her colleagues at the MacDowell Colony, likening
personalities to literature, confirmed her elusiveness, as well as
her charm, when she called her "a lovely book in a strange language."[90] Retreating from threats to her private world, she approached her new literary acquaintances with the same detachment and concern for "connections" that had marked her Vassar
days. For example, though she enjoyed the company of such
writers as Thornton Wilder, Elinor Wylie, Padraic Colum, and
Edwin Arlington Robinson, and drank her share of bootleg gin,
she wrote home from the colony: "As usual after doing outside things rather steadily with people in the late afternoons
and evenings I'm fed up and want to be alone."[91] When Wylie
later invited her for a visit, she reported: "I may go out next
week, and am anxious to do this, for I much value the connection. Elinor is the most distinguished writer I know except
Padraic Colum—and besides Benéts [*sic*] literary influence as
an editor's greatly to be considered."[92] Such a remark is disturbing, not so much for its manipulativeness—success never
comes "naturally," and one can admire Rourke for aggressively

shaping her career—as for its coldness; personal feelings seem absent from consideration. Rourke's repeated subordination of social contact to solitary pursuits—concealing her whereabouts from others, carefully parceling out her time with friends, weighing the advantages of a given encounter—may substantiate a "certain ruthlessness" and a fear of involvement.

Nevertheless, avoidance of other people did conserve strength for writing. Her letters in the late 1920s and throughout the '30s are an impressive record of unstinting devotion to her work. Early in 1928, a projected two-week visit to New York lengthened into more than four months of research away from home. After she finished *Troupers of the Gold Coast*, Rourke returned to Grand Rapids, remaining there for a year to rest and plan *American Humor*. In May of 1929, the Rourkes set sail for England. They stayed abroad for almost half a year, a fact that becomes significant when one recalls that Rourke was engaged in writing a book intended to refute the idea that Americans needed to go to Europe to produce great art. Her work on *American Humor* from the shores of England is only the most salient of the contradictions that mark her ideas about native culture. After several more months with her mother at the American Antiquarian Society in Worcester and in New York, she returned by herself to the MacDowell Colony for further writing.

Lewis Mumford, who had met Rourke on a lecture tour to Grand Rapids in 1927, read the manuscript of *American Humor* for Harcourt, Brace and Company and immediately recognized it as "original" and "penetrating." With its publication in March 1931, Rourke became firmly established as a critic of American arts. She also came closest to achieving a satisfying balance between her commitments to her career and her mother. The 1930s saw the publication of three more books on native subjects—*Davy Crockett* (1934), *Audubon* (1936), and *Charles Sheeler* (1938). Reviewing assignments, which she had made such an effort to obtain in the early 1920s, now came her way automatically. Numerous publishers' advances and a grant

[35]

CONSTANCE DAVIS ROURKE IN 1929
*(Courtesy of Mrs. William J. Butler)*

CONSTANCE ROURKE IN 1934
(Courtesy of Mrs. William J. Butler)

from the Elmhirst Fund eased her financial difficulties, as did the sale of the movie rights to *Davy Crockett*, though the film was never made. Her repeated failure to secure fellowships from other foundations, however, is a sign that earning an adequate income was a continuing struggle. On her visits East, she was entertained at teas and receptions, met such diverse writers as Malcolm Cowley, Matthew Josephson, Edmund Wilson, Henry Steele Commager, Allan Nevins, and William Carlos Williams, enjoyed swing and jazz at Harlem nightclubs, went to the theater and the museums, and enriched many a literary dinner party. But aside from forays to collect material, Rourke spent most of the period between 1930 and 1935 writing in Michigan, moving with her mother in the summers to the lakeshore resorts where she had often gone as a child. She usually took a long morning walk, wrote until noon, read to Mrs. Rourke after lunch, and returned to her work until dinnertime.[93] For recreation she worked in her garden and read detective stories. It was in the mid-'30s that she began thinking about an extended study of all of American culture, and she started to shape other commitments to that purpose. As an organizer of a National Folk Festival in St. Louis in 1934, she gained opportunities to document folk expression from a variety of localities. She extended that work in 1936 by accepting a position as editor of the *Index of American Design*, a branch of the Federal Art Project. A political liberal since her college days—she had backed Robert La Follette as the Progressive candidate for president in 1924—she welcomed the attachment to the New Deal. Her role as supervisor of the compilation of representative American folk forms financed her travels throughout the country and generated countless notes for the book she planned. Similarly, she agreed to write a volume on the Ohio River for her friend Constance Lindsay Skinner's "Rivers of America" series, in large part because she thought she could incorporate the research into her longer project. (She returned her contract in 1938 when that idea no longer seemed feasible and when she developed doubts about the quality of the series.) Her work for the Index took her away from Grand Rapids for such long stretches that in 1936 and 1937 she could hardly be said to have been living at home. But her reputation and achievements must have made her absences easier for both her and her mother to tolerate.

Following her resignation from the Index, she spent most of her time in her home town, involved in her research and in the cultural life of her community. In March 1940, she put other obligations aside to serve as planner and judge of the first National American Art Exhibition at the Grand Rapids Art Gallery. As the political situation in Europe darkened, she became increasingly involved in the local antifascist crusade, the outgrowth of the long-standing commitment to democracy her upbringing and her education had forged. She lectured to women's clubs and church organizations on the need for economic sanctions against Germany, helped to sponsor speeches by H. V. Kaltenborn and Erika Mann, opposed the isolationist Senator Arthur Vandenberg (a Grand Rapids native) and the American Legion, and ultimately urged intervention in the war. Those activities made her the center of a committee of teachers and other concerned citizens, who praised her energy, dedication, and characteristic graciousness. She enjoyed a special relationship with a group of high school and college students, exchanging invitations to parties where discussions of contemporary issues lasted far into the night. One participant later recalled, "Like a magnet she gathered young people to her. . . . [We] never felt conscious of Miss Rourke's age, we never were embarrassed or confused in her presence. She was one of us, she grew with the times and remained always young in spirit."[94] Nationally, she supported Roosevelt in his 1940 race against Willkie, contributing a statement on "What Women Want in the Democratic Platform" to the campaign. When the League of American Writers advocated "an absolute form of pacifism" without polling its members, she resigned in protest.

In the midst of those efforts, she continued her work, bringing to it a serenity compounded of her mother's support and her own faith in the value of her writing. In 1938, she expressed an interest in eventually writing a biography of the colonial painter Charles Willson Peale.[95] By that time, however, she was immersed in research for her multivolume "History of American Culture." She turned to it in the spirit of social service that had guided her years earlier, convinced that a knowledge of popular traditions was as essential in a democracy as settlement houses or experimental schools. The immensity of the undertaking— and the breadth of her mind—were staggering. In keeping with her heritage of evangelical zeal, she meticulously compiled what Margaret Marshall called "her own comprehensive index of American design" on thousands of small blue slips of paper: records of anonymous wall paintings, scrimshaw, cigar-store Indians, Shaker furniture, the shapes of butter molds, New England houses. To this she intended to add her knowledge of folklore and popular songs, of novelists, poets, actors, minstrels, and orators—evidence of enough native culture to convert a generation of disenchanted artists.[96] By March 1939, she had outlined a book of some 200,000 words, divided into five chronologically organized sections emphasizing regional developments in music, the graphic arts, literature, and crafts. She had a third of the study in draft and had already selected many of the photographs for the sixty-four pages of illustrations she planned.[97] Critics like Brooks and Mumford looked forward to the publication of what would be a major contribution to American letters.

That work never reached completion. Coming home one winter night in 1941, after a meeting of the local branch of the Committee to Defend America by Aiding the Allies, Rourke slipped on her icy front porch and broke a vertebra. Afraid of disturbing Mrs. Rourke, she crawled upstairs and waited until morning to seek help. She was hospitalized for several days. On March 23, as she was preparing to return home, she collapsed and died of an embolism. Her mother survived her by almost four years. In 1942, the fragments which Van Wyck Brooks salvaged and edited from her work-in-progress appeared as *The Roots of American Culture*, securing Rourke's own place in the American tradition she had spent her life pursuing.

# 2

# TRADITION

Rourke's diverse books and articles invite many labels: literary or art criticism, cultural history, biography, folklore. But all her writings are works of advocacy, arguing a position in a heated debate among American intellectuals. To read Constance Rourke without appreciating the nature of that debate is to miss much of the explanation for her interests and her conclusions, her language and her tone. At stake was the proposition that America had no cultural traditions on which the artist could draw. Though Americans themselves had taken both the affirmative and negative sides of the controversy from the colonial period onward, an Englishman's contribution to the discussion in the mid-nineteenth century sharpened the issue and pointed out its special urgency. In his inaugural address as Professor of Poetry at Oxford in 1857 ("On the Modern Element in Literature"), Matthew Arnold introduced the concept of an "adequate" culture to describe the demands of the modern age. The confusing spectacle of an increasingly complex world, Arnold maintained, placed new burdens on the artist. He had to interpret the significance of his times, to give meaning to disorderly events. Only with the intervention of the comprehending artist could human values survive; only by creating an adequate culture could society progress. But was

America capable of satisfying those stringent requirements? Or was the country so ridden with materialism that Arnold's prescription lay beyond reach? Did America indeed have a culture at all, or was it only a poor imitation of Europe? Could the artist fulfill his essential function, or was he deprived of the vital resources necessary for any fresh creativity? What was the actual position of the American artist or intellectual? Did he occupy a place at the center of social life? Or was he banished to the periphery, cut off from the mainstream of society?

It was Constance Rourke's achievement that she led her compatriots out of the "wilderness" of those questions by attempting to sketch a native tradition adequate to America's needs. In so doing, she invested that tradition with both the aesthetic and the political dimensions the idea of "adequacy" implied. "The function of criticism has been exalted by critics from Matthew Arnold on . . . ," she wrote in an unpublished essay during the 1930s. "But one thing, surely, it can accomplish, and that is fully to open the perspectives within which . . . contemporary achievements lie: A new and abundant tradition exists in our literature if this can only be extricated from the mass of preconceptions, inferior work, and a widespread belief that our past accomplishment is minor. Tradition, even in new literatures, has always formed a basic soil; ours is rich enough if it can only be fully seen. Out of a living perspective those epics, sagas, allegories, tales in which the imagination offers something for men to live by might come into that startling force and enlargement which would seem their natural destiny in time of revolution." To provide such a perspective, to insure that culture enabled artist and society alike to realize "their highest possibilities"— these were the responsibilities Rourke willingly shouldered as she undertook to explore the American past.[1] But if Rourke was America's "Moses," she followed upon generations of false prophets. Henry James's well-known list of national deficiencies in his *Hawthorne* (1879) typified the outlook of many critics at least until the First World War: he found America wholly inadequate, devoid of the "complex social machinery" required to "set a writer in motion."[2] Along with such others as E. C. Stedman, Hamilton Wright Mabie, and Barrett Wendell, James turned to Europe, and especially to England, for his model of civilization. Though many anglophile critics urged imitation of English literature out of a desire to remedy American culture, the net result of their efforts often seemed a dismissal of America altogether. Repudiating what they termed, in Wendell's phrase, "national inexperience,"[3] they adopted a cosmopolitan outlook receptive to European departures in the arts.

Younger writers partly owed their exposure to Zola, Baudelaire, or other innovative artists to this older generation of American men of letters hospitable toward Europe, yet they largely failed to acknowledge that debt. Instead, in the first decades of the twentieth century, a new group of critics assailed its predecessors for vaunting Europe at the expense of America. In *The Spirit of American Literature* (1913), for example, John Macy, agreeing that American literature seemed impoverished in comparison to England's, nevertheless advocated not a hasty duplication of English achievements but rather the artistic treatment of native subjects. Macy, like Mumford after him, used the metaphor of America as wilderness, but for him the image connoted limitless possibility: "The truth is, the whole country is crying out for those who will record it, satirize it, chant it. As literary material, it is virgin land, ancient as life and fresh as a wilderness. . . . There are signs that some earnest young writers are discovering the fertility of a soil that has scarcely been scratched." Macy placed his hopes for American literature in a "dignified and self-respecting provincialism." Recommending that Americans forego their customary reverence for writers "admittedly dead in the spirit, whose names persist by the inertia of reputation," he called instead for a focus on those works that had a meaning for contemporary life.[4]

At about the same time Macy was advocating the creation of a specifically American literature, though, another writer—

Van Wyck Brooks—had begun explaining why the American "soil" would never yield cultural fruit. He outlined his critique in *The Wine of the Puritans* (1908), amplifying his argument in *America's Coming-of-Age* (1915) and in subsequent articles for magazines like *Seven Arts*, the *Dial*, and the *Freeman*. Because Brooks's formulation of the charges against American culture provoked direct response from Rourke, it warrants some scrutiny.

Throughout Brooks's essays ran a disturbing theme: American society suffered from a split between theory and practice, intellect and daily social experience, literature and life. "In everything," Brooks wrote, ". . . one finds this frank acceptance of twin values which are not expected to have anything in common: on the one hand a quite unclouded, quite unhypocritical assumption of transcendent theory (high ideals); on the other a simultaneous acceptance of catchpenny realities. Between university ethics and business ethics, between American culture and American humor, between Good Government and Tammany, between academic pedantry and pavement slang, there is no community, no genial middle ground."[5] Brooks used the terms "high-brow" and "low-brow" to summarize the "equally undesirable" but omnipresent extremes he found in American life. He traced the origin of those extremes to America's pervasive, unchecked materialism. "For most of us," Brooks wrote, "living means getting a living. We never think what life is—we are continually intent upon what life brings."[6] Our interest in commercial affairs, in acquiring tangible possessions, derived originally from the Puritans' understandable preoccupation with insuring the success of settlements: the virtues "thrift" and "industry" were necessary for economic survival. Eventually, however, the Puritan emphasis on the "machinery of life" became an end in itself. Americans therefore "came to feel suspicious," Brooks wrote, "toward ritual, pleasure, light-heartedness—all those things which an established civilization can support, as symbols of opposition to the stern economic need."[7] As a result, according to Brooks, we pursued art and literature not because of their intrinsic aesthetic value but because of the rest they provided from work.[8] We "associate[ed] happiness with spending money."[9] And we valued efficiency and activity per se more than the kind or quality of the activity, "approv[ing] of a man for the mere fact that he is busy."[10]

The materialism that Brooks assigned to our social life carried with it several consequences for the American character. First, it meant that we were deprived of an inner vitality, never expending our energies in a spiritual direction but always concentrating on the marketplace. "[We] are taught," Brooks noted, "to repress everything that conflicts with the material welfare of [the] environment." As for American writers, Brooks found that "their environment is itself so denatured, so stripped of everything that might nourish the imagination, that they do not so much mature at all as externalize themselves in a world of externalities." The "shame" of this turn away from the inner life to the "universally externalizing influences of modern industrialism," Brooks asserted, "is a national shame."[11]

Our preoccupation with externals, Brooks concluded, had left us without a common spiritual heritage. "We have no myths,"[12] Brooks declared. Nor did we have "a national fabric of spiritual experience."[13] Here the point was not simply that as devotees of commercialism we had neglected the life of the mind. It was rather that we lacked the communal exercise of the imagination that linked man to man through shared assumptions and ideals. Brooks recounted Edgar Lee Masters's description of an American community and took it as normative: "He pictures a community of some thousands of souls every one of whom lives in a spiritual isolation as absolute as that of any lone farmer on the barren prairie, a community that has been utterly unable to spin any sort of spiritual fabric common to all, which has for so many generations cherished and cultivated its animosity towards all those non-utilitarian elements in the human heart that retard the successful pursuit of the main chance that it has reduced itself to a spiritual desert in which nothing humane is able to take root and grow at all."[14] Brooks blamed individualism fostered by the need to win out in the competition of the marketplace for our failure to achieve a "collective spiritual life in the absence of which the individual, having nothing greater than himself to subordinate himself to, is either driven into the blind alley of his appetites or rides some hobby of his own invention until it falls to pieces from sheer craziness."[15] The focus on the external generated only fragmentation and disunity, precluding the development of emotions, passions, and feelings for one's fellow man that Brooks saw as the essence of life.[16]

What, then, was the position of the creative artist in a society barren of spiritual resources? He was, as Brooks depicted him, forced to choose between the service of materialism and a life of loneliness and alienation. Both courses spelled his literary death. Writing subordinated to the demands of commerce Brooks judged vacant and irrelevant, because businessmen required a literature bland and innocuous, diverting but not distracting. Brooks asked, "How then can our literature be anything but impotent? It is inevitably so, since it springs from a national mind that has been sealed against that experience from which literature derives all its values."[17] On the other hand, the outward turn, the individualism, the destruction of community that characterized the American experience were "deadly" to the development of the artist: his creative impulses were sacrificed to his competitive ones.[18] If he were in touch with daily life, but lacked the benefit of supportive tradition, he was likely to become frustrated and channel his thwarted creativity into the grotesque or the humorous, a phenomenon that Poe and Twain best represented. The would-be intellectual was either transformed into a spokesman for business or left to buck the current of materialism alone, with personal difficulties and unsatisfactory art the result.

Brooks's perception of a divided America rang true for many of his contemporaries, who noted similar dichotomies between

"Sunday things" and "everyday things" or, as Harold Stearns put it, "masculine" and "feminine" realms. By 1922, the group of contributors whom Brooks joined in Stearns's anthology, *Civilization in the United States*, found themselves caught between the recognition that "whatever else American civilization is, it is not Anglo-Saxon" and the belief that their commercial, divided society offered them "no heritages or traditions to which to cling except those that have already withered in our hands and turned to dust."[19] Several writers chose images of decay and sterility to express the plight of the arts in America. Freudian critics like Ludwig Lewisohn, Waldo Frank, and, to an extent, Brooks himself added repression and sexual guilt to the features of American life that undermined artistic and human fulfillment.

As they criticized the destructive character of their society, Brooks and others linked the prospects for an adequate culture with the restoration of an "organic" quality to the creative process in America. As Richard Pells has noticed, "organicism" for Brooks signified unity between art and experience, individual and community, intellectual and common man;[20] it represented the antithesis of a division between "high-brow" and "low-brow." Such unity, Brooks thought, was a necessary condition for the creation of art, for he assumed that the artist could thrive only in a supportive environment. Again, the process of natural growth furnished an appropriate metaphor: Mumford, praising Thoreau and Whitman, wrote that they had carried "the potted flower of the scholar's study out into the spring sunshine, the upturned earth, and the keen air";[21] Brooks looked forward to a time when "the dry old Yankee stalk will begin to stir and send forth shoots and burst into a storm of blossoms."[22]

It was to tradition that Brooks and his early followers turned for the rich soil from which an "organic" society could spring. In the "genial middle ground of human tradition,"[23] Brooks found an alternative to the extremes of "high-brow" and "low-brow." Tradition made possible a "cumulative culture";[24] it fostered a mind that related "past, present and future."[25] A consciousness of native traditions might provide the artist with a foundation for his work and at the same time restore him to his rightful place in an integrated community. With those benefits in mind, Brooks called upon Americans to discover what he termed a "usable past." His famous essay "On Creating a Usable Past," which appeared in the *Dial* for April 11, 1918, encouraged Americans to piece together the history of those creative efforts that might be most instructive for the present. As Brooks explained, "The present is a void, and the American writer floats in that void because the past that survives in the common mind of the present is a past without living value. But is this the only possible past? If we need another past so badly, is it inconceivable that we might discover one, that we might even invent one?"[26] When he actually looked at the historical record, however, he saw only a tradition of "tentative endeavor." In James Hoopes's words, "the search which he proposed was not for previously hidden treasure—the few masterpieces, he said, were all too obvious—but for thwarted talents."[27] His *Dial* essay was as pessimistic as his previous writings.

Brooks's call for a "usable past" largely went unheeded throughout the 1920s, though he himself became less negative as he began his investigations of Emerson in the middle of the decade. Some intellectuals simply denied the need for American traditions, rejecting any demand for the creation of bonds between artist and common man. New Humanists like Irving Babbitt, who advocated a return to the study of the classics, saw little value in the American past other than an occasional moral example. H. L. Mencken, quarreling with Stuart Pratt Sherman's description of America's Puritan heritage, complained that "the demand for a restoration of what is called the American tradition in letters is nothing more or less, at bottom, than a demand for supine and nonsensical conformity. . . ."[28] Others grew so disenchanted with the possibilities for art in America that they emigrated to Europe, where they encountered surrealism, dadaism, and competing movements professing to be modern. Still others, however, began to search for traditions at home. Mumford himself has insisted that the theme of *The Golden Day* was not "American artistic failure" but rather the idea that we had once produced writers as great, if not greater, than European ones; the target of his attack was the culture of his own time.[29] In 1927, the first two volumes of Vernon L. Parrington's *Main Currents in American Thought* appeared, a work that set an important precedent for later writers. Parrington's study, although rather rigidly based on his determination to lay bare a tradition of devotion to democracy, sounded a loud affirmation of the nation's cultural achievements.

Nevertheless, Parrington's preoccupations were mainly with writers—with novelists, political theorists, philosophers. No one had yet argued that the discovery of Brooks's "usable past" awaited the critic who ventured outside the realm of letters. But among Brooks's own acquaintances was a writer who would soon do so, and would eventually offer a powerful rejoinder to his critique. This was Constance Rourke. Rourke began the 1920s looking for neither the satisfying artistic life abroad nor the great American novel at home, but for manifestations of what she called "popular expression." Her vaudeville and Paul Bunyon articles signaled the direction of her interests, the outgrowth of her training at Vassar and the Sorbonne. In the summer of 1921, Brooks himself informed her that the *New Republic* was looking for someone to do portraits of "our own eminent Victorians: Mrs. Stowe, H. W. Beecher, T. B. Aldrich, P. T. Barnum, etc."[30] Rourke seized on the topic, envisioned a book rather than a series of articles, dropped Aldrich in favor of Lyman Beecher and Horace Greeley, and focused on the way the American public had transformed her subjects into legendary figures. By 1927, when the results of her research appeared as

*Trumpets of Jubilee*, she was sure that the native imagination had been active and wide-ranging. Her study the next year of the extravagant California gold rush theater for *Troupers of the Gold Coast* confirmed that conclusion.

In 1928, Rourke's investigations led her to the area she thought most revealing of the American mind: humor. In the comic stories that abounded in every region of the country, and that shaped literature as well, were traditions of "spiritual experience" that Brooks and like-minded critics had ignored. New Englanders had created the Yankee, the shrewd yet simple rural lad, too big for his clothing, who spent his days peddling or swapping or gawking. Royall Tyler had made the Yankee, as Brother Jonathan, the mainstay of his play *The Contrast* (1787), and the figure had soon appeared routinely on the stage. For twenty years, starting in 1830, the newspaperman Seba Smith had elaborated the literary version of the Yankee in his character Jack Downing, who commented satirically on Jacksonian politics. Alongside the Yankee, and merging with him over time, was the backwoodsman. Noisier and rougher than his New England counterpart, this Western frontiersman was full of boasts: he was "half horse, half alligator," the "gamecock of the wilderness," an untameable "ring-tailed roarer." The 1830s had been the heyday of the tall tale, which was grounded in the supernatural, and legends clustered around Davy Crockett, Daniel Boone, and the flatboatman Mike Fink. In the old Southwest, a number of lawyers and other observers had produced a series of comic characters reflecting the turbulence of frontier life. A. B. Longstreet had set the pattern with his newspaper sketches collected in 1835 as *Georgia Scenes*. In the same mold was Joseph G. Baldwin's relentless picture of the rapacious legal profession, *Flush Times of Alabama and Mississippi* (1853). Johnson J. Hooper contributed the greedy rascal Simon Suggs; George W. Harris drew Sut Lovingood, a "natural born durn'd fool" from the mountains of Tennessee. Many of these stories first appeared in William T. Porter's *Spirit of the Times*, which in the 1840s had a circulation of 40,000. Eventually they spread all over the nation.

A third element in this comic tradition, joining the Yankee and the backwoodsman, was the minstrel. Realized on stage by white actors such as Edwin Forrest and Jim Crow Rice, the portrait of the slave was at first that of a Yankee in blackface, dressed in "that long-tail'd blue" coat belonging to Uncle Sam. The possibilities of the impersonation caught the attention of Dan Emmett, who drew on the spirituals and dances of Southern blacks for his traveling entertainments. Characters like Zip Coon and old Dan Tucker sang of nonsense and of politics. Minstrel companies grew throughout antebellum America, testifying to a national interest in the theater. The same period saw the rise of strolling players who brought Indian dramas, romantic operas, and especially burlesque to eager audiences. But the "comic trio" remained the permanent basis for American humor.

Constance Rourke appreciated the depth and complexity of that humor. She also perceived that all of those outpourings of the popular mind had been available to American writers from the early nineteenth century on. It was a short step from the Downing Papers to James Russell Lowell's *Biglow Papers*, from the plain speech of the Yankee to the direct, lyrical prose of Emerson and Thoreau. Whitman could use the expansive, flamboyant language of the backwoodsman to sound his "barbaric yawp." Poe's stories gave evidence of his encounters with *Georgia Scenes*, with black culture, with the Western tall tales which often incorporated an undertone of terror. Local legends had fascinated Hawthorne, while *Moby Dick* contained echoes of "The Big Bear of Arkansas" and New England sea lore. In the case of Twain, the influence of the "comic trio" was direct and pervasive: in his writing one met rascals, boatmen, Yankees, "strollers," slaves. Even James, whom Brooks had depicted as a refugee from American subjects in *The Pilgrimage of Henry*

*James* (1925), created a Yankee fable in *The American* and brought the nation's habitual preoccupation with foreign criticism to his treatment of the "international scene." In the twentieth century, poets such as Robinson and Frost, Lindsay and Sandburg, carried on the rhythms and characteristic irony of New England or the exuberance of the West.

These perceptions came together in *American Humor*, Rourke's most important book. The first three chapters establish the identity of Yankee, backwoodsman, and minstrel. A fourth discusses the growth of the theater, and the remaining half of the text treats American literature in terms of its debts to the "comic trio." As a whole, the book was an announcement to readers of Brooks, Mumford, and company that the invention of a "usable past" would be superfluous. Rourke well understood Brooks's assumption that artistic achievement depended on the nurturing function of tradition; in *American Humor* she noted the "solidity, assurance, and justification which traditions may bring."[31] She always respected Brooks and acknowledged the stimulus his ideas provided. No other American critic, she believed, had "given so strong an impetus to the study of popular forces in relation to the artist," because he had approached the question of the creative life in America in terms of an "underlying culture."[32] But, invaluable as she found Brooks's early writings, she also thought them misconceived. As Richard Dorson has pointed out, Rourke largely failed to separate the oral storytelling of the folk from subliterary newspaper and almanac writing, a move that made the comic resources available to Hawthorne or Twain or James seem even richer.[33] With such a unitary, strong heritage of popular expression at hand, how could anyone assert that American culture was inadequate? In the foreword to *American Humor*, Rourke took note of her contemporaries' quarrel with their country and went on to declare her own view: that America possessed a tradition that was "various, subtle, sinewy, scant at times but not poor."

Earlier in the same passage, Rourke remarked that her book

could not be called a "defense," but, as she knew, it was a defense by implication. Never an antiquarian, never merely a collector of tales, Rourke was always fully cognizant of the potential repercussions of her work. As Brooks himself noted in his introduction to *The Roots of American Culture*, she proceeded from the awareness that if she could prove the existence of "an American esthetic tradition," it "might make all the difference for the future of our art and all the difference, meanwhile, for the creative worker."[34] Rourke's stance in *American Humor*, and indeed in everything she wrote, was that of a polite but determined adversary. The politeness appears in her reluctance to mention her opponents by name and to tackle them explicitly; for example, she refers to Brooks only twice in the text, both times in connection with Henry James. But the determination to refute him is everywhere. It is not simply Rourke's concerted display of a "usable past" that works against *The Wine of the Puritans* or *America's Coming-of-Age*. Each of the terms she employed to describe that past cancels out an aspect of Brooks's critique. Because Rourke's language in *American Humor* best reflects the special positive view of the "national character" she brought to all her writing, a closer examination of the book's argument may be helpful at this point.

The important fact about the "comic trio," Rourke suggested, was that Yankee, backwoodsman, and minstrel had each developed from an individual into a generalized type, and so belonged to the realm of myth. With respect to the Yankee, for example, she wrote: "A barrier seemed to lie between this legendary Yankee and any effort to reach his inner character. . . . He was consistently a mythical figure. . . . Plain and pawky, he was an ideal image. . . ."[35] Similarly, a backwoodsman like Crockett became the center of "fabulous stories" that, though remaining fragmentary, "underwent the many changes to which popular legends have always been subject."[36] As for minstrelsy, Rourke noted that "Western myth-making was woven deep in [it], so deep that it can hardly be counted an alien strain."[37] Rourke used the word "myth" interchangeably with the terms "legend," "fable," and "fantasy." For example, she wrote of the Yankee peddler: "He was a myth, a fantasy. Many hands had joined to fashion his figure, from the South, from the West, even from New England. What the Yankee peddler was in life and fact can only be guessed."[38] Her refusal to distinguish between myth and legend, fantasy and fable, means that references to mythmaking accumulate throughout the book until their import is unmistakable: Brooks's statement "we have no myths" could not be further from the truth. As a nation, Americans had consistently engaged in some sort of exercise of the imagination. A typical passage in *American Humor* declared: "Yet a basic tie remained between them [the Yankee and the backwoodsman], even beyond the effects of talk and masquerade, a tie which had been fashioned by the common mind out of which they sprang. Neither invited the literal view or the prosaic touch. The fantasies surrounding them might often be crude and earthy, but they were fantasies. These odd and variegated creatures were firmly planted in the spacious realm of legend."[39] Here the words "fashioned" and "sprang" imply a creative process that is spontaneous, lively, and rich. According to Rourke, American humor was not "literal" or "prosaic" but fanciful. So much for Brooks's spiritually starved Puritan or pioneer.

Moreover, Rourke was careful to demonstrate "the traditional bias toward the inward view"[40] characteristic of native humor, frequently juxtaposing the words "inner" and "fantasy." Noting the American's interest in the conscious mind, she emphasized the quality of self-awareness that extended from tales about the Yankee through the nation's writers. For example, referring to popular stage comedy, Rourke asserted: "With all their rude poetry it was about a mind that these myths centered, a conscious, indeed an acutely self-conscious, mind."[41] She described Thoreau's writing as "the essence of self-consciousness, revealed in Yankee speech," and said of Poe that he "entered another area marked out by the popular comic tradition: that of the inner mind or consciousness." Whitman, too, evinced the same preoccupation, whereas Hawthorne's major subject was "that suppression of individualized feeling, conspicuous in the American temper." James, who concerned himself with unstated motives, joined in the "traditional bias toward the inward view."[42] Yankee, backwoodsman, and minstrel wore masks that gave them blank countenances, but the disguise concealed deep reservoirs of emotion. This national habit of introspection overturned Brooks's stress on externalities, absolving Americans of their "national shame."

At the same time, Rourke distinguished between acting out inner feelings by means of humor and the repression which Brooks had ascribed to a society steeped in Puritanism. If the American shunned the external, he was hardly repressed: Rourke found a tendency running from the Yankee ("Surely . . . no simple son of the Pilgrim fathers")[43] through Poe, Hawthorne, and Melville (who were closer to "rude," "direct and earthy" pioneers than to Puritans)[44] toward unrestrained expression, "not in the analytic forms of Calvinism, but as pure unbridled fantasy and exuberant overflow."[45]

Rourke's focus on exuberance made Americans seem almost childlike, in contrast to Brooks's observation, which Horatio Greenough and George Santayana had made earlier, that "we were founded by full-grown, modern, self-conscious men."[46] Elsewhere in *American Humor* Rourke specifically countered Brooks's statement: "Far from having no childhood, the American nation was having a prolonged childhood, extended as the conditions for young and uncertain developments were extended and spatially widened by the opening of wilderness after wilderness, the breaking down of frontier after frontier. The whole movement westward had a youthful illusory character. . . . Character was drawn in simple and legendary outline, both on and off the stage, in and out of current story-telling."[47] The paraphrase of Brooks, which also occurs in another passage beginning "As a people the Americans are said to have had no childhood,"[48] indicates, despite her disclaimer, the polemical nature of Rourke's book. Though her explorations of native culture placed her in the service of Brooks, she accepted only half of his instruction to "Discover, invent a usable past," for she believed the hidden treasure was there to be unearthed. Because America's childhood had furnished a substantial tradition that only awaited discovery, its invention was unnecessary.

On the question of the divided state of American society, Rourke took an equally adamant stand. She disagreed both with Brooks's general characterization of the rift between "highbrow" and "low-brow" and with his specific assignment of the intellectual to a place outside the dominant culture. Her repeated use of words like "mind" and "consciousness" not only established the American's spiritual nature but also worked against Brooks's description of the intellectual's marginal role. For if, as Rourke maintained, self-conscious reflection was a characteristic native trait, then the intellectual, who valued such reflection, stood at the center of American life. Rourke's demonstration that an interest in the mind joined intellectual and common man alike was proof of national unity, undermining Brooks's dichotomy.

Rourke made the same argument against the "high-brow"/ "low-brow" distinction by demonstrating the ways in which American writers had drawn upon patterns of folk humor in creating literature. This effort serves several functions, not least of which is to provide evidence that American "high culture" and folk culture are built on the same base. As Rourke wrote, "A homogeneous world of the imagination had been created in which popular fancies and those of genius were loosely knit together."[49] That statement tacitly repudiated the notion of a split in American society, thereby contradicting Brooks's description of a division between "American culture and American humor." That the writings of Thoreau, Poe, and Hawthorne, of Melville and James, of Whitman and countless lesser figures reflected the mythic strain in American humor or drew upon patterns of language and ideas developed in the popular comic tradition proved that there was an underlying unity in the nation's life.

Rourke's emphasis on a unified America comes across nowhere more clearly than in the subtitle of *American Humor*, "A Study of the National Character." In *America's Coming-of-Age*, Brooks had called for "that secure and unobtrusive element of national character, taken for granted, and providing a certain underlying coherence" as a way of becoming "a great people."[50] *American Humor* argued that we had already developed such a character that Americans possessed common traits which invalidated distinctions like "high-brow" and "low-brow." That assumption determined Rourke's analysis of the "comic trio." Yankee, backwoodsman, and minstrel represented different areas of the country; Rourke's claim that they tended to blend into one another was an assertion that the national heritage transcended sectional differences. For example, she noted that "the ancestry of the backwoodsman bore a close resemblance to that of the Yankee," and that later on "[i]f the backwoodsman became Yankee, the Yankee of legend also absorbed the character of the backwoodsman."[51] Even though some features distinguished one figure from another, "in stories and on the stage each took on qualities and even appearances of the other; they fell into many of the same roles."[52] Moreover, Rourke explained, later folk figures created by an urban imagination, such as the "b'hoy" who swaggered down the streets of New York, exhibited traits shared by the "comic trio"; in them "the pioneer mythologizing habit remained unbroken."[53]

Brooks had drawn a picture of American culture as commercial, divided between intellectual life and experience, devoid of social cohesion and plagued by individualism, and above all fundamentally inhibiting to the exercise of the imagination. In *American Humor* Rourke replied by describing the national character in terms of mythmaking capacity, habitual self-

[58]

consciousness, exuberance, and underlying unity, traits that indicated a basic spiritual health.

That argument required a particular conception of the nature of culture and myth. Unless the measure of an adequate culture included the accomplishments of the folk, Rourke could not report that America passed the test with flying colors; unless mythmaking certified the well-being of the artist, she could not look to the nation's aesthetic future with assurance. And, as Rourke sometimes forgot, neither a folk tradition nor the presence of myth by itself guaranteed progress for society as a whole. Here it is sufficient to note, however, that she was convincing. Brooks, who by the 1930s had retracted his earlier denunciations and turned with enthusiasm to the delineation of a New England literary heritage, admitted in *Days of the Phoenix* (1957): "In part from reading Emerson, I was already prepared to take a more sympathetic view of our old writers and the country, but in certain respects my horizon was indefinitely broadened by Constance Rourke's eager and eloquent studies. She was already preparing for the general history of American culture of which she finished parts before her death; and she wrote, from time to time, to tell me of the proofs she found that America had its own definite aesthetic tradition." [54] Rourke herself elaborated on her framework in the biographies—Audubon, Crockett, Sheeler—that pointed the way to the book she never completed. As the Depression dispelled the confident mood of the boom years, others joined her in a positive view of American culture. For many, the desire to discover the sources of economic failure gave impetus to a search for the "real" America. The idea that theirs was a divided society seemed, in the face of visible social disunity, urgently to require refutation. Popular historians like Constance Lindsay Skinner, poets like Stephen Vincent Benét, documentary writers and authors of WPA state guides settled the American intellectual's longstanding quarrel with his homeland by embracing its past. Critics as different as Bernard DeVoto and F. O. Matthiessen,

separated by temperament, by primary interest, by their dis-
parate relationships to academic and popular audiences, took as
their common task the creation of a widespread appreciation of
native traditions. By the late 1930s, Rourke was far from alone
in her treatment of American subjects; in her own words, she
belonged almost to a "guild" or "coterie."[55]

Yet Rourke differed from other writers who investigated native culture in ways that make her own work especially "usable" for the historian. She began her explorations before virtually anyone else; as she might have put it, she was a pioneer.
No other critic treated all of the particular topics she addressed:
folklore, myth, the public figure, humor, the "practical arts."
Moreover, Rourke was uniquely single-minded. The persistence
with which she claimed that America had its own artistic traditions is striking; however far she ranged in subject matter, she
argued the affirmative side of her debate with the early Brooks
over and over again. Her position as free-lance writer facilitated
this exclusivity of interest. In contrast to a critic like Matthiessen, bound to academia, or to one like DeVoto, committed to
journalism, Rourke adopted an independent vantage point from
which she could explore America's past without the infringe-
ment of other professional obligations. The characteristics of
the search for a "usable past," sometimes diluted by a preoccupation with literary form (as in Matthiessen's case) or diffused
in varied, polemical writing (as in DeVoto's) are magnified in
Rourke's work.

The contradictions, the defensive moves that informed the
discovery of native culture, are magnified as well. Rourke's attitude toward the American past was more ambiguous than she
acknowledged, and her affirmative stance at times more the result of wish than belief. Though the positive strain dominates
Rourke's writing, in places her work betrays the suspicion that
Brooks, in his early essays, had correctly assessed America's
deficiencies. As she turned from subject to subject, she invoked

definitions and concepts that allowed her to refute Brooks's charges while assuaging her own doubts. That double purpose, which shaped many aspects of Rourke's approach, is clearest in her shifting interpretation of the idea of "culture."

# 3

## CULTURE

In the spring of 1940, when she was deep in research for her "History of American Culture," Rourke sounded out Lewis Mumford about the advisability of transforming the lengthy introduction to that study into a separate volume that could be issued without delay. The subject of the introduction was a question—"What is a Culture?"—and Rourke thought her answer of sufficient theoretical importance to warrant a book of its own.[1] Mumford convinced her to keep theory and evidence together, with the result that her views survive in print only in her posthumously published essays. Nevertheless, enough of her notes and drafts remains to illuminate the way she redefined "culture" to allow for the practical, unpredictable, democratic achievements of the American people.

Rourke's formulation belongs in the context of contemporary developments in anthropology, which entailed a movement away from evolutionism (represented by Edward B. Tylor and Lewis Henry Morgan) and toward historical particularism (pioneered by Franz Boas and primarily represented for Rourke by Ruth Benedict). In 1871, Tylor, an Englishman, had published *Primitive Culture*, which became a standard text for several decades thereafter. Subscribing to Herbert Spencer's premise that social growth paralleled biological growth, Tylor postulated an evolutionary model of cultural change. He coupled this "biological reductionism"[2] with a belief in a universal standard of progress. The result was a stage theory in which cultures followed discrete steps that could be classified, arranged, and compared. As Marvin Harris quotes Tylor, " 'The institutions of men are as distinctly stratified as the earth on which he lives. They succeed each other in series substantially uniform over the globe, independent of what seem the comparatively superficial differences of race and language, but shaped by similar human nature acting through successively changed conditions in savage, barbaric, and civilized life.' "[3] Lewis Henry Morgan, widely regarded as the father of American anthropology, had proposed an even more elaborate developmental scheme in his *Ancient Society* (1877). Dividing "savagery," "barbarism," and "civilization" into lower, middle, and upper segments, Morgan defined the consecutive technological advances that had enable human beings to pass from one stage to the next. Subsistence by means of the bow and arrow, for example, characterized upper savagery, whereas a society that had learned how to make pottery would be considered to be at the level of lower barbarism. Morgan also outlined five forms of family structure, ranging from group marriage and incest to monogamy, and described the organization of politics and economics in each period. For both Tylor and Morgan, whether a culture progressed by inventing its own new institutions and customs or by borrowing them from other societies was less important than the general sequence through which all of mankind passed. Rourke's response to the question "What is a Culture?" was largely phrased in the negative: it was not Tylor's and Morgan's series of stages toward civilization.

Rourke did not discuss Tylor and Morgan directly, but in her outline for "American Culture" she took up the work of the journalist and historian Edward Eggleston, to whom she imputed the evolutionists' model of cultural growth. In 1901,

Eggleston had published *The Transit of Civilization from England to America in the Seventeenth Century.*[4] Like Tylor and Morgan, Eggleston assumed that certain attainments—his categories were medicine, speech, conduct, education, economic arrangement, and "mental outfit"—functioned as tests of a society's progress toward greater and greater maturity. Rourke observed that for Eggleston culture involved a succession of developmental stages.[5] Unlike Tylor and Morgan, however, Eggleston was a confirmed "diffusionist"; he believed that culture spread by "transit" from a center of civilization to a less mature area. Eggleston's history attempted to set forth a concrete example of that process of cultural development: he recorded and applauded the extent to which English traits had been "carried" to the New World. The same hierarchical view governed his novel *The Hoosier School-Master* (1871), which described frontier society in transition from savagery and lawlessness to literacy and cultivation, under the influence of imported refinements.[6]

As Rourke was aware, Dixon Ryan Fox, in *Ideas in Motion* (1935), elaborated and generalized Eggleston's model of the "transit of civilization." Like Eggleston, Fox proceeded from Spencer's, Tylor's, and Morgan's premise that societies evolved from the simple to the complex,[7] and took Europe to represent the culmination of that evolution. Fox went beyond Eggleston's description of a single instance of transit. "Four stages are discerned," he wrote: "first, when foreign practitioners of the [professional] specialty are received by the pioneer community; second, when the native youth go to the old country to attend upon instruction; third, when institutions of the special learning are established in the new land, though still dependent on the metropolis for the equipment of their teachers; fourth, when the institutions have sufficiently developed to maintain themselves."[8] Fox applied his model not only to the migration of "carriers" (like foreign soldiers and visiting professionals) from Europe to America, but to the movement from east to west within American boundaries as well. For Fox, the frontier was synonymous with a decline in civilization, because "the delicate plant can not immediately take root in a wilderness."[9] (Once again, organic imagery seemed an appropriate description of cultural development, but for Fox the "seeds"[10] had to be transplanted.) As Rourke recounted it in "The Roots of American Culture," the "transit theory" proposed that "if we dipped deeply and often enough into the major European streams we might hope to witness their rise among us. . . . What we might hope eventually to possess was an extension of European culture, that is, if the process of diffusion was not too greatly impaired by forces peculiar to American life [like the frontier]."[11] In Eggleston's words, "In human history nothing is educed from nothing; that which is exists by virtue of far-reaching roots struck deep into the mold of that which was. Pioneers especially have no time to invent; necessity rarely brings forth anything better than imitation and adaptation."[12] That idea of the growth of culture made America, as Rourke said, "a frontier of Europe."[13]

Rourke brought to her reading of Eggleston and Fox the idea of "cultural lag." As originally formulated by William Fielding Ogburn in *Social Change with Respect to Culture and Original Nature* (1922), "cultural lag" described a situation where "there is a rapid change in a culture of interdependent parts and . . . [where] the rates of change in the parts are unequal."[14] Ogburn limited his concept to circumstances in which technological growth created lingering institutional anachronisms; he was not concerned with art. For Rourke, however, "cultural lag" pertained to the way America's achievements in the fine arts trailed behind Europe's—a usage quite remote from Ogburn's. Because, as Richard Pells has pointed out, the notion of "cultural lag" gained currency among diverse intellectuals in the 1930s,[15] Rourke's use of the phrase may well point not to a reading of Ogburn but merely to her familiarity with popular versions of his work.

Rourke's attack on the theory of "cultural lag" also obscured the battle lines between evolutionists and other writers who had begun to oppose Tylor's and Morgan's views. Although Ogburn accounted for cultural change by the diffusion of traits from one place to another, he discarded any "inevitable succession of stages."[16] Thus, in assailing "cultural lag," Rourke was in a sense attacking her allies, the antievolutionists. This confusion, coupled with her failure to provide an explicit definition of "culture," may simply reflect the incomplete state of Rourke's notes, but it also suggests that she invoked anthropological terminology where useful as a weapon in her defense of America, without an anthropologist's understanding of the principles and issues involved.

Her imprecision notwithstanding, Rourke detected an acceptance of "cultural lag" at the heart of Eggleston's and Fox's "transit theory" (despite the fact that Eggleston wrote well before Ogburn). As Rourke read them, Eggleston and Fox argued that because of the slow evolutionary process, some societies, debilitated by the need for economic survival or suffering merely from newness, would be less civilized than others. With the assistance of "carriers" of culture and the passage of time, however, laggard civilizations could eventually catch up to more advanced ones.

Rourke's outline indicates that she had planned to introduce her long history with a detailed rebuttal to the "transit" model, a part of which found its way into her essay "The Roots of American Culture." She judged the implications of evolutionism and the idea of "cultural lag" objectionable for several reasons. First, the "transit" theory seemed to her an essentially "static," "unvital" view of culture, as if there were a single set of societal traits that signified maturity and could be transferred from one place to another without modification. True, the model involved development, and hence, it would seem, was not static; but for Eggleston and Fox the evolutionary movement was prescribed, inevitable, and free from the influence of specific time and place. As in Tylor's and Morgan's view, the stages of growth were discrete and essentially unalterable. Rourke argued that the idea of a gradual rise toward higher and higher civilization was an inaccurate description of cultural development. She noted that some eastern institutions sprang up full-blown on the frontier, and that at times European ideas first took root on the frontier and only later moved east. Rourke characterized the growth of a culture in terms of "syncopation" rather than steady rhythm, with jumps toward and away from European forms, "regressions" or backward turns to more primitive institutions, and rearrangements of established patterns. In particular she took Fox to task for invoking Tennyson's line "I am a part of all that I have met" as a description of the impact of "carriers" on a culture; Fox ignored the fact that some experiences, once "met," were rejected, whereas others received a disproportionate stress.[17] The "transit" model overlooked what Rourke called the "complexity of cultures" and the existence of "special soils" that led to "great variations in cultural directions."[18]

For Rourke, not all cultures developed in the same way. She was vague about the determinants of a given culture's characteristics, setting them down in her outline simply as environmental, economic, and psychological influences. In "The Roots of American Culture," she made the following remark, which leaves the reader wondering exactly what she thought did "determine": "And while it cannot be sweepingly said that 'sky determines,' that is, that cultures are basically conditioned by environmental factors, nevertheless these factors were forces mingling with others in our early settlements."[19] Rourke's point, however, was that, given the variable impact of environment, one was wrong to expect that growth would be the same everywhere. More important, one was mistaken in faulting a culture for its failure to exhibit strength in any given area. In her notes, Rourke commented that the "fact that a single form cannot be translated [from one culture to another] means nothing at all." For example, she observed, English painting, and particularly portraiture, "remained in the provincial stage" for a long period, "but we do not in consequence deny [the] stream of culture to the British." A better example was that of Scotland, where, Rourke said, there was even less painting and only a small body of literature. Nevertheless, no one could dispute that there was such a thing as Scottish culture, "resting upon Scott, Burns, a body of folksong and legend, a body of intellectuals in Edinburgh. . . ."[20] Rourke asserted that America required the same allowances. Because American circumstances were so different from those in Europe, it followed that a unique culture, not a pale imitation, would result: "Strange horizons, a totally unknown continent, extremes in climate—these created a rigorous and electric medium within which all experience was shaped and colored. . . . Essential patterns of thought, emotion and imagination were freshly twisted, emboldened, pulled into new dimensional forms; and it is the resultant configuration that must concern us rather than the separated parts of their antecedent sources."[21] In contrast to the notion of "cultural lag," Rourke put forth the concept of the "new course" of cultural development, determined by new conditions.

In this pluralistic view, Rourke was heavily influenced by contemporary anthropologists like Franz Boas who subscribed to historical particularism.[22] Rourke's chief debt was to Ruth Benedict, a student of Boas. According to Margaret Marshall, Rourke knew Benedict as early as 1931, when they both attended a dinner at the home of the critic Eda Lou Walton, and may well have met her before then, because both were at Vassar between 1905 and 1907.[23] In 1934, Benedict published *Patterns of Culture*, which argued for the cultural relativism Rourke's position implies. Benedict advanced for anthropologists two principles that Rourke was to insist upon for critics. First, Benedict stressed the importance of seeing culture as a totality. As Rourke quoted her in "The Roots of American Culture," " 'A culture, like an individual, is a more or less consistent pattern of thought and action. . . . The whole, as modern science is insisting in many fields, is not merely the sum of all its parts, but the result of a unique arrangement and interrelation of the parts that has brought about a new entity. . . . The importance of the study of the whole configuration as over against the continued analysis of its parts is stressed in field after field of modern science.' "[24] Rourke's repeated use of the phrase "whole configuration" was a direct borrowing from Benedict. Just as Benedict sketched the "pattern" of the Kwakiutl, so in conceiving "A History of American Culture" Rourke can be seen as attempting to provide a description of the unique American "pattern." The influence of Benedict might also account for Rourke's frequent use of the word "pattern" throughout *American Humor*.

Second, Benedict emphasized the concept of "cultures" rather than "culture," implicitly arguing that no one society was "higher" than another. In Rourke's words, Benedict maintained that " 'anthropologists are turning from the study of primitive culture to that of primitive cultures, and the implications of this change from singular to plural are only just beginning to be evident.' "[25] For Benedict, this relativism allowed for the possibility of radical social change,[26] because American culture was in no way sacred or intrinsically better than any other system of organization. For Rourke, the implication was the reverse: reassuringly, America, though different from Europe, was not inherently inferior to it.

Rourke did not go so far as to make a total separation between European and American culture. She sensibly recognized our foreign debts, conceding that, as "transit" critics had suggested, we had at times exaggerated our "special experience." Flamboyantly proclaiming our uniqueness, we had sometimes considered our deficiencies as singular, without taking into account parallel European shortcomings. There was a sense, Rourke wrote, in which we had not regarded Europe enough: we had not always seen the way "the strains which we most criticize [in ourselves] are part of large movements in Western civilization," and were not our defects alone. (Her mention of self-criticism is a probable reference to Brooks, because her notes continue, "Separation of art and the artist from society by no means peculiar to us.")[27] Europe should provide perspective, Rourke thought, reminding us of the way both our achievements and our failures had been conditioned by our emergence in a particular phase of Western development. For example, Rourke asserted, "We were born into a world in which the intellectual approach with intensive inner scrutiny was becoming dominant,"[28] circumstances that left a deep mark on the American character. Conscious of America's relationship to Europe, Rourke criticized Brooks for not regarding the "international scene" (presumably as he treated it in *The Pilgrimage of Henry James*) as a "natural and even traditional American subject."[29] Still, whatever our borrowings from abroad, modern anthropology dictated that we regard European civilization only as a shaping force, not as an example for imitation.

Benedict's framework allowed Rourke to draw evidence about the development of American culture from a source that many of her fellow critics had considered inadmissable: the history of the frontier. It was not only Fox and the "transit" theorists who disparaged the frontier as uncivilized. In *The Golden Day*, Mumford had announced: "the life of the pioneer was bare and insufficient: he did not really face Nature, he merely evaded society. . . . [Man] can reside for long in the wilderness only by losing some of the essential qualities of the cultivated human species."[30] As Warren Susman has pointed out, Mumford's sentiments were echoed by other intellectuals—for example, Brooks and Harold Stearns—who, like Mumford himself, had detected a harmful split in American life; for them, the frontier "became the scapegoat for all that was wrong with contemporary America."[31] Rourke was aware of the size and prominence of this group and sensitive to the importance of the controversy, noting that the frontier had been "the nub" of an emotionally charged "discussion as to our culture." But she preferred the example of another writer—Frederick Jackson Turner—to the disaffection of Mumford or Brooks. For Rourke, Turner's paper "The Significance of the Frontier in American History" (1893), though proposed long before Benedict's work, was ahead of its time in its implicit view of the factors that determined cultural patterns. Rourke had outlined for "A History of American Culture" a section beginning with an elucidation of Turner's thesis, followed by a discussion of antagonistic viewpoints like Eggleston's and Fox's, and culminating in a reply to Turner's opponents that contrasted the "transit" theory with her own and Benedict's.

According to Rourke, Turner's argument that American democracy was the product of a series of encounters with unsettled territory—encounters that influenced social institutions, political forms, and intellectual traits—rested on all the correct assumptions about cultural growth. His model took into account the effect on American life of unique circumstances, principally relating to the environment. As Rourke pointed out, Turner dealt with "contours and character of land, watersheds, the fall line, climate, racial strains, motives in social groups giving a special bias to communal life." Moreover, his thesis rejected the idea of a linear progression from the primitive to the civilized. In her notes Rourke quoted Turner at length: " 'Thus American development has exhibited not merely advance along a single line, but a return to primitive conditions on a continually advancing line, and a new development in that area. American social development has been continually beginning over again on the frontier. This perennial rebirth, this fluidity of American life, this expansion westward with new opportunities, its continuous touch with the simplicity of primitive society, furnish the forces dominating American character.' " Here Turner evinced an understanding of exactly that syncopation that Rourke criticized Eggleston and Fox for neglecting. Whereas Fox's stages implied that "the frontier was all one experience," Turner's stress on the backward turn and on flexibility was in keeping with Rourke's contention that cultures did not evolve uniformly. Rourke admitted that, like Fox, Turner employed the term *social evolution* "as though American civilization were repeating the stages of European civilization." Rourke claimed, however, that he actually meant "something else," that the implications of his thesis worked against the idea that societies developed in a fixed way and that we were misreading him if we took him as a proponent of that view. In fact, Rourke concluded, Turner was "close to anthropological theory as to the differences of cultures"; in other words, he anticipated Benedict. On a page headed "conformity of Turner's underlying ideas to concepts in contemporary anthropology," Rourke jotted: "cultures not culture," followed by the remark "not absolutes in culture: relativity."[32]

Rourke did not accept Turner "in full" or unquestioningly. She conceded that he did not "elaborate the return to primitive conditions," nor did he dwell on the "setbacks" that occurred on the frontier. Though she did not say so explicitly, she seemed aware that Turner had a stake, by virtue of his midwestern origins, in proving the positive effects of the frontier, a bias that impeded his treatment of unsavory features of pioneer life. For Rourke, Turner's statement about the prevalence of frontier democracy was "too sweeping"; she cited the presence of an early homeless class as evidence that undemocratic forces were at work as well. In addition, Turner's commendable relativism did not prevent him from an excessive concern with the conventional fine arts. He was, according to Rourke, mistakenly bent on proving that the frontier had nourished cultural achievements worthy of European recognition.[33]

Rourke, also a midwesterner, did not herself fully escape the temptation to make the frontier conventionally acceptable. But she was less squeamish about its negative aspects because her theory of culture afforded her a comforting way to deal with unlovely attributes of the American past. Arguing that we were set on a course different from Europe's, and insisting that we must evaluate cultural patterns as totalities, she was free to assert that the verdict was not yet in on American civilization. Given our incompleteness and the necessity of viewing the whole configuration, frontier violence, lawlessness, poverty, and economic ruthlessness would quite possibly fall into place as minor (though deplorable) aberrations in our development. Furthermore, the assumption that American culture constituted a special pattern permitted Rourke to perceive even those features of frontier life as possible catalysts for fresh growth: new directions might come from anywhere, because we could not be held to a preexisting, Europe-centered model.

Thus in 1932, when the critic and historian Bernard DeVoto issued *Mark Twain's America* as an attack on Brooks's *The Ordeal of Mark Twain* (1922), Rourke found that most of her sympathies lay with DeVoto. Brooks had argued that the crudeness and pervasive materialism of pioneer existence had damaged Twain's artistic sensibilities; unable to do serious creative work, he was forced to write humor instead. DeVoto thought this interpretation the product of Brooks's hopeless incapacity to appreciate the richness and vitality of Western history. In a remark to Rourke that reveals the limits of his concern with the need for an adequate culture, he disparaged Brooks as a zealous "social reformer."[34] Delighting in the very roughness that Brooks deplored, DeVoto judged Twain psychologically healthy and his work a brilliant, authentic, and literarily masterful appraisal of the human condition in general and of frontier life in particular. Rourke was inclined to agree. She never surrendered her respect for Brooks's reassessment of native traditions, and dismayed DeVoto by saying, in a review of *Mark Twain's America*, that Brooks had created a climate in which a realistic view of the frontier could flourish. Her own commitment to "social reform" prevented her from harping, as DeVoto did, on Brooks's "delusions" and "inexcusable ignorance."[35] Nevertheless, DeVoto's ideas, Rourke thought, provided a "healthy antithesis" to Brooks's, for Brooks had never been able to see the positive consequences of even the raw side of the frontier:

> In referring to Turner's theory as to the nature and influence of the frontier Mr. Brooks has spoken of our societies as always beginning *de novo*, and as preventing Americans, even in the settled areas, from retaining "a firm hold upon civilized values." But while it is true that losses have inevitably attended the development of our new societies "civilized values" were sustained there in far greater measure than could be guessed from Mr. Brooks's portraits in monotone of the frontier, and he has failed to recognize that the entire overturn could mean the beginnings of a fresh synthesis in which "civilized values" might be freshly created.[36]

*American Humor*, as DeVoto gleefully put it, took a "delightful, and unanswerable, crack at poor Brooks" by announcing that it was "a mistake to look for the social critic—even manqué—in Mark Twain."[37] The same understanding—that the frontier might actually have furnished rather than destroyed the basis for America's distinctive pattern—informed Rourke's biographies of Crockett and Audubon and would have shaped a good deal of her uncompleted general study as well.

A second idea, equally heretical to "transit theorists," also became a cornerstone of Rourke's theory of culture. This was the belief that the accomplishments of the "folk" were more important than isolated masterpieces. According to Rourke, the evolutionary hierarchy slighted the freshness and vitality that could exist in the beginning stages of a culture's development; it dispensed with possibly productive new forces by dismissing them as "barbarism or degradation." By focusing on "peaks of achievement," the hierarchical approach overlooked the possibility that more important cultural attainments might lie in the "valleys." Without denying the role of genius in the growth of art, Rourke noted: "In a nascent culture such as ours, peaks of achievement have occurred and must have their place, but if our concern is with the whole dimensional pattern minor figures may also become symbols of a dominant creative effort. Not merely the individual but the culture of a group, a town, a region may be significant of main tendencies."[38]

Rourke found support for that position in the work of two eighteenth-century writers: Johann Herder and Giambattista Vico. As Rourke paraphrased him, Herder demonstrated in *Ideas for a Philosophy of the History of Mankind* (1784–91) that "the folk-arts laid a base for the fine arts in form, spirit and expression, that folk-forms were the essential forms in any communal group, and that these tended to shape and color sophisticated or conscious art even when they were not specifically drawn upon."[39] Foreshadowing anthropologists like Benedict, Herder maintained no single standard of culture as absolute, and operated instead from a relativistic perspective that merely described the attributes of diverse cultures without evaluating them.[40] Similarly, in *The New Science* (1725), Vico asserted that popular traditions of language and myth were the most accurate indices of cultural history. He emphasized the social origin of myth and legend, and looked at the creation of culture as an ongoing collective activity, rather than the sum of individual efforts. Both Herder and Vico, in Rourke's view, furthered the study of popular values and understood the importance of treating a culture as a whole. They saw in folk forms "distinctive national patterns," for which they accounted in terms of variations in "environmental conditions" and "experiences."[41]

Ironically, given the usefulness of his writing for Rourke, Vico proceeded from a stage model of cultural growth in which the "primitive" or "folk" level was basic. Believing that there were laws of human development that formed the structure for a "new science," he postulated three steps—Rourke called them "the intuitive, the metaphysical, the scientific"—through which all mankind had passed.[42] Vico also detected a cyclical pattern in the succession of civilizations, a series of inevitable rises and falls. Those aspects of Vico's thought do not undermine his assertion of the importance of popular traditions, but they indicate an evolutionism directly opposed to Rourke's picture of the "new course."

Moreover, at times Rourke does not seem entirely to have rejected the evolutionist strains in Vico's theory. Rourke's concept of cultural growth admitted movement from the primitive to the complex, but it denied that such movement followed a single line through fixed stages or that the process culminated in an externally imposed set of achievements defined as "civilization." Yet, attracted as she was by the notion of the importance of primitive expression, Rourke sometimes inadvertently implied evolution according to rigid laws. In her unpublished essay "The Decline of the Novel," she characterized the replacement of novel writing with "semi-primitive forms" like the epic and the allegory as part of a recurring "rhythmic cycle";[43] her phrase seems directly drawn from Vico. The following passage from *American Humor* reflects even more clearly Rourke's tendency to wander toward the evolutionist camp. Restating the theory of the "new course," she began: "the pace of each [English and American literature], and perhaps the direction, has been wholly different; the movement of each has necessarily been conditioned by profound differences in the national history." But later in the passage Rourke continued: "By one of those ellipses which sometimes occur in the life of nations as well as in that of individuals, a stage may have been omitted in American development, that which would have allowed a slow accumulation and enrichment." By remarking that a stage might have been skipped, Rourke implicitly affirmed the existence of some sort of standard developmental progression. It is not far from this affirmation to the view that some cultures are ahead of others in their passage through such stages—or in other words, that there is such a phenomenon as "cultural lag." Indeed, Rourke's next paragraph introduces the notion of "maturity" in literature, a status that the English novel represented but that had not yet been attained by Americans: "A full and imaginative penetration of contemporary life [as in the novel] would seem to be required if maturity in literature is to be reached." The section concludes with the reassurance that in turning to legend we were on the right path. One can almost hear Rourke saying at this point to European critics, "Give us time—we'll get there." The passage leaves the impression that Rourke has sketched a process of evolution from a primitive state to civilization, a process in accord with the theories of Vico but quite out of line with Benedict and with most of what Rourke had to say elsewhere.[44] One sees a similar assumption, reflecting Herder's influence, in Rourke's description of folklore as a "prelude" for literature.[45]

Nevertheless, the contradictions in Rourke's interpretation of Vico and Herder are less noteworthy than the way their stress on popular expression confirmed the commitment to democracy she had inherited from her mother and renewed during her years at Vassar. Because the culture of the folk was "the broadest, most enduring, most fundamental strain" in American civilization, the study of their "practical" arts promised the greatest rewards for artist and citizen. John Dewey had said as much when he rejected the conventional emphasis on history, literature, and the classics as narrow and aristocratic and argued instead that the test of a subject's value be whether it incorporated "experience in which the widest groups share."[46] For generations, however, an alternative view had held sway: the concept of the arts as "luxuries," as the possessions of the rich. In "The Roots of American Culture," Rourke traced the history of that pernicious idea. In an effort to symbolize his newly acquired wealth, she noted, the Renaissance gentleman, exemplifying Thorstein Veblen's theory of conspicuous waste, had detached the fine arts from "the homely practical arts and the homely crafts." Even further refinements had occurred under the system of patronage, whereby the *literati* "sedulously cultivated the art of letters as a luxury." The dilettante also appeared, "concerned with the more delicate fringes of esthetic expression."[47] Finally—and worst of all—the "luxury" concept made its way to America, where it coincided with "the first broad accumulation of colonial wealth," and where its "print went deep." Fortunately, Franklin, Washington, Jefferson, and Adams, knowing that, to retain its vitality, art in the new nation had to be connected to the "common life," prepared the way for a replacement of the luxury ideal with standards more appropriate to a democratic society. Franklin, Rourke maintained, had foreshadowed functionalism by recognizing that "practical arts might have beauty if they perfectly accomplished their ends" and that " 'nothing is good or beautiful but in the measure that it is useful.' "[48] The Founding Fathers' concern with "the arts as common utility," she argued, "provides a broad chart for an approach to American culture which by no means excludes the fine arts or the derivative forms of expression but which keeps the center of gravity within that social complex out of which the arts must spring."[49] Without elaboration, Rourke noted under the heading "What is a Culture?": "Luxury concept wrong in a democracy: culture like wealth seeping down from the top (the seepage theory as wrong in culture as in economics)."[50] Her phrase "the social complex out of which the arts must spring" echoed Vico and Herder; translated to the American scene, it referred to the practical pursuits of the common man.

The democratic implications of Rourke's rejection of the "luxury" concept come into sharp focus when her view is set against T. S. Eliot's explicitly antidemocratic approach in *Notes Towards the Definition of Culture* (1948). Eliot, with whose earlier work Rourke was familiar, proclaimed the possibility of distinguishing between "higher and lower cultures," between "advance and retrogression."[51] Though Eliot shared with Benedict and Rourke a regard for "the pattern of the society as a whole," he insisted on designating as superior the "more conscious" culture of an aristocratic governing class.[52] For Eliot, cultural "advance" depended on the extent to which the priorities and values (particularly Christian values) of the "higher" minority culture withstood the incursions of "mass-culture" and the success with which "the classes" transmitted "traditional," "orthodox" attitudes from generation to generation. Eliot's idea of culture lent itself to the perpetuation of class distinctions: in his view, as Roger Kojecky has phrased it, "to argue for the maintenance of culture was to argue for a society's or a group's established way of life."[53] In contrast to Eliot, and to numerous academic critics who shared Eliot's premises, even if afraid to express Eliot's frankly antidemocratic conclusions, Rourke understood cultural growth as a process that took place from the bottom up. The power to determine the character of the fine arts rested with the folk who, far from needing the protection from "boredom" and "despair" with which Eliot sought to provide them,[54] supplied the foundation for the whole culture.

In consequence, Rourke planned to demonstrate in her comprehensive history as much as she could of native folklore and folk art, along with other types of popular expression. She had intended to consider as part of "the immense scope of our culture" "Indian, regional, Negro" as well as "nationalized elements." Her essays in *The Roots of American Culture*—on the arts of the Shakers, on shapenote singing in the South, on the rise of theatricals—only hint at the types of investigations she proposed to pursue. In addition, her list of native achievements included "new forms" like the idea of the stream of consciousness (which Rourke credited to William James), Indian treaties, "the epical in the modern world," "social autobiography," and radio drama.[55] She had written drafts of chapters on science and education. Rourke knew that those practical activities, along with lumberjacking stories and cowboy songs, would not be taken as manifestations of a rich culture on the hierarchical model of "transit" theorists like Fox or critics like Eliot. But from Herder and Vico, as well as Benedict and Turner, she knew that such a model was incorrect.

Rourke's interpretation of "culture" in terms of popular expression, as opposed to the idea of the arts as "luxuries," led her to reject a companion principle that had dominated past evaluations of America: the contention that classic forms (as, for example, in architecture) represented the height of aesthetic achievement. Historically, the classic ideal had become associated with "luxury" because, in Rourke's words, "wealth alone could acquire the impressive manifestations of classic art."[56] Rourke repeatedly decried the "long domination of the classic ideal," defining it as "the study of relative proportions" and ascribing to the classic style a preoccupation with "rules, standards, and conscious precepts."[57] In a passage (greatly condensed from her notes) in "The Roots of American Culture," she explained: "The extended spell of the classic ideal, first taking shape in the Renaissance with sprawling vigor in England, declining, then greatly revivified in the mid-eighteenth century, meant a fixing of norms or patterns in the arts and their further separation in practice and in critical approach from one another."[58] Rourke summarized the appeal of classic art and architecture in *Charles Sheeler*: "Perhaps its forms were appropriated the more eagerly because they seemed to give permanence or balance in the midst of the hasty turmoil of pioneering, or to assure us that we might cultivate these qualities. The idea was afloat that we were to emulate the Golden Age in our rising civilization."[59] Unfortunately, the classic ideal degenerated into empty formula: Rourke pointed to the "thin mirroring of classic forms in the eighteen thirties and forties." Blind to the unique configuration of our culture, we had persisted in submitting to foreign standards, with disastrous results. For, as Rourke put it in her notes, "there is no such thing as a not-so-good classic. If that special coordination, freedom, control —balances which we recognize as classic—[are] not achieved,

then the effect [is] not classic." She added: "What this indicates so far as . . . classic imitation in this country is concerned
is that the result isn't anything at all, [it is] a waste, a dead
loss: [it is] not to be counted as within our expression in any
genuine sense, [but] only to be reckoned with as an indication
of uncertainty, a fringe, not anything like a core."[60]

The outcome of the assumption that American culture should
strive to fulfill the classic ideal was a case study of what happened when criteria for measuring cultural achievement were
extrapolated from one set of social circumstances to another:
bad art was the inevitable result. Rourke may have been especially cautionary on this point because of the hold classicism
exerted over the New Humanist critics of her own time. As they
strove to impose order and rationality on a world increasingly
given over, in their eyes, to pragmatism, disorder, and destructive democracy, New Humanists such as Irving Babbitt and
Paul Elmer More embraced the classic tradition, and did so
with an elitism that surely offended Rourke's Progressive in-
stincts. But the sense of inferiority resulting from America's
halfhearted classic expressions was sufficient grounds for concern: Americans labored under the notion that because they
had not duplicated European styles, they were "culturally un-
developed or unworthy." "From Emerson to contemporary critics"—and here Rourke must have had Brooks firmly in mind—
"we have searched for causes of our failure," assuming without
question that it "*must* be a failure in ourselves," and never
stopping to consider that "there might be something wrong with
[our] underlying ideas."[61]

Nor had we ever examined the dominant belief, espoused by
anglophile critics like Barrett Wendell, among others, that we
should produce literature like Europe's. The assumption that we
would "move into the great sweep of English literature" was
just as wrong and detrimental as the concept of the arts as "luxuries" or the unthinking devotion to the classic. (In fact, Rourke
asserted that our importation of the classic ideal made it "in-

evitable that these ideas should invade our concepts of literature,"[62] though she did not explain the precise connection between the demand for classic forms in the visual arts and the
standards exacted of writers.) Here again we had operated
under the mistaken supposition that our pattern of cultural
development was independent of our special condition. Our expectations had been wrong in two ways: first, because we had
assumed that we would produce literature at all, and second,
because we had looked for duplications of European forms.

Rourke asserted that we had made the wholly unwarranted
equation of "culture" with "literary culture." The belief that a
culture had to be literary, she noted, ran "extremely deep" in
our consciousness, so that "individuals for example who possess
great skills, [which are] special, [and] rooted in life, who do
not possess literary culture, do not regard themselves as cul-
tured." It was true, Rourke argued, that the Puritan emphasis
on early popular education had led to an inevitable interest in
literature, and that we had a tradition (as in Emerson's idea
of the American Scholar as leader) of viewing writing as our
"primary art."[63] But in spite of those tendencies, she maintained, "in spite of the obvious ties with Britain, in spite of our
abundant literacy, in spite of what Emerson was to call our
'enormous paper currency of words,' perhaps after all the American genius is not literary. Henry James, writing of Hawthorne
a hundred years after the nation was founded, thought that it
was not. The governing idea that ours is a literary culture, or
any similar preconception, may throw our judgments awry."[64]
In her notes Rourke expanded this point, remarking that "we
may only have adopted literary tools, literary experience, without those special propulsions which mean the distinctive command of an art."

Bernard DeVoto made a similar argument in *The Literary
Fallacy* (1944), though apparently without Rourke's consciousness of anthropology. DeVoto's target was identical to Rourke's:
the faulty equation of "literature" and "culture." His definition

of the "literary fallacy" referred to the belief, which he found rampant among critics like Brooks, "that a culture may be understood and judged solely by means of its literature, that literature embodies truly and completely both the values and the content of a culture, that literature is the highest expression of a culture, that literature is the measure of life, and finally that life is subordinate to literature."[65] DeVoto went even further than Rourke in repudiating such a view. Given the way writers of the 1920s had, as he thought, misrepresented the country, portraying it as dominated by a "mediocre mob," he was quite willing to concede that America's strengths lay elsewhere. Rourke was more tentative, reserving her conclusions for the time when greater familiarity with the nation's traditions would make it possible to assess the American pattern as a whole.

But even if America turned out to be a literary culture, we were wrong to expect that its literature would take a European —and specifically British—shape. In Rourke's view there might never be any sustained production of "great American novels" because novel writing grew out of specific social conditions missing from our "configuration." England had had "the great sweep of the novel [with its] abundance, complications, density"; in contrast, we had produced, in Poe and Hawthorne, for example, "the tale or the greatly simplified story." That form lent itself to psychological themes absent from English novels of the same period.[66] In the critical treatment of Melville we had most blatantly subjected our literature to an inappropriate standard, "subsuming his works under the heading of novels" and criticizing them "for the failure to achieve the complexities of plot, characterization, and realism of the English novel." Rourke insisted that Melville never attempted that form. Instead, he was writing epics about "journeys into the unknown," concerned not with the "complexities of civilization" but with "eternities" and "spiritual forces."[67] Melville's books, Rourke concluded, were "notably different from [those of] Dickens,

Thackeray, the Brontës, or Jane Austen," and must not be judged inferior to theirs because the difference is an index of a wider difference in cultural pattern.

Rourke took as another reflection of the fact that our literature was on its own course variations in the degree of influence certain novelists exerted in America and abroad. For example, though Americans read both Dickens and Scott with great enthusiasm, Scott became a source of literary inspiration whereas Dickens did not. There was "no extensive work which even attempted the kind of realistic social panorama which is the heart of Dickens's novel[s]," giving them "a rich complication of plot." (Instead, Rourke remarked, Dickens affected painters like Bingham and Blythe rather than writers.) She tentatively suggested that Scott's impact stemmed from elements of national consciousness and a sense of the past that appealed to us as a new nation. Dickens's writing, on the other hand, was founded on a "close and many-sided knowledge" of a "stabilized society" that we were unable to duplicate. Hence we produced Cooper and Simms, resembling Scott, and Hawthorne, Poe, and Melville— resembling no one. Those contrasts in the record of the novel, Rourke argued, should in no way lead the American to adopt a defensive posture. She noted that "the novel did not exist in the Elizabethan period because in an essential sense even its materials did not exist." The same materials—the complexities of an established social life—were absent from the American scene: "Dreiser's hand-to-hand combat with form, style, language, and even with his own basic intentions may stand as a symbol of the failure of the American writer to master the novel when its full materials were lacking. . . ."[68] But Dreiser's failure was not to be charged against American culture in general, which, though possibly nonliterary, offered abundant achievements in other areas.

Rourke's substitution of relativism for an evolutionary sequence and of frontier and folk life for the "luxury," classic, and literary ideals was her greatest contribution to the study of the American past. Her fresh approach released scholars and critics from a prison of inappropriate standards, erroneous expectations, and misleading comparisons. Rourke would never have maintained that American culture was wholly adequate, or that its artistic future was secure. However often she praised native folklore in *American Humor*, for example, "for purposes of candor" she also noted its deficiencies: it was "coarse," "fragmentary," "full of grotesquerie or brutality," incomplete. Nor was American literature as satisfactory as it might be: she described it as "scant, fitful, sporadic."[60] For the introduction to "A History of American Culture," Rourke projected a summary of our "disabilities" to accompany her discussion of our strengths. Her notes refer to American snobbery, uprootedness, lack of discipline, and lack of self-criticism. She was not blind to our shortcomings; in fact, one of her tasks was to point them out in order to spur improvement. Yet Rourke's awareness of these deficiencies did not prevent her from insisting that, given the abundance of its "practical arts," America had produced enough. Her own investigations of the frontier and the folk had demonstrated that much, and signaled the beginning, she might have said with justifiable pride, of a new freedom to explore and celebrate a uniquely American aesthetic tradition.

In her essay "A Note on Folklore," which appeared posthumously as part of *The Roots of American Culture*, Rourke suggested some specific ways scholars might exercise that freedom. Instead of regarding folk materials as quaint survivals or as "regression," social and literary critics might together learn to take stories or songs or carvings on their own terms. "To say, as has been said, that a given folk-novel is not heroic or that it fails to illuminate life on a large scale," Rourke protested, "is to apply, very flatteringly, standards which are seldom applied to other fiction." More productively, critics might recognize what folklore had to offer both the writer and the student of American culture, particularly with respect to form and language. An understanding of the "rise and pressure" of "primitive forms" (the monologue, the tale) and "semi-literary modes of expression" (the sketch, the chronicle) in the development of American literature would permit experimentally inclined writers to leave the constraints of the novel behind without feeling that they were breaking with the past. A knowledge of the characteristic rhythms of folk speech would similarly function as a resource for artists groping toward a sure sense of "the American language." If scholars would focus, for example, on the conjunction of the chronicle play and the choral drama in Marc Connelly's *The Green Pastures*, or on the reverberations since the nineteenth century of Seba Smith's slow, quiet, Yankee satire, they might come to apprehend "certain essential movements of the American mind." Such undertakings would help to foster "a full perception of our culture or cultures" and create the basis for criticism "of a most radical, refreshing kind."[70]

This promising theory, a testimony to the wide scope of Rourke's vision, has not worked entirely well in practice since the publication of "A Note on Folklore." As Richard Dorson has pointed out, Rourke's recommendations licensed numerous critics after her simply to search for the presence of folk humor in literature, and unfortunately to perpetuate her failure to limit the term "folklore" to oral tales.[71] When, however, seven years after Rourke's death, John A. Kouwenhoven issued *Made in America* (1948), he took her insights in a more fruitful direction. Kouwenhoven's description of what he called America's "vernacular" style—the patterns of popular art shaped by democratic institutions—demonstrated the rich possibilities of Rourke's approach. He cited numerous specific debts to Rourke: she was "the first to call attention to" the literary role of Shaker pamphlets and the vein of Yankee humor in Emerson; she taught him about the connections among revivalism, oratory, and Western comedy; she led him to look to form rather than subject for evidence of the vernacular in native painting.[72] Elsewhere, Kouwenhoven acknowledged an even more important lesson of Rourke's: "The fact that we are heirs to much of England's culture, including its language, does not necessarily mean—as Constance Rourke long ago pointed out—that we have, like the English, expressed ourselves most fully in literature."[73] Kouwenhoven's examination of the style of clipper ships and balloon-frame buildings, of landscape architecture, of automobile and machine design, as well as of vernacular influences in literature, made *Made in America* almost the book Rourke had intended to write. Here was an adequate culture in a place where most scholars (Lewis Mumford excepted) had never bothered to look. Had the professors of American Studies followed Kouwenhoven's suggestion, in 1964, that they occupy themselves less with words than with things, Rourke's work might even have furnished the guidelines for an entire movement devoted to the history of popular culture—a prospect that still remains unfulfilled.

Yet original as Rourke's writing was, she did not quite free herself, as Kouwenhoven did, from the concept of art as "luxury" and from classic and literary ideals. There are tensions in her insistence on discarding European yardsticks that the advocate of popular traditions must ultimately reject. For while she pronounced an emphasis on "peaks of achievement" irrelevant to a democratic society, she simultaneously strained to prove that we had attained those artistic heights. A deep, unresolved ambivalence about the expectations of "transit" theorists who looked for great novels and portraits—not great tall tales and furniture—creeps into her unpublished manuscripts and colors *American Humor* and her biographies as well.

It is significant, first of all, that "A History of American Culture" was initially entitled "In Defense of American Literature"; only later did Rourke decide to broaden the project. She first intended merely to argue that though it was correct to suppose that we would produce literature, our efforts in that direction had never been properly understood. The same concern with demonstrating that we were literary (despite the protestation elsewhere that we might not be) permeates the chapter on literature she eventually drafted for the expanded study. Mingled with her disparagement of genteel literary clubs, for example, is an attitude of pride in the amount and intensity of their activity. She wrote of early societies like the Drones and the Belles Lettres Club, "Quite clearly the prevailing idea was that the art of literature could be cultivated and acquired. It was a polite accomplishment. Little essays were written and read before the assembled membership. . . ." Here her tone ("little essays") is slightly contemptuous, and her description of the societies emphasizes the frivolity of their discussions. Yet she concluded the section with this laudatory comment: "Though the New York literary groups were the dominant groups, though the societies undoubtedly gave a shaping hand to our early literature, they were part of a broadly scattered movement throughout the country. Literary magazines were founded with energy and immediacy. . . ."[74] In part the point of Rourke's literature section was to indicate the scope of early American writing, whatever its quality. Her fragmentary notes read: "No doubt about the spread of literary effort, expression, interest— a torrent, the more remarkable when the period is considered. There is no such spread, surely, in the provinces of England or France. Notable, extraordinary . . . even passionate . . . many sided . . . the hungry wish for literary enjoyment and sophistication . . . the implications as to literacy . . . a marked tendency . . . a trait of character . . . certainly literacy a widespread phenomenon."[75] In spite of her commitment to the "practical" arts, Rourke was plainly pleased with her conclusion that there was greater concern with literature in America than in parts of Europe.

Rourke recognized all too clearly that literary activity did not insure artistic merit. As she wrote of our first novels, "The weakness is obvious." But when she described several early "socalled novels," ostensibly to demonstrate their value at least as social and psychological documents, she found that they qualified as literature and even surpassed European developments: "In the most difficult of all areas, the psychological, we had zigzagged off beyond English beginnings, taking a distinctive direction."[76] A similar stress on the way we had outdone English literary forms occurs in *American Humor*. We had achieved the special combination of the epic and self-scrutiny. "In literature," Rourke was pleased to observe, "the scope was new and strange which could include the epical scale in free expression and at the same time reveal the conscious and indwelling mind."[77] Rourke's notes for "American Culture" indicate that she thought this combination an important advance worthy of emphasis as a native contribution to world civilization. Elsewhere discarding the foreign standard of culture that required literary excellence, she nevertheless invoked it in pointing out our singular attainments.

Rourke's treatment of Washington Irving in the draft for "American Culture" illustrates this tension at work. She was quite clear, at first, about Irving's merits: "Washington Irving said that he wouldn't write novels because he didn't care to emulate Scott, but from the work which he has left us we may say with certainty that he could not have done so if he had tried." Nonetheless, Irving managed in the legend of Rip Van Winkle to produce significant literature. Rourke was careful to point out that the vitality of Irving's Knickerbocker stories sprang from their connection to the folk: "drawing upon the folk imagination, touching it with his own," Irving sketched "one of the American immortals." But Rourke would not let Irving's achievement go at the revitalization of folklore. She concluded her discussion of this admittedly deficient American writer with a statement that captures a recurring theme of her work. Referring to the Rip Van Winkle story, she wrote, "This was myth, it was legend, it had poetry; in the rolling of ninepins in the Catskills . . . poetry . . . be it noted, not in verse, but in prose. . . ."[78] The juxtaposition of the phrase "it had poetry" with the assertion that Irving created myth or legend endows

[89]

those folk forms with the status of literature. That is, Rourke was not wholly willing to count folktales as evidence of culture on their own terms; rather, myth had to be dignified as poetry. The need to dress up folklore to look like literature lies just below the surface of *American Humor*. An inventory of the terms Rourke used to describe native folktales reveals that her most common descriptions imply a kinship to literary forms. Here, too, are striking, repeated characterizations of folklore as poetry. The Crockett legends, for example, were not just popular stories; instead, they approximated literature because they were "striated by a naturalistic poetry," and "even distantly approached the realm of the epic." Rourke's discussion of Lincoln provides an even clearer example: "Poetry belonged to most of Lincoln's stories—an earthy poetry; he used the fable, the allegory, the tale grounded in metaphor. The artist was often at work there: but with all the praise bestowed upon them, upon the Gettysburg speech and in a less knowledgeable fashion upon his other writings, Lincoln has rarely been described as a literary figure."[79] Rourke recognized the difference between a folklore with poetic overtones and full-fledged literature: hence the phrase "an earthy poetry" or, elsewhere, "rude poetry." At times she acknowledged that folk expression "did not belong to literature" but only "used the primary stuffs of literature. . . ."[80] In other places, though, she relinquished that awareness and blurred the distinction, equating such diverse efforts as the Crockett story and *Moby Dick*: "For more than a century the poetic temper had been dominant in the country, nourished by a sense of legend. The American imagination had invested the commonest preoccupations and homeliest characters with an essential poetry. Now as the areas of a literature were fairly defined the poetic strain arose as the major strain."[81] If folklore was literature, literature was in a sense folklore. The perception of the common poetic element permitted Rourke to unite her favorite writer, Henry James, with American humorists: "Poetry indeed overspread much of James's writing. Like that of the popular fabulists, it was packed with metaphor. . . . Few writers have had so deep a sense of the poetry of character. . . ."[82] Rourke's description of folklore and literature in identical terms was of course one more aspect of her response to Brooks; it denied any division between "high-brow" and "low-brow" and refuted his portrait of the materialistic American. But it also served to placate those who remained unconvinced that the "practical" arts deserved the same consideration as the fine arts.

Rourke made concessions to "peaks of achievement" critics in works other than *American Humor*. Though she deplored as misguided Turner's concern to portray the frontier as a center of literary culture, for example, her *Davy Crockett* evinces a similar tendency to spruce up Western life for the sake of conventional expectations. The very traits that she implied her relativistic view could accommodate—poverty, wanton killing, crude manners, lawlessness, political shenanigans—were the ones she banished from her biography of the "coonskin Congressman." Her perspective emerges from a comparison of her Crockett with Parrington's, which had appeared in his second volume of *Main Currents in American Thought* (1927). After noting the way ambitious Whig politicians had seized on the "simple-minded frontiersman" to appropriate some of Jackson's rugged, self-made image, Parrington separated the man from the "picturesque propaganda" surrounding him. "The real Davy," wrote Parrington, "was very far from romantic. An honest picture of the Tennessee democracy in its native habitat would reveal few idyllic features. It was a slovenly world and Davy was pretty much of a sloven. Crude and unlovely in its familiar details, with its primitive courtships and shiftless removals, its brutal Indian campaign and fierce hunting sprees, its rough equality, its unscrupulous politics, its elections carried by sheer impudence and whisky, [Crockett's] autobiography reveals the backwoods Anglo-Irishman as an uncivilized animal. . . . Wastefulness was in the frontier blood, and Davy was a true frontier wastrel."[83] Rourke's Crockett, in contrast, exhibits none of those features. With Parrington clearly in mind, she dismissed the contention of historians that the Crockett myth was the creation of canny Whigs: "But the politicians who possessed this singular imaginative power have not been identified." In place of that view, she offered one of Davy Crockett as so generous, sincere, witty, competent, and lovable that he could not help but have enormous popular appeal. His courtship of his wife Polly is not "primitive," but rather takes place at an innocent "frolic" where the women shun "fashion's mold" in favor of more virtuous homespun.[84] Because Polly is "fair-haired, blue-eyed," and a quick dancer, Davy logically decides to marry her that evening. Interestingly, though Rourke drew her discussion of the frolic from Crockett's autobiographical *Narrative of the Life of David Crockett* and the fanciful, less historically accurate *Sketches and Eccentricities of Colonel David Crockett* (Parrington's source as well), she omitted a more worldly episode of the courtship that both those books recounted: Davy, wandering in the woods one evening, coincidentally comes across Polly, who is also lost. The two make their way to a house. "Here we staid all night," Davy announces. "I set up all night courting."[85] Whether the incident actually occurred or whether Crockett and his collaborators introduced it to illustrate Davy's prowess with women is not as important as Rourke's partial reporting: she has excluded any material that might make Parrington's version credible. Likewise, her Crockett never engages in "shiftless removals," but instead always moves on for admirable reasons: he wants his boys to "grow up in new country"; he feels his independence and self-reliance threatened by land that is "getting too much filled up."[86] As for fighting Indians, Davy does so reluctantly and only to protect whites from merciless, unprovoked attacks. The voters elect Crockett not because he buys them drinks, as he does throughout the *Narrative* and *Sketches and Eccentricities*, but because of his guilelessness, his "good nature and his story telling."[87] In sum, far from being a "sloven" and a "wastrel," Rourke's Davy Crockett is a model of middle-class virtue. Whereas Parrington called Crockett a "game-hog" and concluded that "his family must have had Gargantuan appetites to have consumed one-tenth of the meat that fell before his beloved Betsy," Rourke portrayed him as the concerned provider merely hunting to take care of his wife and children: "This meat won't last long with ten in the family."[88] On one expedition, the account of which Rourke adapted from the *Sketches*, he fells a bear, a buck, and a panther in quick succession, impressing some visiting strangers: " 'That took courage, Colonel,' cried one of the strangers admiringly. But Crockett was looking at his dogs. They were badly mauled."[89] Humane and selfless, caring nothing for praise and little for sport, the Davy Crockett in Rourke's book would be as much at home in a parlor or Sunday School as in the canebrakes. He is a domesticated Crockett who only "fills the part" of the back-woodsman at times when he "could not resist" the role.[90]

This domestication suggests that Rourke was more comfort-able with a middle-class Crockett than an "uncouth" one, that despite her assertions to the contrary her interest in creating an adequate culture sometimes required heroes who conformed to Tylor's or Eggleston's standards for civilization. It is true that Parrington's wastrel is an extreme, drawn from a reading of the *Narrative* that attributed all the unsavory elements of frontier life to Crockett and any humorous or picturesque details to his collaborator. We know, for example, that Crockett was literate and well-acquainted with the conduct of government, but in-tentionally posed as ignorant to woo poor voters.[91] Still, Rourke went to the other extreme. She used only those episodes about Crockett that made good—that is to say, harmless and conven-tionally respectable—stories. Thus, from the tales in *Sketches and Eccentricities*, she picked one emphasizing Crockett's hu-mility, in which his supporters, mistaking his opponent's carpet for a quilt on the floor, dismiss it as a "piece of pride." On the other hand, she neglected the famous anecdote immediately preceding the carpet story, which depicts the wily Crockett using the same coonskin to buy round after round of whisky for the voters. Similarly, out of the Crockett Almanacks, those compilations of fantastic stories starring Crockett that appeared in the Southwest from 1834 to 1858, she chose the appealing description of the animals' joy at the skillful hunter's death and the charming account of the way Crockett thawed out the earth and came home with sunrise in his pocket. Alternatively, she might have incorporated Crockett's boast that he could "swallow an Injun whole without choking if you butter his head and pin his ears back,"[92] or related the legend that he killed an Indian and boiled his body for a tonic to cure an ailing bear. But such stories, incompatible with the glorification of a middle-class Crockett, lay beyond the pale. "Sometimes I think there's two Davy Crocketts," Rourke has Elizabeth Crockett "sagely" remark in her book—and there were: the full man and the myth, complete with occasional racism and cruelty; and Rourke's pristine version. Franklin J. Meine noted in his introduction to a collection of Almanack materials that Rourke used them "freely" in her biography, but he did not say how freely: that, paralleling her concern to demonstrate America's propensity for literature, she drew on the Crockett sources to construct a frontier "gentleman" worthy of a "peak of achievement" critic's respect.

*Audubon* shows the same strains in Rourke's relativistic definition of culture. In her concern with depicting Audubon as a serious painter, she sometimes came close to the defensiveness for which she had rebuked Turner. "Crudeness has often been attached to the frontier as by a stereotype," she remarked, "and the notion that men had no concern there with matters of the mind has had widespread currency."[93] The activities of Audubon and his like-minded companions fortunately proved, however, that refinement was also a feature of the frontier. It is interesting that Rourke devoted so much attention not to a figure whose accomplishments were primarily "practical"—Audubon is not noted for painting birds on furniture—but to a man whose work is fit for, and indeed hangs in, art galleries. For Rourke, Audubon's cultural significance ultimately derived from his conventional artistic achievements. The same point can be made about Rourke's choice of Charles Sheeler as her exemplary "artist in the American tradition." Though she emphasized that Sheeler used the forms and subjects of the American folk heritage, she thought it important that he was schooled in Europe as well as in America, that he invited the label "artist" without debate over the definition of the term. She was not content to say that the Pennsylvania barns he painted were by themselves works of art. Rather, they needed Sheeler to make them so, using the recognized tools of paint and canvas. At the conclusion of *Charles Sheeler*, Rourke took pains to accord Sheeler's work universality, as if his epitomizing the special American configuration were not enough to make him worthy of consideration:

> Though its revelations as to American traditions in art are particularly wide, and though these must be stressed since no one else has made them, Sheeler's work remains securely placed outside these considerations. Significantly, many of those viewing it for the first time do not mention its subject matter, but try to phrase the impact which they feel in terms of emotion. There is justice in the circumstance that he is now seldom mentioned as a painter of the American scene though he has produced genuine discoveries in this direction. Rightly, his work has come to be judged in terms that are less transitory.[94]

The tendency to look to European critics despite the proclamation of their irrelevance emerges in a somewhat different way in the draft of Rourke's introduction to her multivolume study. She had planned to begin the book with a fictional sketch of a young man abroad, busy espousing to inquisitive foreigners

[95]

the belief that America stifled artistic endeavor. He is, as Rourke later pointed out, the vehicle for the early ideas of Van Wyck Brooks. Noting her character's need for an adequate culture, Rourke wondered which aesthetic alternatives would free him from the burden of our alleged materialism. She posed several possibilities: symbolism, primitivism, dadaism, surrealism. Each movement constituted, in Rourke's view, a drive to alter or break with artistic tradition. Moreover, each involved a theory developed in and applied to the European situation. If the "young man," allying himself with those movements, looked at the American past, "he [would] continue consciously to carry the inevitable incubus of European traditions and of contemporary European theory."[95] As one might expect, Rourke began her discussion of such European approaches by noting their deficiencies. Symbolism, her first example, seemed to offer a "tradition apart from the chaos of contemporary life—American life." But, citing Edmund Wilson's *Axel's Castle*, Rourke described the "dangerous and destructive" forces within symbolism—the way the movement caused its own disintegration: "the symbolists, completing their ivory towers, [had] at the same time wrought tools with which these may be levelled, since the imagination cannot be given new flexibility and freedom to remain imprisoned." Rourke's critique of symbolism turned on the movement's tendency to sabotage itself by encouraging experimentation that might lead to its own overthrow.

Given Rourke's stance toward self-conscious, theoretical artistic movements divorced from social life—and especially European movements when applied to America—her dismissal of symbolism is not surprising. But her next claim is: that the symbolist outlook was fundamentally an American one. "Mr. Wilson," Rourke wrote, "has shown Poe to have been a progenitor of this movement. . . . Poe with Hawthorne gave early expression to a personalized and sometimes wholly singular fantasy." Rourke traced an American symbolist tradition through

William James and Gertrude Stein, and concluded: "Thus with
its stress upon the inner monologue and upon the isolated individual, symbolism may be said to [form] a sequence from a
major American tradition and even in some measure to have
sprung from this, whatever the bias given to the movement by
a notable school of European writers. Our young poet, seeking
to escape the pressure of the American environment, will be
turned back to this if he cares to consider anything more than
the surfaces of symbolism. With all his doubts and his revolt
and his scorn he is tethered to one of the major American experiences."[96] Having first rejected symbolism, here Rourke re-
possessed it by noting its essential American qualities.

The rest of Rourke's introduction repeats the characterization
of European artistic movements as extreme forms of basically
American tendencies. Rourke noted the impulse toward surrealism in American humor, literature, and especially in films such
as those of Walt Disney. Moving to primitivism, Rourke declared that if "our young man decides to throw in his lot with
certain European artists who have turned to the primitive he
will of course discover that he was forestalled in this some three
hundred years ago by Thomas Morton of Merrymount and by
early American seekers for Indian scalps and by Yankee sailors
who basked on South Sea islands with brown maidens." Like
symbolism and surrealism, primitivism was fundamentally
American. So, too, Rourke next argued, was the contemporary
interest in biography. Despite the attention paid to Lytton
Strachey, there existed a strong native tradition in biography
writing, stretching from the first anonymous life of Davy Crockett through the character delineations of Edward Ellis in the
1870s and '80s to Henry Adams, the poetry of Vachel Lindsay,
and the work of Carl Sandburg on Lincoln and Lloyd Lewis on
Sherman. (For Rourke, the tradition culminated in the biographical efforts of Van Wyck Brooks, and it is at this point in
her text that she introduced the bulk of her remarks about him.)
Thus the refuge that Europe seemed to promise was merely illu-

sory—a message that would carry more force in the late 1930s with the spread of fascism abroad. Turning to Europe was no escape from America; in so doing, Rourke wrote, "our young man [would] be tripped and caught by the snares of a native tradition. . . ."[97]

Yet by pointing out the American strain within them, Rourke in effect embraced the very European movements she set out to reject. It is as if she were saying, first, that such movements had no value, and then hedging by adding, "And, anyway, even if they do have value, they are essentially American." As a result, she could legitimize American culture by establishing its crucial relationship to European art. If European aesthetic developments were really American at base, then America's achievements did meet the expectations of those who measured culture only in terms of the fine arts. We did not need to defend furniture as a valid cultural attainment when we could argue that lofty theories about literature and painting, remote from the "practical" arts, belonged to us as well. Claiming European artistic developments for the American side was a variation on Rourke's tendency—manifest in her treatment of literature, of "poetry" in *American Humor*, and of Crockett, Audubon, and Sheeler—to conform to imported criteria all the while she was disavowing them.

Rourke's model of cultural development is thus ridden with a tension between two sets of expectations. In her simultaneous rejection and adoption of foreign standards, she exhibited all the characteristic coloration of the provincial, following (as she might have said) in a long-established tradition. She had noted the same discontinuity in *American Humor*. "The new American rejoinder," she said of the Yankee response to British criticism in the colonial period, "was double: first that all refinements might be found at home; then that they didn't matter." She was attuned to the fact that "the noisy assertion of American superiority suggested an underlying doubt that this superiority existed."[98] Nevertheless, she herself was similarly at once imitative and heedless of comparisons, cowering and boastful. Her uneasy glances in opposite directions indicate that she was not always convinced by her own rebuttal to the early Brooks's attack on American life; she felt the force of Brooks's critique even while refuting it.

For though Rourke understood, as Brooks did not, that America's distinctive culture originated in the achievements of the folk, it was not so clear precisely how those folk traditions would engender an organic, unified society. Brooks, even when he lauded the American past, never abandoned his belief that social change would proceed from a "high" art devoted to a criticism of life.[99] Writers who lacked that perspective, Brooks thought, were guilty of the "apotheosis of the low-brow." Rourke was not nearly as explicit or sophisticated about the political uses of culture as Brooks was, but, having read him, may well have had the troubling sense that a James novel provided more meaningful values "for men to live by," more insight into the possibilities for human fulfillment, than a Crockett Almanack. Although her commitment to relativism was the dominant element in her theory of cultural development, the ambiguities in her approach strategically allowed her to take account of that contingency.

Nor did Rourke's detection of the importance of the folk automatically solve the problem of the place of the artist and critic in modern America: small comfort that movements like symbolism had a native cast if they were basically superfluous. It was only when Rourke added to her definition of culture the particular achievement of the American folk—a tradition of mythmaking—that the connections the nation's intellectuals had long sought came into view.

# 4

## M Y T H

"We are a nation of myth makers," Constance Rourke wrote as the opening sentence of an incomplete, undated essay on American theatricals, parts of which appeared in different form in *The Roots of American Culture.* "We have created a great store of myths and legends," she added, "whose richness we hardly know and have hardly touched. Perhaps no country has created so many mythological figures in so short a time. . . . We have indeed a whole mythology—a very rich mythology, which we are just beginning to explore."[1] Though she never defined myth precisely, the presentation of evidence supporting her characterization of the American as mythmaker was one of the central tasks of Rourke's work. She not only found in American myths the "spiritual experience" that Brooks had pronounced absent; she took from its gathered mythology the assurance that America's art and culture rested on a secure foundation. In the end, her discovery of native myths furnished Rourke a way of joining a divided society and lent a new, saving dimension to the role of the critic in American life.

Rourke's preoccupation with myth pervades *American Humor.* In addition to her portrait of the "comic trio," Rourke included as part of her analysis of the national character such remarks as:

Popular declamation of the [18]30's and '40's has often been considered as bombast when it should be taken as comic mythology.

If it [the burlesque of the 1840s and '50s] punctured romantic feeling, it kept a breathless comic emotion of its own. Invading current fantasies, it employed fantastical forms. Indian myths might traipse across the stage in grotesque and balloonlike guises, but they only became mythical again with a broader and livelier look.

The accumulated American myth....

These mythical figures partook of the primitive....

As though comic myth-making were a native habit, formed early....[2]

References to legend, fable, and epic, which all strengthened Rourke's rebuttal to the early Brooks, fill the book as well.

Rourke saw her demonstration of the American propensity for myth as a central argument of *American Humor*, and one of that work's contributions to scholarship. When, in an allegedly original *Scribner's* article in 1936 on "Humor and America," Max Eastman asserted that American literature derived from the nation's mythological tales, Rourke wrote him with justifiable anger: "I believe that I am right in saying that there was no basis for this conclusion until I had gathered together the research which underlies my first five chapters."[3] His book from which the article was drawn, *Enjoyment of Laughter* (1936), credited her influence, but Rourke never got over her sense that Eastman had pirated her findings. In a warmer exchange with

Bernard DeVoto, she announced: "I feel that the outlining of the element of fantasy as continuous in American humor is something specially my own. So far as I know this has not been done before. . . . I believe that even the use of the word "fantasy" in relation to American humor is entirely my own. As a rule I am not very strong on acknowledgments, but the drawing together of these materials and the tracing of a sequence required so much pioneering, first hand effort, that I am inclined that way at this point."[4]

Rourke's comment to DeVoto appeared in a letter she wrote him about his proposed discussion of *American Humor* in *Mark Twain's America.* In the spring of 1932, he had informed Rourke that he was planning to dispute in a footnote what he saw as her undue emphasis on fantasy at the expense of realism. The draft of his remarks touched off a long and revealing correspondence. What made frontier humor funny, DeVoto told Rourke, was the recognition of familiar individuals and scenes. Even the tall tale, he maintained, functioned as a vehicle for the "realistic portrayal of character." Therefore, though he respected and admired her book, he felt compelled to insist: "That is why I must dissent from the basic argument in Miss Constance Rourke's 'American Humor'. . . . [S]he asserts that the mythic element is the basis of all American humor—that American humor is unrealistic in that it deals with abstracted, conventionalized types derived from fantasy. . . . There were a vast number of characteristic themes but I cannot see that the individual treatments of them are anti-realistic. . . . In my opinion, an overwhelming weight of evidence contradicts Miss Rourke's thesis."[5] DeVoto modified that statement considerably in light of Rourke's reply, in which she took issue with his view that she had called American humor "anti-realistic." On the contrary, Rourke claimed, she had pointed out the faithfulness of our humor to observable detail. But, she countered, "It seems to me that the transition into fantasy was typically made." "I do honestly feel," she concluded, "that the realistic element is not the dominant one in Mark Twain."[6] Rather, Twain and others had drawn not highly differentiated figures but impersonal, generalized sketches divorced from specific historical circumstances—sketches that "belonged to fantasy rather than to actuality."[7]

This controversy is hard to arbitrate. DeVoto and Rourke each recognized that fantasy and realism coexisted in American humor and that they differed only about which was the stronger element. In the face of certain statements in *American Humor*, it is difficult to construe Rourke's distinction between "unrealistic" and "anti-realistic"—a distinction DeVoto did not make—as anything but a way to dodge his criticism. For example, her scattered phrases "full of circumstance" and "faithful drawing," which she said were among those indicating realism, pale beside a pronouncement like this one: "It was not a realistic spirit that was abroad. The world of burlesque was still the familiar native world of phantasmagoria."[8] On the other hand, on some subjects Rourke knew more than DeVoto did. She reminded him that Yankee humor was characteristically quiet, that words such as "slantendicular" and "catawampously" had no place in New England speech, that, even granting his view of frontier tales, he was leaving the theater, oratory, and the minstrel out of account.[9] In the end, as both Rourke and DeVoto realized, the debate between them was a standoff. But their exchange raises interesting questions. If the proposition that Americans were mythmakers required elaborate proof, did Rourke's efforts to amass such proof govern, in addition to *American Humor*, her other writings on behalf of a "usable past"? And if the primacy of myth was a matter of interpretation, what factors explain her attraction to that point of view?

Part of the answer to the first question appears in Rourke's plan for the opening chapter of her "History of American Culture." There she outlined a lengthy section on Hakluyt's *Voy-*

*ages* that emphasized the place of those narratives in the literature of legend. Although Rourke recognized the practical aspect
of the *Voyages*—"they were written for the benefit of traders
and explorers who roamed the seas on behalf of the great mer-
cantile houses"[10]—she found them pervaded by myth. Sometimes they centered on the great wealth that lay in store for
adventurers to the New World; Rourke acknowledged that
myths could operate in the service of "greed." Other tales developed, however, around the balmy climate or weird features
of the unexplored continent. For Rourke, Hakluyt provided
proof that America was born in a mythic vision. By electing to
begin her history with a discussion of the *Voyages*, Rourke was
implicitly asserting the presence of the mythmaking habit in
America from the very start. Her reading of the early maps of
explorers substantiated that view. In notes that are unfortunately only richly suggestive, she described maps as symbols, as
imaginative forms. Though they were functional as tools for
exploration, Rourke saw them also as graphic art, containing
not merely realism but also fantastic elements like drawings of
sea monsters. For Rourke, the map was an instrument for the
introduction of the "legendary temper" to America—a temper
that, she contended, had remained a permanent part of the
national character.[11]

Subsequent passages in "American Culture" reiterate the
mythmaking tendencies Rourke detected in our earliest stages.
The conclusion of her lengthy, theoretical introduction general-
izes about our "special form of myth-making interspersed with
criticism." "Myth was created in its clearest forms," she wrote,
"in the perennial Yankee who first appeared (so far as we
know) in *The Contrast*, who meandered his witty way down the
years and came into considerable stature in *The Connecticut
Yankee*: the form of Mark Twain's skit is that of the myth, the
fable, the allegory. Myth is no less present in the highly intellectual social scrutiny of Henry Adams."[12] In the substance

of the text itself, Rourke applied the term "myth" variously to the literature of Washington Irving, the development of folk art, and the landscape painting of the Hudson River School, to take only a few examples. The sections on lumberjacks and cowboys demonstrate the way in which those craftsmen, as Rourke thought they were, became the subject for myth and legend. In fact, taken as a whole, Rourke's "History of American Culture," her most ambitious undertaking, may be seen as a record of and a tribute to the wide-ranging American inclination toward myth.

Rourke had documented this tendency on a smaller scale in her earlier articles and biographical studies. Her *New Republic* piece on Paul Bunyon marked the first analysis of Bunyon as a mythical creation. The figures she discussed in *Trumpets of Jubilee* sometimes captured public attention to the extent that they became legendary. Rourke concluded the book with this comment on P. T. Barnum: "Fittingly enough, he has become a myth. His history grows into fable, mixed with the caprices of the time—not the great fable, perhaps, but a portion of what might be called the American legend."[13] More important, *Troupers of the Gold Coast*, *Davy Crockett*, and *Audubon* each dealt with an object of extensive mythmaking. In fact, as she explained in Stanley Kunitz's and Howard Haycraft's *Twentieth Century Authors*, Rourke chose her subjects for biography not merely because they were fascinating personalities but precisely because they stimulated the popular imagination.[14]

Thus in her treatment of Lotta Crabtree, for example, Rourke did not merely recount the story of the actress's life. Rather, she highlighted the way in which "Lotta," Lola Montez, and others attached to the theater of the California gold rush period became protagonists in a body of colorful tales. She wrote of Lola Montez, "Legend enveloped that strong-fibered personality."[15] As interested in the myths constructed around Montez as in the facts of her biography, Rourke intertwined historically accurate accounts of her appearance with a catalog of her fanciful attributes:

Most often she has been described as having black hair and black eyes; but her hair, which curled almost childishly back from her face, was bronzed with dark shadows, her eyes were blue. She was called a "tigress," "a modern Amazon," and was said to have the wit of a pot-house, with the carriage of a duchess; yet she could romp with children and look like one of them. She could also take on the aspect of a blue-stocking, offering the contents of her amazing memory with a pedantic air. . . . She was often said to be the daughter of Lord Byron, and perhaps invented the notion. What was she truly?[16]

Rourke's question reflects her concern with more than the details of Lola Montez's character; she took the Montez legends as further proof of a canon of American mythical figures. Similarly, she spent several pages at the end of the book recounting the stories concocted about Lotta Crabtree after her death. While still alive, "Lotta" had been the object of mythmaking: "The newspapers had carried stories of romance about her. . . ."[17] With the contest over her will, legends grew even more rife: one woman, claiming that she was Crabtree's daughter, offered an intricate, melodramatic tale of secret marriage and abandonment. For many people looking back on the gold rush days (a time, Rourke remarked, "full of elegance and fantasy"), Crabtree "seemed the positive embodiment of a glittering era."[18] Therein lay her appeal for Rourke: she was a product of and a credit to the active American imagination. Kenneth Lynn (who has so persuasively demonstrated Rourke's achievements) has disparaged *Troupers of the Gold Coast,* concluding that Rourke's "enthusiasm for the color and zip of American popular taste seemed to be overwhelming her capacity to judge both its merit and its significance."[19] Yet for Rourke it was precisely by the proportion of "color and zip" that "merit" and "significance" ought to be measured.

The same delight in discovering a figure of mythic proportions accounts for Rourke's treatment of John J. Audubon. Audubon's career ably served several of Rourke's purposes simultaneously, among them her desire to locate an artist on a frontier supposedly barren of cultural achievements. But, in addition, Audubon furnished another example of the American propensity toward myth. Of mysterious origin and strange habits—he would disappear into unknown regions of wilderness and emerge some time later with sketches of strange beasts—he offered rich material for the mythmaker. Rourke's attention to the popular legend that Audubon was really the lost French Dauphin is not so much a mark of her "gullibility," as Stanley Hyman would have it,[20] as the result of her interest in displaying Audubon's mythic proportions. The "Dauphin" legend secured Audubon's place in the annals of American mythology, and implicitly celebrated the American mythmaking capacity.

Rourke's interest in documenting a native habit of mythologizing is even plainer in *Davy Crockett*. Hyman called this book "Miss Rourke's only thorough failure": "the book is a jumble of the real Crockett and the legend; a sequence of dramatized anecdotes, including Crockett's children speaking 'tall talk' around the house, strung-together Crockett fables from the *Almanacs*, with little interest in the real man and his significance."[21] The historian James B. Shackford found the intertwining of biographical detail and apocryphal story so extensive as to render Rourke's account "relatively useless."[22] Those descriptions are partly accurate: the book lacks clear demarcation of fact and fantasy. But Rourke's blurring of myth and reality was functional, for her purpose was to heighten and clarify Crockett's position in the realm of imagination, not politics. She was less interested in "the real man and his significance" than in his transformation into a folk hero, and a middle-class one at that—

or rather, it was in the transformation that she located Crockett's true significance. Hence, myth and historical anecdote shade into one another:

> Before this last adventure is traced another story about
> Davy Crockett must be told—a tale that has a gala
> touch of light opera, yet is singularly life-like. This
> appeared in "Col. Crockett's Exploits and Adventures
> in Texas," which was published early in the summer
> of 1836. The book was said to be based on a diary of his
> journey, kept by Crockett. A pattern of evidence may
> yet be woven to prove that it had a basis in fact. In the
> main story Crockett often speaks as he might have
> spoken. Passages of his journey are lighted that other-
> wise remain dim. The principal adventures might
> have occurred. The tale was—and remains—part of
> the spreading Crockett legend; it is part of the Texas
> legend, and so must have a place in this narrative.[23]

This passage introduces the story of Crockett's travels to Texas with a bee hunter and other "strange companions." Shackford, citing clear proof that a hack newspaperman named Richard Penn Smith wrote the *Texas Exploits*, chided Rourke for refusing to draw the same conclusion; she had the evidence, and "saw but refused to believe."[24] Yet Rourke's unwillingness to diminish the Crockett myth is understandable, for her intention in *Davy Crockett*, as she remarked in a draft of her statement for *Twentieth Century Authors*, was to portray "a folk figure, bringing together for the first time a body of legend which had developed in the Crockett almanacs of 1834–58, as well as in oral legend in Kentucky, Tennessee, and in the Ozarks."[25] With respect to that goal, she could hardly be said to have failed.

    A survey of Rourke's writing, then, reveals a persistent theme: "we are a nation of myth makers." Lola Montez is Byron's daughter, Audubon is the Dauphin, Crockett carried "sunrise in his pocket," Paul Bunyon used boulders for marbles. These stories indicated both a characteristic habit of mind and a rich tradition, dominating our cultural heritage. But our mythmaking patterns were neither obvious nor readily accessible. They needed to be uncovered, and Rourke's decision to set herself the task of excavating our myths provides a further clue to the nature of her search for a "usable past." The explanation for Rourke's attraction to myth requires examination of her understanding —or, better, her unconsciously deliberate misunderstanding— of the relationship between myth, art, and society.

Among the major sources for Rourke's conception of myth were the writings of Herder, whose work had licensed her to count folk art as an achievement of American culture. For Herder, myth, in Richard Chase's phrase, was "the folk spirit speaking."[26] Without myth, there could be no art, and art, as Gene Bluestein has noted, was Herder's primary concern: "His work was permeated by one overriding conception, namely, to discover the source for the creation of a distinctly German literary tradition. [He identified] that source in the folk traditions of the common people. . . ."[27] Rourke's affinity with Herder's purpose is striking. Working backward from Herder's premise that the absence of myth spelled doom for the fine arts, Rourke set out to discover a native mythology in order to guarantee the future of American culture. Though Herder did not imply that the presence of myth necessarily insured the development of art, she tended toward that view. At least she hoped such a sequence was inevitable, and devoted herself to providing the requisite mythic base.

Rourke's intellectual encounter with a later group of writers on myth—the so-called Cambridge School of classicists— strengthened her understanding that the fine arts were contingent upon the existence of a rich tradition of mythmaking. The Cambridge School—dominated by Sir James G. Frazer, ex-

panded in the work of Andrew Lang, E. S. Hartland, Gilbert
Murray, F. M. Cornford, and others—exerted greatest influence
on Rourke through the books of Jane Ellen Harrison. Yet whereas Harrison is the only member of the group whose work Rourke
cited directly, she was aware of several other studies along similar lines. Stanley Hyman's remark in *The Armed Vision* that
Harrison was the only member of the Cambridge School "with
whose work Miss Rourke seems to have been familiar" (an assumption that led him to announce that she might have done
better "with another background and a great deal more learning")[28] is simply inaccurate: Rourke's library contained at least
three books by Andrew Lang and ten, counting several transla-
tions, by Gilbert Murray.[29] Nevertheless, Harrison's *Ancient
Art and Ritual* (1913) provides sufficient indication of the impact of the Cambridge School upon Rourke.

Harrison's purpose was to demonstrate that ritual, and the
myths contrived to explain it, were, in her words, "rudimentary
art." For instance, Harrison argued, the drama developed out
of the Greek fertility dance, or *dromenon*, once the religious
faith and desire for immediate action accompanying the dance
had disappeared. Two aspects of Harrison's theory held special
appeal for Rourke: her depiction of mythmaking as a communal
enterprise and her understanding, as in Herder's view, of myth
as the precursor of art. The festivals that Harrison discussed occurred on dates "of importance to the food-supply of the community, in summer, in winter, at the coming of the annual
rains, or the regular rising of a river."[30] Given the social origins
of ritual, and hence of all art, the artist emerges not as Brooks's
isolated individual but as one who draws sanction and sustenance from the wider community.

*American Humor* reveals prominent traces of Harrison's
ideas. Most suggestive is Rourke's explicit reference to early
Greek religious rituals in her discussion of American revival
meetings:

Once again personal emotion was submerged in a
coarse and crescent patterning of communal emotion;
and the flight was toward legend. Around the simple
outline of the divine comedy these people continually
wove innumerable small new fables and beliefs. Once
again, too, the movement was toward the theater. The
orgiastic forest revivals with their pagan spirit and
savage manifestations bore a not altogether distant resemblance to the Eleusinarian mysteries out of which
the Greek drama had developed. A fantastic basic ritual was often present in later cults, such as has been
a prelude to the theater or the drama among primitive
peoples. A minor religious theater could have been
drawn from the celebration of almost any one of these
new sects. All their modes were outward, rhapsodic,
declamatory, full of song, verging upon the dance,
adorned with symbolic costume. . . .[31]

This passage owes a large debt to *Ancient Art and Ritual.* Com-
pare, for example, Rourke's emphasis on collective emotion and
the social character of ritual (its "outward" quality) with Harrison's remark that "it is not [primitive man's] private and personal emotions that tend to become ritual, but those that are
public, felt and expressed officially, that is, by the whole tribe
or community."[32] Rourke's focus upon the primitive or pagan
element in revival meetings—and in this passage her reference
to Greek drama—reflect a desire to discover an American counterpart of Greek cultural forms. Similarly, many elements of
Harrison's characterization of Greek dances invade Rourke's
discussion of black minstrelsy: the stress on ritual as communal
activity, the notion of the redirection of individual emotion, the
interest in the minstrel performance as primitive or ritualistic.
For example, she traced the "walkaround," the climactic dance
of the minstrel show, back to "the communal dancing of the

African."[33] A passage that concludes by arguing for the legendary quality attending the Negro character in minstrelsy—his emergence as a "type" rather than a closely delineated individual—begins:

> Primitive elements were roughly patterned in minstrelsy. Its songs, its dances, its patter, were soon set within a ritual which grew more and more fixed, like some rude ceremonial. Endmen and interlocutors spun out their talk with an air of improvisation, but this free talk and song occupied an inalienable place in the procedure. In the dancing a strong individualism appeared, and the single dancer might step out of the whole pattern; the jig dancer might perform his feats on a peck measure, and dancers might be matched against each other with high careerings which belonged to each alone: but these excursions were caught within the broad effect. Beneath them all ran the deep insurgence of Negro choruses that flowed into minstrelsy for many years, even after its ritual grew stereotyped and other elements were added; and the choral dancing of the walkaround made a resonant primitive groundwork.
>
> Within this ritualistic design certain Negro characters were permanently limned. . . .
> [Jim Crow, Zip Coon, Dan Tucker] all revealed the Negro character: yet they showed that greater outline and more abstract drawing which reveals the world of legend.[34]

When this passage is set against a section of *Ancient Art and Ritual* concerning the process by which actual persons became the basis for abstract personification, Rourke's affinity with Harrison becomes clear:

. . . from many actual men and women decked with leaves, or trees dressed up as men and women, arises *the* Tree Spirit, *the* Vegetation Spirit, *the* Death.

At the back, then, of the fact of personification lies the fact that the emotion is felt collectively, the rite is performed by a band or chorus who dance together *with a common leader.* Round that leader the emotion centres. When there is an act of Carrying-out or Bringing-in he either is himself the puppet or he carries it. Emotion is of the whole band; drama doing tends to focus on the leader. This leader, this focus is then remembered, thought of, imaged; from being *per*ceived year by year he is finally *con*ceived. . . .

Had there been no periodic festivals, personification might long have halted. But it is easy to see that a recurrent *per*ception helps to form a permanent abstract *con*ception. The different actual recurrent May Kings and "Deaths," *because they recur*, get a sort of permanent life of their own and become beings apart.[35]

The May King in the Greek ritual dance is akin to the interlocutor or solo jig dancer in the minstrel show: both express collective emotion and so owe their force to the group they represent; both turn into abstract types rather than individual personalities; both persist despite the passage of time; both ultimately belong to the realm of legend. From the attributes Rourke ascribed to the interlocutor one can readily deduce the antithetical terms in which Brooks criticized American society —its lack of social unity, its inability to move beyond the concrete demands of the business world, and, again, its absence of tradition and "spiritual experience." Rourke's reading of Harrison afforded her a striking refutation of all those charges.

Harrison's theory also provided Rourke with a way of defending America even if, as she sometimes seems to have suspected, Brooks were correct. The view of myth as originating in primitive ritual allowed her to make an additional, important claim: that America was a nascent culture. Like the ancient Greeks, we possessed all the mythic material on which artistic achievements were based. Rourke wrote in "American Art: A Possible Future": "Through [our folklore] our early fantasies and mythologies are coming back to us, showing the secure beginnings of a native poetry and a native language."[36] But the presence in America of forms similar to Greek ritual signified that it was too early to demand completions. As Rourke remarked after noting that Americans were mythmakers, "This is only to say that we are a young people, with a riotous imagination. All peoples in their youth invent mythologies."[37] Rourke's reference to "all peoples"—an assertion that America is not unique—runs directly counter to her argument, drawn from Ruth Benedict, that we had our own special "pattern of culture." Rather, in her characterization of Americans as "young," Rourke worked from Frazer's and Harrison's evolutionary model of cultural development, without perceiving that it was exactly the model that Benedict and other followers of Boas rejected. Despite her statements to the contrary elsewhere, Rourke's conception of myth as the primitive basis for art betrays a concern with meeting European standards and represents a concession to Brooks: our youth excused our inferior efforts. In mythmaking, we were only taking the first step that all cultures must take, and, with patience, we might ultimately rival the Greeks.

Yet Rourke did not limit her use of the term "myth" to Herder's and Harrison's sense of "primitive, necessary, universal foundation for culture." Sometimes Rourke discussed mythmaking as if that activity constituted not the basis for art, but rather art itself. Early in *American Humor*, Rourke repeated Henri Bergson's formulation of the origins of the comic: it " 'comes into being just when society and the individual, freed from the worry of self-preservation, begin to regard themselves as works of art.' " "With his triumphs fresh and his mind noticeably free," Rourke added, "by 1815 the American seemed to regard himself as a work of art, and began that embellished self-portraiture which nations as well as individuals may undertake."[38] Rourke's characterization, following Bergson, of the mythic Yankee, backwoodsman, and minstrel as artistic achievements was as effective a rejoinder to Brooks as the idea that we were a nascent culture. Americans were unique. In a few brief years of national life, without a long period of primitive, pre-artistic expression, they had managed to create a special aesthetic form. This view did accord with Benedict's theory. Margaret Mead's comment that Benedict "saw primitive cultures as in themselves works of art to be preserved for the world"[39] could describe equally well Rourke's attitude toward the American's creation of mythical figures. Benedict's model furnished the relativistic perspective from which mythmaking could be judged as significant as painting, while her nonevolutionary approach admitted the possibility that by 1815 the young nation had already produced its own art.

Rourke's double view of America as both primitive and specially advanced, a view informed by two quite different conceptions of myth, exactly parallels her provincial stance toward a literary ideal. By absolving a "young people" of its obligations to meet European expectations of culture, she implicitly adhered to imported standards. By proclaiming the mythmaking American's early, unique triumph as artist, however, she dismissed those standards as irrelevant.

In her view of mythmaking as itself a type of art, Rourke may well have owed a debt to writers who looked upon myth not as primitive activity eventually outgrown, but rather as the persistent, fundamental dimension of modern literature. Some even went so far as to equate myth and art.[40] For example, William Troy, a friend of Rourke's and a reviewer for the *Nation* throughout the 1930s, wrote about such figures as Joyce and Lawrence in terms of the patterns of myth their work embodied. For Troy, who was heavily influenced by Jung and Frazer, myth offered the only salvation of culture. "In a regenerated Myth alone," he wrote in 1938, "we may hope to find a beckoning image of the successful alliance of the twin virtues of love and justice."[41] Elsewhere, Troy noted, "conscious preoccupation with the myth has never been so widespread and intense as [it is] at the moment. . . ."[42] He was not alone in that perception. The existence of a movement committed to the exploration of myth in literature is most easily documented by the statements of its opponents. Philip Rahv, writing in 1953 but reflecting back on a long period of "myth criticism," referred to "present-day mythomania" and declared that the advocates of myth kept arguing for its "seminal uses" in the face of opponents stressing its "regressive implications."[43]

The presence on the critical sense of scholars bent on identifying the mythic probably enriched Rourke's own interest in the subject. Yet her failure to distinguish between myth as art and myth as the product of primitive ritual is a sign that she herself did not participate in the debates Rahv described. Rourke occupied a similar relationship to the attempts of anthropologists throughout the 1920s and '30s to clarify the nature of myth in primitive society. From 1925 to 1940, the period of Ruth Benedict's editorship, every volume of the *Journal of American Folklore* carried at least one article or review on the myths or legends of a particular cultural group. Benedict published her own *Zuni Mythology* in 1935; as her friend, Rourke was almost surely aware of the book. She may also have known the work of Bronislaw Malinowski, whose reference in "Myth in Primitive Psychology" (1926) to the "incredible mythological controversy"[44] then engaging a wide range of social scientists indicates a charged atmosphere surrounding attention to myth. But Rourke, though probably more attuned to the mythic because of such controversy, nevertheless stood outside it. She used the term "myth" naïvely.

Yet Rourke's imprecision served her well. It allowed her to discover everywhere in the American past doubly strong evidence of a condition Herder, Harrison, "myth critics," and anthropologists all associated with mythmaking: a unified society. That discovery—a direct challenge to Brooks's depiction of a divided America—carried important, positive consequences for the development of art, for the role of the artist, and for the spiritual well-being of the whole culture.

However she defined the term, Rourke's acquaintance with writers on myth had taught her that it sprang from the needs of the community as a whole. Hence her references to myth and mythmaking were closely interwoven with remarks about the social character of American culture. Rourke's repeated use of words like "collective," "communal," and "social" were partially meant to counter the description of American civilization as irredeemably individualistic; such language worked against the claim that we were incapable of dealing with anything beyond the concrete, single, material. But that emphasis was also intended to signify the existence of conditions that had already generated myth, and that guaranteed the development of art.

The social element in American life is a pervasive theme in the notes for Rourke's "History of American Culture." For example, her sketches for a survey of differences among areas like the Spanish Southwest, New England, and Virginia in the colonial era all end with the vague but suggestive instruction to "test" each list of regional characteristics "by communal elements." She announced the theme of the section covering the years between 1830 and 1860 as the "rise of the legendary temper through communal forms." She had planned a full discussion of communitarian experiments like Brook Farm and the Shaker settlements, assigning to the spirit of perfectionism that dominated such efforts an interest in the "whole aspect of life" rather than merely in the individual. Her outline for a treatment of reform movements of the time includes the note "Social elements throughout" as a reminder of her intended focus.[45] The general plan for the section on the period from 1860 to 1910 projects the "underlying idea" as "the social theme, the typical, the broadly social expression" and contains as guidelines such phrases as "society . . . the type . . . ways of social living . . . not as yet the closely drawn individual for all the emphasis upon the 'I' who was after all the generic 'I.' " A fragment on the place of women in the same period concludes with the phrase "note the social elements."[46] Those directives clearly reflect the legacy of "social criticism"; they all extend Laura Wylie's classroom method to the study of America.

In *American Humor*, as in the draft for "American Culture," Rourke often linked references to communal or social properties with mention of legend, myth, or the "type." Consider, again, this sentence: "Once again personal emotion was submerged in a coarse and crescent patterning of communal emotion; and the flight was toward legend."[47] The import of that juxtaposition was reassuringly double-edged. It implied, first, that we had been sufficiently united to permit legend to arise. But it also suggested that where legend appeared, a coherent society must exist. Rourke took the latter tack in her treatment of Lincoln, which she based in part on Lloyd Lewis's *Myths After Lincoln* (1929). Noting the popularity of anecdotes about Lincoln after his death—the way he became a center of folk expression—Rourke located a resurgence of the American disposition toward collective exercise of the imagination in an age when one might least expect it: the turbulent post-Civil War era. She offered a reading of the 1860s and '70s that, as she herself pointed out, contradicted the prevalent view of the period as a time when "cultural forces were in abeyance," when cleavages ran deep and economic changes produced turmoil and disruption. The current view among historians, Rourke observed, was to stress the achievement of economic reformers like Henry George "as all that can be salvaged out of the confusion and noise of a rising industrial civilization." Instead, Rourke salvaged a great deal more: she found in the existence of "myths after Lincoln" evidence of a unified America. The same was true of the development of songs and stories about the Quantrill gang and other

Western figures, or, on the darker side, the growth of the pag-
eantry and ritual of the Ku Klux Klan. Those expressions,
Rourke planned to emphasize, arose "in small towns, country
places . . . ," and incorporated themes typically belonging to
folk forms: "death, resurrection, [a] messiah. . . ." Without denying the power of industrialism in the post-Civil War period,
Rourke discovered in this outcropping of the "legendary, myth,
primitive poetry, [and] folk song" "broad continuances" related less to the urban than to the rural scene: "Undoubtedly
this industrialism was a potent factor during this period . . . undoubtedly we saw the rise of the city. . . . [But] there were other
industries in less mechanized forms . . . which gave rise to continuances in expression . . . fresh forms. . . . Broad dominances
still of the open country, untouched land, what men did with
it . . . earlier strain in life, labor, expression, culture continued,
renewed, transformed. . . ."[48] Rourke's detection of "continuances" signified a basic unity with the past, a unity created and
perpetuated by the spread of myth and legend in a period often
thought of as fragmented. But whether, as in this example,
myth revealed the absence of divisions, or, as elsewhere, coherence portended myth, for Rourke the presence of both throughout the history of American culture boded well for the future
of art.

Moreover, originating in a unified society, myth promised to
foster even stronger social bonds. Rourke had recognized the
integrative aspects of myth in *American Humor*. Noting the
way in which Mark Twain had used the fantasies of the Yankee,
Californian, and backwoodsman, giving his work "nation-wide
scope," she added: "The wide reach may be unimportant for
judgments of intrinsic quality, but its significance may be great
among a people seeking the illusive goal of unity and the
resting-place of a tradition."[49] Elsewhere she observed: "Laughter created ease, and even more, a sense of unity, among a people who were not yet a nation and who were seldom joined in
stable communities. These mythical figures partook of the prim-

itive; and for a people whose life was still unformed, a searching out of primitive concepts was an inevitable and stirring pursuit, uncovering common purposes and directions."[50] Finally, summarizing the nature of American humor, she wrote, "Its objective—the unconscious objective of a disunited people—has seemed to be that of creating fresh bonds, a new unity, the semblance of a society and the rounded completion of an American type."[51] In fact, in his critique of *American Humor*, Bernard DeVoto found Rourke "in danger of finding too much unity" in her characterization of native humor as fantasy, and guilty of "pushing [her] original folk motif so far that it may discount individual originality and saltation."[52] Though Rourke rightly denied the specific charge, claiming that she had differentiated among varieties of humor, DeVoto had indeed sensed an impulse in her that a broad concept of myth could satisfy.

But myth could accomplish even more: it could supply that crucial link between the folk and the artist in danger of alienation from society. A sense of participation in socially created myths could break the spell of isolation from the dominant culture, substituting a share in the collective imagination for the lonely confines of personality. Rourke incorporated into her reassuring concept of the connections among myth, artist, and society T. S. Eliot's idea of the function of tradition. For Rourke the terms "myth" and "tradition" shaded into one another, because she saw the creation and perpetuation of myths as the American's principal traditional activity. At the end of *American Humor*, she quoted directly from Eliot's "Tradition and the Individual Talent":

> The writer must know, as Eliot has said, "the mind of his own country—a mind which he learns in time to be much more important than his own private mind." ... The difficult task of discovering and diffusing the materials of the American tradition—many of them still buried—belongs for the most part to criticism;

the artist will steep himself in the gathered light. In the end he may use native sources as a point of radical departure; he may seldom be intent upon early materials; but he will discover a relationship with the many streams of native character and feeling. The single writer—the single production—will no longer stand solitary or aggressive but within a natural sequence.[53]

Though Rourke knew, with Eliot, that the future of art depended on the existence of a strong tradition, in this passage she emphasized the "relationship" that tradition constructed between the potentially isolated artist and "his own country" by demanding, in Eliot's phrase, the "continual extinction of personality."[54] No image better captures the hope the discovery of a tradition of mythmaking offered Rourke than her phrase "the artist will steep himself in the gathered light"; it promised warmth, abundance, clarity, immersion, illumination of place and direction.

There was nothing in this comforting embrace that gave the artist the sort of social responsibility Arnold and Brooks wanted him to exercise. But Rourke's reference to the critic suggested, at least in the abstract, how he might assume that responsibility. For if he accorded myths the power to insure art and social coherence, he could also charge himself with the important obligation of explicating and disseminating them to a culture dependent on them for sustenance. That view rescued the critic from the position of expendable, ineffectual commentator on someone else's work and awarded him an indispensable function—one that Rourke's Progressive training had inclined her to welcome. The discovery of myth, with its ramifications for society, was the key to the transformation of criticism into social service: by assembling myths in proper perspective so that they fostered the highest aesthetic and human values, the critic—and the critic alone—could satisfy the need for an adequate culture. In the most explicit, albeit fragmentary, reference Rourke made to Brooks's sense of disunities within American life, she wrote in her notes, "Two levels, highbrow, lowbrow, to bring them together," followed by the phrase "what a set of writers could do."[55] Because her remark falls in a section of "A History of American Culture" calling for nonacademic explorations of native traditions, the "set of writers" Rourke had in mind would seem to have consisted of critics like herself. That the explication of our myths promised not "comfort" or "solace" but long and difficult effort—"a concerted archaeology"[56] requiring self-less dedication—glorified the role of the critic all the more. It is interesting, along these lines, to look more closely at the passage that was to precede Rourke's acknowledgments in "American Culture": "Those of us who have embarked upon these controversial subjects in this generation almost constitute a guild; we often do not know each other except by our writings, yet we make a coterie." The words "guild" and "coterie" endow Rourke's critical efforts with a stature and dignity that the average American, if he knew of her activities at all, would probably not confer upon them. Her words reflect the hope, if not the fact, that she occupied a distinct and exclusive place in American life.

Finally, Rourke's own history suggests that writing about myth may have earned her another sort of distinction and exclusivity. Her description in her letter to her mother of "something wild" and mystical inside her are signs of a personal involvement in mythmaking, an involvement she brought to bear on her subject matter. As an expert in fantasy in her own right, she was predisposed to find it in the national character at large, even where, if one believes DeVoto, it might not exist. A remark she made in an effort to convince DeVoto that the heroes of tall tales were types—"there are too many things one doesn't know about them and never could know from the sketches"—strikingly resembles the observation that she herself was "impossible ever to know completely."[57] Emotion seldom crept through this assumed disguise,"[58] she said of the "comic trio's" propensity for self-consciousness and introspection, for the "inward turn," but the same could be said of her similarly self-conscious behavior as she established connections among her fellow critics. The mask she ascribed to the Yankee, backwoodsman, and minstrel was one she also wore and valued. For mythmaking was an activity beyond Mrs. Rourke's reach. Her reference to Eliot notwithstanding, Rourke may have achieved, through fantasy, what her deference to Mrs. Rourke obstructed in real life: the conviction that she was a unique individual. When Rourke wrote to DeVoto that "the outlining of the element of fantasy as continuous in American humor is something specially my own," she might have been stating more than her belief in the originality of her scholarship. Yet Rourke could hardly have afforded to release her own store of the submerged emotion she said Poe, Hawthorne, and others had examined. To have done so would have been to disturb the careful balance of control, compliance, and independence at the heart of the most important relationship in her life. Mrs. Rourke, after all, had always encouraged that "suppression of individualized feeling" her daughter had found "conspicuous in the American temper."[59] Aware of the power of fantasy, Rourke turned to a means of dealing with it that was safe—writing. An analysis of Americans as mythmakers was an acceptable form of expressing her own psychic experience. It allowed Rourke to assert her special knowledge of what she called "inner and secret feelings,"[60] and hence to claim an identity of her own, while behaving in a way of which her mother could only approve.

Like her willingness to consider America as primitive, Rourke's attraction to the intellectual and emotional benefits of myth—for the artist, the critic, and for society as a whole—tinges her defense of American culture with a tentative quality, as if she were worried that Brooks had been right after all. To ward off that conclusion, she set about to safeguard the permanence of an American mythology, drawing upon the legends surrounding figures like Crabtree, Crockett, and Audubon. But on the chance that those fables might be too sparse, Rourke also looked for traditions in virtually every movement in American thought about which she wrote. This is perhaps the most heavy-handed feature of Rourke's work, and it betrays her need to discover an adequate culture even if she were forced to create it on her own. For example, Rourke wrote in the draft for "A History of American Culture": "Our participation in the World War was in a sequence, not a departure. It focused, of course, one of our major preoccupations, our concern with the opinion of Europe, the wish to measure up to it. . . . At varying times, and in many ways we had had this experience before."[61] Of course, America had not previously fought a war of the magnitude of World War I, nor does the statement that its participation was traditional illuminate very much about the nature of its involvement. Instead, Rourke was merely seizing upon whatever she could find in the way of continuities between past and present in order to accumulate as many as possible. That same tendency colors her discussion of the native element in such European artistic movements as symbolism and surrealism. Likewise, Rourke's focus on traditional elements invades her discussion of Marxist literary criticism. However much she disagreed with Granville Hicks and other advocates of proletarian literature, her unfailing impulse to establish traditions led her to find characteristic American aspects even in moments that she strongly disliked: "Its [Marxist criticism's] intellectual bias, its self-consciousness are by no means alien to us. Its emphasis upon the duties of the writer and the relationship of literature to society has had firm root among us. We have again in Marxian criticism our perennial conviction as to the primary importance of the arts."[62] Indeed, cultural criticism in general receives the same treatment. Though all her work was set against those writers who argued that America had nothing to offer the artist, Rourke noted that "the whole approach [of total rejection] may be considered a trait of our culture."[63] Thus she labeled even her archest intellectual opponents "traditional," enabling her to count still another school of thought as proof of America's vitality. This willful, boundless fabrication of traditions extends in less extreme form to habits of mind like subjectivity,[64] interest in biography,[65] and an impulse toward communal organization.[66]

Those efforts made Rourke a mythmaker herself, engaged in strengthening the basis for art and social unity. In this role, which influenced her writing style as well as her choice of subject, she was not alone. Many writers in the 1930s, suffering from a keen awareness of a disintegrating society, turned to myth as a way of restoring order to what seemed an irrational world. Warren Susman has characterized the period of the Depression as a Jungian age, an era dominated by "a search for metaphysical certainty, a search for a sense of transcendent being, a collective identity deeply responding to deeply felt needs and aspirations. . . . It was an age which consciously sought new heroes, new symbols, even new myths" as a means of coping with what many perceived as the exposure of the American way of life.[67] As Richard Pells has perceptively explained, their need to understand the meaning of the Depression impelled Carl Sandburg, Archibald MacLeish, authors of WPA guidebooks, and even Brooks, among others, to explore the American past; in Pells's words, they transformed the past into "precisely the sort of compelling 'political myth' that could comfort the populace in an age of chaos and uncertainty."[68]

But to place Rourke, as Pells has done, in the company of those who, because of the psychological consequences of the Depression, looked for native myths is to misrepresent Rourke's early—and most significant—writing. The theme of myth appeared in Rourke's published work as far back as 1920 (the year of her Paul Bunyon article); by the time she began *American Humor*, the depiction of Americans as mythmakers had already become her central preoccupation. Whereas the Depression may have heightened her awareness of the unifying function of myth, adding to her sense that she was performing a crucial task, in Rourke's case economic crisis bore no causal relation to intellectual concern.

In the years following Rourke's death, a number of scholars —F. O. Matthiessen, Henry Nash Smith, R.W.B. Lewis, and Leo Marx among them—took the concept of myth in a direction that would have pleased her: toward explaining the special character of American life. We now identify those figures as the founders and guiding lights of the American Studies movement. For a time in the 1950s and 1960s, in fact, a concern with depicting and analyzing various mythical constructs—the vision of the West as regenerative "virgin land," the notion of the American as a new Adam, the pastoral ideal, the symbolism attached to Andrew Jackson, the image of Northerners and Southerners as "Yankee" and "Cavalier"—seemed to constitute a definable American Studies "method."[69] Hopeful observers detected in the "myth and symbol" approach the promise of systematic, fresh insight into the nation's past. More recently, under the impetus of the "new social history," some writers have rightly reassessed that approach, questioning the precise connections between the myths evident in literary sources and the aspirations and behavior of all Americans. Such criticisms, however necessary, have popularized the idea of a "myth and symbol" school while discrediting it, with the result that one is inclined to label anyone concerned with native myth a practitioner of "American Studies." It is tempting, therefore, to see Rourke as a forerunner of the movement and even to praise or blame *American Humor* for subsequent investigations of the American as mythmaker. The temptation is all the stronger because, just as she would have applauded a work like Matthiessen's *American Renaissance* or Marx's *The Machine in the Garden*, so did those books explicitly acknowledge the value of some of Rourke's perceptions: Matthiessen hailed *American Humor* as "the most successful instance of her sensitive kind of cultural and folk history"; Marx commended the way she had noted the pastoral quality in the fable of the "contrast" between America and Europe.[70] In addition, beyond those specific debts, the first members of the American Studies movement owed to Rourke part of their excitement about exploring American subjects and their certainty that such explorations had become legitimate academic pursuits. Nevertheless, it is a mistake to confuse a common interest in the nature of American culture and a common vocabulary ("myth") with common meaning and intent. Significantly, none of the American Studies writers, praising Rourke, mentioned her portrait of the American's mythmaking tendency as the starting point for their own concerns. For in Rourke's work, the idea of myth, however freighted with proving America a spiritually healthy, unified society beneficial to artist and critic, did not carry the same burdens that Matthiessen, Lewis, Smith, or Marx attached to it.

A comment Rourke made about Charles Sheeler clarifies the relationship between her use of myth and that of the "myth and symbol" scholars. Sheeler, Rourke argued, was a painter in the American tradition not because he chose American subjects— "subject alone is never a solution for the artist"—but because he adopted characteristically American forms, drawing his barns and factories with the spare, clean lines of Bucks County architecture and Shaker furniture or translating the craftsmanship of wrought iron farm tools or pottery jugs into shapes on canvas. "It is by the use of form that the individual artist makes his art distinctive," Rourke wrote. "It is the consistent print of form in successive periods which gives a national tradition its character."[71] That insight prompted Stanley Hyman to call the Sheeler biography Rourke's most mature and important book, but, had he looked more closely, he might have seen the same assumption implicitly at work in *American Humor*, where Rourke's preoccupation was with the form of myth. Rourke placed Sinclair Lewis in the line of American humorists, for example, not because of his "grasp of an immediate life"—his depiction of Main Street—but because he was "primarily a fabulist." Describing American literature generally, she linked Poe, Hawthorne, Melville, and Whitman as writers who had all employed "primitive or anterior forms, the monologue, the rhapsody, the tale, the legend, the romance."[72] These remarks leave aside the content of the fable or tale, for tradition inheres in the act of mythmaking, not in the recourse to a particular mythical figure. Subject matter is secondary. Whereas Smith, Lewis, and Marx became concerned with tracing the growth of a single American myth, Rourke was only interested in demonstrating continuities in form by tabulating myths on many themes. This is not to say that any myths would do, given her reluctance to abandon "transit" theory altogether. But there is no need for one overriding myth, and so in *American Humor*, despite the appeal of unity, Yankee, backwoodsman, and minstrel remain distinct. Emerson or Thoreau or Frost might have absorbed elements of Yankee speech or mentality, but they did not reproduce anecdotes about peddlers. The subjects of some writers, notably Twain, were closer to popular myth than others, but, as with Sheeler, that affinity alone did not make them traditional. It took the American Studies movement to shift the delineation of native mythmaking from form to content and to argue for one pervasive mythic tradition.

The transition from Rourke's use of myth to Smith's or Marx's was gradual. Matthiessen, closest of the American Studies founders to Rourke in time—*American Renaissance* appeared the year she died—was also closest in approach. In fact, though he taught many of them in his position as professor of history and literature at Harvard, Matthiessen does not strictly belong in the ranks of the "myth and symbol" writers because his interest in myth only surfaces in the last chapter of his massive book. There he relied heavily on *American Humor*, and especially on Rourke's treatment of Crockett, to demonstrate the "myth-making faculty" of nineteenth-century Americans. He borrowed Rourke's account of Crockett as a "frontier Prometheus" carrying "sunrise in his pocket" and noticed the debt of

Thoreau, Emerson, Whitman, and Melville to the tall tale. "His own accents," Matthiessen said of Melville, "were at times closer than he probably realized, to those of Crockett himself."[73] Matthiessen's purpose, like Rourke's, was to chart mythmaking in both popular and literary expression. Yet his handling of myth differed from Rourke's in two important respects that foreshadowed later developments. First, he assigned to his subjects a conscious interest in the power of myth. Emerson not only laced his writing with symbols; as Matthiessen demonstrated, he understood the need for " 'a theory of interpretation or Mythology.' " "Thoreau's greater concentration," Matthiessen wrote, "carried him to explicit statement of the connections between symbol and myth," connections that proceeded from his desire to expand existence beyond the bounds of present time and narrow locality. Whitman and Melville likewise knew that "the infancy of a human being recapitulates the infancy of the race, and that myths are collective dreams."[74] Second, more self-aware than they appear in *American Humor*, Matthiessen's writers also gravitated toward what he called "the myth of the common man." Emerson, and Thoreau even more, objected to Carlyle's disregard for the stature of the workingman, and found their own "representatives" among " 'the simplest and obscurest of men.' " Whitman was most committed to the view that the myth of the age waited "in the souls of the armies of common people." When Matthiessen turned to Crockett and frontier humor, he emphasized the way the material filled out "the contours of the myth of the common man," catching a "quality of homely existence." Describing in heroic terms a blacksmith's cousin in one of George Washington Harris's *Sut Lovingood* tales, Matthiessen likened the character to Emerson's "central man" and to the demigod figure of Bulkington in *Moby Dick*. Thus *American Renaissance* went beyond *American Humor* by linking native mythmaking to a specific, compelling theme.

Matthiessen's sights remained chiefly on literature, however, as did R.W.B. Lewis's in *The American Adam* (1955). Though Lewis shared Rourke's understanding of myth as a "collective affair," he departed from her stress on the popular imagination by restricting the creators of myth to "the best-attuned artists of the time."[75] Acknowledging the influence of Matthiessen, Lewis took another step away from Rourke by devoting his entire book to an analysis of what he termed "the American myth": the story of an innocent Adam thrust into a vast new world. But Lewis did more than identify the content of a unitary native myth as "Adamic." By claiming that the heroes of such works as Cooper's *The Deerslayer*, Brown's *Arthur Mervyn*, Hawthorne's *The Marble Faun*, and Melville's *Moby Dick* evolved from the conception of an American Adam, Lewis invested that conception with the power to explain the nature of American fiction. Neither Rourke nor Matthiessen had gone so far in spelling out the influence of a single myth. Moreover, at certain points Lewis expanded the explanatory dimension of myth even further. Remarking on the recurrence of a literary Adam long after Hawthorne and Melville had concluded the story of his fall, Lewis speculated on one reason for the hero's endurance: "We may suppose that there has been a kind of resistance in America to the painful process of growing up, something mirrored and perhaps buttressed by our writers, expressing itself in repeated efforts to revert to a lost childhood and a vanished Eden, and issuing repeatedly in a series of outcries at the freshly discovered capacity of the world to injure."[76] By moving outside fiction and observing that the Adamic myth reflected and even contributed to the shape of the American character, Lewis broadened his enterprise from literary to cultural criticism. Rourke, too, had postulated an interaction between national experience and native myth. The Yankee arose, for example, when "a deep relish for talk had grown up throughout the country, on solitary farms, in the starved emptiness of the backwoods, on the wide wastes of the rivers."[77] But for Rourke, the interaction was all in one direction: conditions sometimes accounted for the appearance, if not the content, of various myths, but myths did not create conditions. Rourke never explained historical events in terms of the impact of the idea of the peddler or the frontiersman. Lewis, however, in his phrase "perhaps buttressed by our writers," implied that the connections might run the other way as well, that myth could determine the course not only of literature but also of life.

This suggestion, tentative and chastened in Lewis's work, had already received extensive play from another American Studies scholar by the time *The American Adam* appeared. When Henry Nash Smith wrote *Virgin Land* in 1950, he carried the "myth and symbol" approach away from fiction, toward cultural history, and even further from Rourke's mere observation of mythmaking. Smith's primary purpose was to trace the "impact of the West . . . on the consciousness of Americans" and "the principal consequences of this impact in literature and social thought down to Turner's formulation of it." Like Matthiessen and Lewis, Smith focused on a particular myth, which he labeled "*the* myth of mid-nineteenth-century America": the ideal of the independent yeoman farmer tilling the garden of the world.[78] The yeoman ideal, Smith argued, appeared in the agrarian doctrines of Jefferson, informed James K. Paulding's poem *The Backwoodsman*, colored Cooper's picture of social structure, and contributed to the gloomy tone of Hamlin Garland's *Main-Travelled Roads*, to cite only a few of Smith's examples. In this effort, Smith was much like Matthiessen and Lewis, though they had their own ideas of "*the* myth" of the age. Similarly, the first part of *Virgin Land* described the evolution of another of the "fixtures of American mythology": the hunter and trapper represented variously as Daniel Boone, Leatherstocking, Kit Carson, and the dime novel hero. But Smith accorded myth more explanatory power than possibly any other American Studies writer before or after him. For in Smith's formulation, the myth of "virgin land," arising out of the historical circumstance of the unsettled West, also affected historical developments. His announced purpose notwithstanding, Smith moved in the last part of his book from a discussion of the literary consequences of myth to its effects on politics and reform. The yeoman ideal, Smith insisted, became a mainstay of the Republican platform in 1860 and explained the passage of the Homestead Act two years later, because their adoption of the symbol enabled Republican orators to win "the undefined but powerful force which the imagination of the masses of voters always exerts in political crises." Smith's politicians were even more conscious of the need for myth than Matthiessen's writers: in Smith's view, the Republicans "meant to capture" myth and symbol to "command" Northwestern farmers. The "myth of the garden," according to Smith, had "exerted a conservative influence on the slavery controversy" while fostering a "humanitarian concern for the white laborer and landless farmer." By the 1870s, Smith observed, the agrarian myth was having a negative influence on the campaign to revise laws governing the public domain—but an influence nonetheless.[79] Here Smith has left the depiction of mythmaking activity, or even the content of a specific myth, far behind; from observations about the impact of the West on myth he has undertaken to describe the impact of myth on the West. At this point Smith is open to all the questions about the American Studies "method" that have by now become familiar: Do myths really determine political behavior? How do we know whether the "masses of voters" actually shared their leaders' conceptions? Should we not take account of class differences? What is the relationship between symbols and myths and the world of facts? Does Smith assume, in Bruce Kuklick's phrase, that ideas "exist independently of the people who think them"?[80]

One can raise the same issues about Leo Marx's *The Machine in the Garden* (1964), the book that proclaimed that American Studies had come of age. Marx, a student of both Matthiessen and Smith, followed their techniques in exploring native attitudes toward technology. More concerned with literature than Smith was, Marx nevertheless described "pastoralism" as "a significant force in American life" and treated the myth of the garden as an ideal relevant to "American experience."[81] Again, one might ask, whose experience? But that question exposes the difference between Rourke and later writers. For Rourke never ventured to account for experience in terms of myth at all, nor did she forsake form for any special mythic content. Kuklick's summary of one purpose of the American Studies movement— "to demonstrate the way in which . . . 'collective' images and symbols can be used to explain the behavior of people in the United States"[82]—surely describes the tendency from Matthiessen to Marx yet hardly applies to Rourke. There is no progression from myth to behavior (outside of the writing of literature) in *American Humor*; Rourke's use of myth stopped short of historical explanation.

As such, Rourke was only an intellectual second cousin, not an immediate relative, of the American Studies scholars, a position that exempts her from negative judgments of the "myth and symbol" approach. Her attention to myth in *American Humor* served as an inspiration rather than as a model. If Rourke's concept of mythmaking was free of certain explanatory encumbrances, however, it was still charged with numerous other functions. From Herder, Harrison, and Eliot, Rourke had learned that myth was the basis of art. She knew as well that myth could provide emotional comforts beyond its intellectual appeal: it promised to unify artist and society, "high-brow" and "low-brow." In addition, the idea of the primacy of myth placed the future health of American culture in the hands of the critic, giving him a role of crucial social importance. In Rourke's case, writing about myth may also have allowed her the safe expression of her own encounter with fantasy. Those diverse hopes came together in Rourke's effort to discover "usable myths." In that convergence her reach was even greater than that of the American Studies movement, for she wanted nothing less than to make, as she wrote in *Trumpets of Jubilee*, "a world out of a wilderness"[83]—a world in which culture would flourish, the artist would prosper, and the critic would reign.

# 5

---

## STYLE

---

When the reviewers acclaimed
*American Humor* in the spring of 1931, they hailed not only
the book's interpretation of native culture but also its delight-
fully lively style. "Miss Rourke," wrote her friend Eda Lou
Walton in the *Nation*, "is one of the few truly scholarly critics
who write a beautiful prose. She is able so naturally to fuse her
documentary evidence with her critical exposition as to convince any reader that her book . . . was written for pure pleasure."[1] "Charming qualities" and a "freshness of feeling," Van
Wyck Brooks later noted, were a hallmark of Rourke's style in
her biographical studies as well.[2] A glance at any of Rourke's
writings is enough to corroborate those observations. Carefully
wrought descriptions of Crockett's surroundings enrich her discussions of his life on the frontier; striking metaphors explain
the character of the Yankee, backwoodsman, and minstrel;
imagined conversations enliven the story of Barnum, Greeley,
or the Beechers. Rourke's acknowledgments reveal that she immersed herself in her subject matter, riding through the "en-
chanting country" of Audubon's home in Louisiana or retrac-
ing Lotta Crabtree's California journeys for what Rourke liked
to call "living research." The results showed in her vivid recreation of mood and look and atmosphere. "Cool spaces sometimes

caught the eye where lupine grew in wet grassy valleys," she wrote with typical sensitivity in *Troupers of the Gold Coast,* "small as jewels within the rising heights of the Sierras, and quickly gone."[3] Yet Walton, Brooks, and others, considering Rourke's prose, have never gone beyond praise. Her special amalgamation of scholarship and popular style was inextricably related to her concern for American culture. It deserves examination not simply as an illustration of beautiful writing but as a strategy for achieving the mythmaking, tradition-conscious, unified society Rourke valued.

The opening section of *American Humor* provides a good example of Rourke's style generally:

> Toward evening of a midsummer day at the latter end of the eighteenth century a traveler was seen descending a steep red road into a fertile Carolina valley. He carried a staff and walked with a wide, fast, sprawling gait, his tall shadow cutting across the lengthening shadows of the trees. His head was crouched, his back long; a heavy pack lay across his shoulders.
>
> A close view of his figure brought consternation to the men and women lounging at the tavern or near the sheds that clustered around the planter's gate. "I'll be shot if it ain't a Yankee!" cried one. The yard was suddenly vacant.[4]

This passage, which is like a glimpse into the past through a pair of binoculars, is a refreshing beginning to a scholarly work on the themes and patterns of American humor in folklore and literature, for its style could hardly be called academic. Instead, Rourke has undertaken to spin a yarn. She is telling a story— and creating a myth. Her fictionalized narration has several components: the use of the vague, passive "was seen" that re-

moves the reader's expectations of historical accuracy; the in-
clusion of details of appearance, movement, and setting ("the
lengthening shadows of the trees") designed to establish an impression of fantasy rather than to bolster an argument; the reliance on direct quotation to supply dramatic effect. The nature
of the stylistic device becomes clearer when one considers other
ways of beginning the book. For example, Rourke might have
written, "The Yankee, the backwoodsman, and the minstrel
have formed the basis for American humor. The Yankee was
traditionally a peddler who traveled throughout the country-
side; he was frequently the object of suspicion by local towns-
people." She might have documented the statement by estimat-
ing the number of peddlers on the road in 1800 or describing a
typical trade route. Walter Blair's discussion of the Yankee in
his *Native American Humor* (1937) indicates the alternative
Rourke rejected: "The term 'Yankee,' in widespread use to de-
note an American, dates back to about 1775. . . . His simplicity,
his penury, and his cautiousness are details of a sketchy portrait. . . ."[5] But Blair's straightforward and rather dry treatment
was incompatible with Rourke's purposes. Arguing that the
Yankee was a mythical creature, she adopted a form that guaranteed the persistence of that myth. Her use of the language of
fiction both corroborated and insured the validity of her argument. We see her once more as a mythmaker herself, this time
employing style to amplify the Yankee's mythical attributes
and create them anew. Perhaps by recording myths in the man-
ner of the mythmaker, Rourke could crystallize them once and
for all, so that they remained part of a permanent tradition.

The same reliance on fictional style as a way of revitalizing
myth appears in Rourke's treatment of Audubon:

On an autumn evening Dr. Rankin stopped there [at
Audubon's mill] for a bit of talk with Audubon. They
came out together, and suddenly Audubon noted a

[137]

flock of small birds winging their way southeast over
the river. "What are they?" he cried. Without waiting
for an answer he unhitched his horse from a tree,
mounted, and was off. How long he was gone or where
he went nobody knows. The story is that he pursued
the flock through Kentucky, through Tennessee and
over the mountains into North Carolina, returning at
last with two small birds for a trophy.

There were many such stories. He was said to have
followed an unknown species of woodpecker on foot
for many miles to the south, scrambling through
thickets, swimming rivers, penetrating far down into
the Cumberlands.[6]

The quoted exclamation, the use of words like "suddenly" and
"without waiting for an answer" that allow the reader a sense
of direct observation, and the introduction of connotative
phrases like "scrambling through thickets" transform Audubon
from a historical figure into a colorful "character." Audubon's
legendary quality is likewise enhanced by Rourke's description
of him in the "garb" (itself a word belonging to fantasy) "of a
common French sailor, blue dungarees and a short jacket with a
red madras handkerchief wound around his head and large gold
earrings in his ears. His beard and mustachios were his own,
but they flowed and curled so abundantly that they looked as
though he had fastened them on with glue for a masquerade.
He looked gayer, wilder than any common sailor. . . ."[7] Though
Rourke announced in her bibliographical note that the "traditions" about Audubon had "salience and strength,"[8] her portrait of him indicates a desire to strengthen those traditions even
further by perpetuating the view of a "gay," "wild," fantastic,
mythical Audubon. She could, after all, have written a sober
history of the artist's life and work, sticking only to bare fact.
But her interest was more in vivid impression than minute de-

tail, more in myth than in biography. The same interest governed her style in her other biographical studies: hence, for example, Crockett's children "speak tall talk around the house."

Apart from creating vivid characters, Rourke used style as an instrument of mythmaking in her less admirable practice of tentative phrasing. The words "seems" and "as if" appear frequently throughout *American Humor*. For example, she wrote: "The Revolution, with its cutting of ties, its movement, its impulses toward freedom, seemed to set one portion of the scant population free from its narrow matrix." Similarly, Rourke observed: "But queerly enough, the backwoodsman indulged in conduct resembling that of the Yankee when under the fire of criticism, as if after all there were a tacit bond between them." A few more examples will suffice to indicate how such words fairly dominate Rourke's style in the book:

The two figures [Yankee and backwoodsman] seemed to join in a new national mythology. . . .

In the *Knickerbocker History* and in *Rip Van Winkle* Irving created a comic mythology as though comic myth-making were a native habit, formed early . . .

He [the legendary Indian] seemed an improbable and ghostly ancestor.

This primitive drawing was maintained as though some essential search were under way for an intrinsic substance.

[Emily Dickinson's] language is bold, humorously and defiantly experimental, as if she had absorbed the inconsequence in regard to formal language abroad during her youth. . . .[9]

Faced with her repeated use of words like "seems," "as if," and "as though," the impatient reader may want to ask what *really* happened. But Rourke's failure to write concretely may be read as a further sign of her desire to create myth. Her language lends an aspect of imprecision and unreality to her writing, removing her discussion from the realm of fact to that of possibility.

Sometimes Rourke's interest in mythmaking even led her to take liberties with her sources. In *Audubon*, for example, she doctored the story of a meeting between Audubon and Daniel Boone to heighten the drama and romance of the episode. Though the originals of Audubon's journals have not survived, making it impossible to retrieve his own account of the event, there are interesting discrepancies between Rourke's version and the works she cited in her bibliography. Audubon's *Ornithological Biography*, Maria R. Audubon's *Audubon and His Journals*, and Lucy Audubon's *The Life of John James Audubon* all report that Boone and Audubon returned from a shooting match and retired to their room for the night, whereupon Audubon asked the famous hunter to talk about some of his adventures. After Audubon had gotten into bed and Boone had made himself comfortable on the floor, Boone related the tale of his narrow escape from some Indians when his squaw captors became drunk on whisky. To mark the spot, Boone added, he cut chips out of a sapling, and when he returned years later, he amazed witnesses by identifying the very same tree even though bark had covered over the notches. This anecdote, colorful enough, becomes even more so in Rourke's book. She removed the encounter between Audubon and Boone to a campfire, where the two men sit with other hunters. Interpolating a direct quotation and "tall talk," she has one of the audience say: "Tell us how you flusterated the Injuns, Dan'l."[10] Boone complies, using "Injun" for "Indian" throughout his speech. Rourke has deliberately romanticized the setting of Boone's narration, transforming it from a private conversation to a public performance and adding fanciful lingo to emphasize Boone's and Audubon's mythic stature. Only after describing the campfire scene did she retire Boone to his blanket on the floor.

By this effort, as well as her fictionalized, evocative, and sometimes vague prose, Rourke saw to it that Americans would have enough myths to sustain an adequate culture. But myth-making, especially out of the material of the frontier, could be a touchy enterprise. Though Rourke added backwoods language to the Boone story, she left out backwoods violence, for in her sources, although not in her retelling, Boone says of the squaws: "I now recollect how desirous I once or twice felt to lay open the skulls of the wretches with my tomahawk."[11] Like her transformation of Davy Crockett into a middle-class hero, the omission bespeaks a concern with the acceptability of native traditions. Rourke's double-edged definition of culture meant that she had to strike another of her delicate balances: between a view of frontier life as exciting enough to fuel the imagination, but not so raw and rough that it entirely flouted conventional standards for civilization. If her style helped to create a sufficient number of myths, it also made sure that those myths would pass muster.

A comparison of part of Bernard DeVoto's writings on the frontier with Rourke's contemporaneous treatment illuminates that stylistic strategy. Both DeVoto and Rourke discussed the Western boatman, for example, but in very different terms. "This image," wrote DeVoto in *Mark Twain's America* (1932),

is a sun-scorched man in a red shirt and a blue capote with a white fringe—swarthy, powerful, obscene. Shirt and capote were display: in most weathers the boatmen worked naked to the waist. . . . They warred inimitably upon one another and then allied for the spoliation of the tender when the boats tied up beside the little towns. They swaggered down the streets while the citizenry trembled. They drank what pleased them: they levied on shops and poultry runs; they

marched upon brothels where white whores worn out
in the cities competed for their favors with young
black wenches and mulattoes.

Sometimes, DeVoto continued, the boatmen were attacked by
pirates, who, if beaten, "fled backward while the victorious
crews pushed them off with rifles and brandished knives. The
boats moved on. The boatmen tied up their wounds. A song
floated across the chocolate water: 'Hard upon the beech oar/
She moves too slow/All the way to Shawneetown/Long while
ago.' A jigging tune, the words far decenter than most. Cairo lay
ahead. There would be fillies of whisky, an awed citizenry, and
wenches. The boats drifted on." [12] DeVoto's language here is as
concrete as the blow from a boatman's fist. He is somewhat engaged in the same mythmaking effort that occupied Rourke: the
deliberately inflated phrase "the spoliation of the tender" gives
the boatman's activities the stature of heroic exploits, while the
use of the subjunctive mood ("Cairo lay ahead. There would be
fillies of whisky . . .") sets the reader's imagination to work all
over again. But DeVoto's emphasis is on what he called "frontier hardness," a view supported by his language and by the relentless rhythm of his sentences. His list of the boatman's actions ("They swaggered . . . they drank . . . they levied . . . they
marched upon brothels") is itself written in a swaggering pace
and communicates the power of its subject. Figures of speech do
not intervene to mediate the reader's confrontation with this
whoring, obscene, violent roarer. The matter-of-fact, stark sentence "The boatmen tied up their wounds" reinforces the point
that bloody battles were routine occurrences, as does the image
of the boat simply drifting on after the encounter.

Neither the blood nor the bawdiness bothered DeVoto in this
context, determined as he was to present the "reality" of frontier life for the benefit of Brooks and his effete, tender-minded
literary coterie. In fact, DeVoto celebrated the "masculine," un-
inhibited features of the boatman's personality. His remark that

the words of the "Shawneetown" song were "far decenter than most" is an insider's comment, as if he were giving his audience a wink of the eye, for he knows the other songs. And why not revel in this raw, raucous heritage? The boatmen were alive, vibrant, outrageous, captivating—and in the tales that developed about them, funny.

Yet when Rourke took up the same subject, she did so in a way that bore little resemblance to DeVoto's. Discussions of the boatman occur in both *Davy Crockett* and *American Humor.* "The red-shirted riverboatmen," Rourke said in *Davy Crockett,* "kept up a running repartee with men ashore or on other boats along the river. Like the wagoners they consorted together, had their own lingo, their own way of bantering, their wit, which was quick, and their songs, which were both rowdy and sentimental. Thousands of them were now afloat on the western rivers, noisy, quarrelsome, full of sport, gathering for short holidays at taverns when a journey was ended, and then away again up or down the rivers." Later in the passage, Rourke commented, "on open easy water the boatmen would sing out—" and quoted the first two lines of the Shawneetown song. "The air was full of boatmen's songs and full of talk," she added. "Flatboats passed, plying the rivers as shops or 'doggeries,' drawing alongside the arks to sell food or spirits or fancy notions to travelers."[13] The first thing to notice in Rourke's description is the contrast between the characteristics she ascribed to the boatmen and the traits DeVoto enumerated. Most striking, of course, is the way Rourke has dropped out the sex: there are no "brothels" or "wenches" in her version, and she has introduced the sentimental Shawneetown song as typical. What DeVoto confronted as "obscene," Rourke transmuted into "rowdy." Her relativistic definition of culture had its limits, and whoring was beyond them. But there is more going on here than Rourke's neglect of details that did not meet certain cultural requirements. The difference between Rourke and DeVoto is not simply a question of content—that he includes sex while she does not.

[143]

Even when they are talking about the same scenes, the same behavior, Rourke's account comes out less graphic, more lyrical, and so more comforting. The phrase "on open easy water" has the ring of serenity. DeVoto's boatmen drink; Rourke's gather "for short holidays at taverns." "War" for DeVoto is a "quarrel" for Rourke. Her boatmen are playful, cheerful, and rather innocent: they are "full of sport," they "banter" and "consort." This abstract, almost quaint language (also apparent in "spirits or fancy notions") softens the "frontier hardness" that delighted DeVoto but that Rourke, retaining some allegiance to a hierarchical view of culture, could not accept. It is important to observe that Rourke had achieved the softer effect stylistically: the image of the benign boatmen arises from her choice of words as well as from her selective focus.

The technique is even clearer in her treatment of the boatmen in *American Humor*. "At the great bends of the rivers where the horns sounded their warning of the swift approach of the heavy boats," Rourke began, "the Ohio was like sheets of crystal, so clear that the eye could see to a depth of twenty feet or more. In the early spring, gum tree and locust, dogwood and redbud drifted. The notes of the mocking-bird floated out: everywhere was the fresh faint odor of wild grape."[14] At this point one is reminded of Amy Reed's instructions to her earnest student: the description is a model of concern with "sensual experience." And it works. The reader imagines the stillness of the river, its pleasing clarity, the appealing fragrances in the air. There are no noises except the musical sound of the bird, which is not obtrusive but instead "floats out," as the driftwood floats. All of the elements of the scene naturally belong there and harmonize with one another. This is a pastoral vignette. Rourke's style is vivid, evocative, and extremely effective—but the effect is to recreate a mood of tranquility and peace. Rourke has reinforced that mood by following the passage with a poem about a "simple boatman," which appears without introduction or comment so as not to jar the reader out of his reverie. The wording

of the poem could not be further from the language of the boatman himself: "How oft in boyhood's joyous days,/Unmindful
of the lapsing hours,/I've loitered on my homeward way/By
wild Ohio's bank of flowers;/ While some lone boatman from
the deck/Poured his soft numbers to the tide. . . ." Though she
added that "the boatman blew his magic horn and improvised
sentimental songs," the lyrics she provided are composed, not
improvised, and represent a literary view of the boatman, not
his own rough speech. It is true that Rourke thought the boatman more pensive than DeVoto did, remarking that "he slipped
into a highly posed melancholy." She found in him the intro-
spective nature she knew so well in herself. Yet her style also
perpetuated the elusiveness, the indirection she associated with
the "inward view" and exhibited in her own personality. Even
when she described the trait about which she and DeVoto agreed
—the boatman's physical prowess—she chose words that insured no disturbance of the gentle image she had drawn: "He
had answers for every landing-stage, could provoke talk where
none seemed to be forthcoming, and reenforced his repartee by
muscular evidence."[15] "Muscular evidence" refers to the same
swaggering and slashing that DeVoto identified. But it is a eu-
phemistic and ambiguous phrase—what muscles? what evidence?—and stands between her audience and a full compre-
hension of the actions involved. Rourke's next sentence, which
labels the boatman "a prime wrestler and a crack shot," does not
undo the softened effect. In the context of the magic spell she
has herself woven, the reader hardly remembers that Rourke is
telling him about men who freely terrorized one another.

Rourke's depiction of the boatman can serve as an emblem of
the way she approached frontier humor in general. An even better illustration of her stylistic tactics emerges by comparing the
newspaper humor of the old Southwest to her treatment of it,
with one important caveat. The writings of the newspaper
humorists—Longstreet, Baldwin, Hooper, Harris, William T.
Thompson, T. B. Thorpe—are among the richest manifestations

of the American comic sensibility. It is easy—but wrong—to assume that Rourke discussed them at length, because so many books in the 1930s focused on frontier comedy. *Mark Twain's America*, Franklin J. Meine's anthology *Tall Tales of the Southwest* (1930)— compiled under DeVoto's editorship for Alfred Knopf's Americana Deserta series, the outsized section in Walter Blair's *Native American Humor* (1937), Blair's and Meine's *Mike Fink: King of the Mississippi Keelboatmen* (1933), and Richard Dorson's excerpts from the Crockett Almanacks (1939): this flood of attention turned such material into the canon of American humor. (Dorson himself recognized the resulting distortion and tried to redress the balance in *Jonathan Draws the Long Bow* (1946), a study of New England folklore.) Rourke had met Meine in 1929 and found him knowledgeable and generous, and she in turn deserves a great deal of credit for stimulating interest in Southwestern humor, but she did her own work before that humor dominated the field. Rourke understood her position as historians have not; she is often classed with De Voto, whereas she accused him in their correspondence of "making Southwestern humor characterize American humor generally." Rourke also drew a distinction, unlike Meine, between "the true tall tale with its stress upon the supernatural" and the "less inflated" newspaper sketches (though, again, not between oral and subliterary humor). Her balanced overview, more accurate than Meine's or DeVoto's, meant that she consigned her analysis of the newspaper writers to less than three and one-half pages of *American Humor*.

Within that analysis, moreover, she argued that even those more "prosaic" stories were fantasies, in contrast to DeVoto's stress on their realism. But although she had sufficient intellectual justification for compressing her discussion and skirting realistic details, a return to the tales themselves makes one wonder if she did not slight them with a sense of relief. For here are characters much like the boatman: they drink and gamble, they are often cruel, violent, or obscene, their speech is rough and their manners rougher. Hooper's Simon Suggs makes himself captain of a ragtag Indian-fighting militia and court-martials the widow Haycock for screaming.[16] In T. B. Thorpe's "The Big Bear of Arkansas," which DeVoto thought a classic example of the realistic tall tale, part of the humor derives from the narrator's scatalogical allusions juxtaposed with references to the magnificence of the bear: "I went into the woods near my house, taking my gun and Bowie-knife along, just *from habit*, and there sitting down also from habit, what should I see, getting over my fence, but *the bar*! . . . I raised myself, took deliberate aim, and fired. Instantly the varmint wheeled, gave a yell, and *walked through the fence* like a falling tree would through a cobweb. I started after, but was tripped up by my inexpressibles, which either from habit, or the excitement of the moment, were about my heels. . . ."[17] Joseph G. Baldwin's sketches for *Flush Times of Alabama and Mississippi* (1853), first published in the *Southern Literary Messenger*, catalog the "general infection of morals" on the frontier: "The pursuits of industry neglected, riot and debauchery filled up the vacant hours. . . . [A little boy would] give a man ten dollars to hold him up to bet at the table of a faro-bank."[18] As Walter Blair noted, Longstreet's "The Fight," part of his 1835 collection *Georgia Scenes*, carries the "humor of physical discomfiture to extraordinary extremes": "I looked, and saw that Bob had entirely lost his left ear and a large piece from his left cheek. His right eye was a little discolored, and the blood flowed profusely from his wounds."[19]

Even more extreme, perhaps, and the best case in point, is George Washington Harris's creation, Sut Lovingood. The first Sut yarn appeared in the *Spirit of the Times* on November 4, 1854, setting the precedent for the earthy, fast-paced tales that followed over the next fifteen years. The stories relate the adventures and pranks of Sut Lovingood, who speaks in the first person and in the vernacular of east Tennessee. M. Thomas Inge, the editor of one Sut collection, has noted the character's "prejudice, brutality, cowardice, sensuality, coarseness, and vulgarity," though he credited him with a love of freedom and an intolerance for hypocrisy.[20] For Edmund Wilson, however, Sut's sadistic streak and physical cruelty overshadowed any possible virtues. "One of the most striking things about *Sut Lovingood*," Wilson observed in *Patriotic Gore*, "is that it is all as offensive as possible. . . . I should say that, as far as my experience goes, it is by far the most repellent book of any real literary merit in American literature."[21] Sut's usual pastime is revenge for some affront, often because he considers the perpetrator self-important or pretentious, but also, as Wilson pointed out, for any other reason that happens to irritate him. In "Trapping a Sheriff," he arranges to compensate a friend for the adultery between the friend's wife and Sheriff Doltin by stripping Doltin to his shirt and shoes, tying a noose around his neck, attaching one end of the rope to a ball of turpentine-soaked twine, igniting it, and then hooking two clawing cats onto his shirttail. Perhaps there is loyalty to the betrayed husband here, but there is mainly wanton glee in grizzly torture:

The tupentine lit up a bright road ahine him, kivered wif broke down an' tore up briars, an' his white shut, an' the cats' eyes 'zembled a flag ove truce, kivered wif litnin-bugs. I think I never seed es meny cat's-eyes in es many places afore, tu be no more cats than thar wer; tails too, wer ruther numerous, an' sorter swelled, an' claws a plenty. The noise he made soundid jis' like a two-hoss mown-mersheen, druv by chain-lightnin, a-cuttin thru a dry cane brake on a big beat. An' thar wer wif the noise a ondercurrent ove soun, like tarin starched muslin; this, I speck wer the briars an' cats a-breakin holts.[22]

The humor in this passage, as in many of the Sut stories, partly arises from Sut's innocent, wide-eyed pose—his understated "like tarin starched muslin" and "I speck" when he knows the cats and briars are ripping the sheriff's shirt, and skin, to shreds. In fact, he characteristically plays the innocent to his victims, in this case by telling the sheriff "Bulge squar fur the briars; they won't foller in thar" just before releasing the cats. Sut appears as simply a boyish prankster who could not resist a "good one" and who is not really responsible for the consequences of the havoc he has set in motion. The implication that Sut is standing around with a "Who, me?" look on his face makes it possible to take the view that his practical jokes are indeed jokes, all in fun.

That was Franklin Meine's position in *Tall Tales of the Southwest*. Meine saw Sut as "simply the genuine naive roughneck mountaineer, riotously bent on raising hell."[23] He also enjoyed what he called the "Rabelaisian touch" in the yarns—the scenes and images that revolve around physicality or sex. "Mrs. Yardley's Quilting," for example, in which Mrs. Yardley is trampled to death by a horse at Sut's instigation, contains a disquisition on the sexual abilities of widows: "They cum clost up tu the hoss-block, standin still wif thar purty silky years playin, an' the naik-veins a-throbbin, an' waits fur the word, which ove course yu gives, arter you finds yer feet well in the stirrup, an' away they moves like a cradil on cushioned rockers, ur a spring buggy running in damp san'."[24] Another tale, one that still seems funny, perhaps because the woman is triumphant, involves Bob Dawson's discovery, on his wedding day, that he has married a "substitute": " 'She looked at me, feelin' in her bussum the while, an' said, "Robert, my love, when I come to look at you clost, your eyes seem larger, an' rounder than I thought for, an' more bulgin—they bulge as much as these palpitators," drawin' forth a pair ove somethings like sugar bowl leds, knobs an' all. When she flung 'em on the table, they bounced a time or two.' "[25] " 'False calves, false breasts, false teeth, false eye, false hair,' what next?" Dawson asks himself, and does not wait around for the answer. Language pertaining to bodily discomfort is a mainstay of Sut's speech. In "Dad's Dog-School," where the entire story turns on the pain Sut's father suffers in a ridiculous dog training attempt, Sut's mother is busy picking bugs out of her children's hair: "Mam cracked an insex vigrusly atwixt her thumbs, an' then wiped her nails ontu her gown along her thighs. . . ." Later Sut says of Dad: "Hit looked just like he'd swaller'd a terbacker-wum, dipp'd in aquafortis, an' cudn't vomit." [26]

Whereas Edmund Wilson found such language "excessively sordid," [27] to Meine it was an index of Harris's artistic abilities and a source of *Sut Lovingood*'s appeal. Interestingly, DeVoto, Meine's mentor in these matters, once suggested a "translation" of Lovingood's dialect into standard English, but presumably because he wanted to make Sut's earthiness more accessible. As DeVoto explained in *Mark Twain's America*: "The folk are everywhere bawdy and obscene. . . . The antiquarian who at last surmounts the all but insuperable difficulties in his way and gives us a study of the bawdy American folk will endlessly amuse himself and do art an immortal service." [28] But Constance Rourke, DeVoto knew, was not that antiquarian. *American Humor* had appeared the year before and contained not one example of a bawdy story, nor did it display much of the "emphatic, coarse, vivid, violent, uproarious" frontier comedy DeVoto relished. Though Wilson grouped DeVoto and Rourke together (along with F. O. Matthiessen) as writers who had recently taken an interest in *Sut Lovingood*, Rourke's handling of the yarns and other frontier newspaper humor is so different from DeVoto's as to make Wilson's remark misleading.

Rourke's section on the Southwestern writers in *American Humor* entirely avoids the material that Wilson found so objectionable. It begins with an example of the genre, a description of Ovid Bolus from Baldwin's *Flush Times*. Rourke's choice is significant, for out of all the newspaper sketches she might have quoted, she selected a passage concerning neither sex nor crude horseplay nor violence but rather the much more respectable pastime of lying. Beyond its palatable content, moreover, an excerpt from *Flush Times* had an additional advantage. Baldwin, more than most of his fellow journalists, was indebted to the essay style. He wrote in conventional literary English, not in the rough talk of an illiterate mountaineer or wandering sharper. Thus the quotation fits smoothly between Rourke's own polished paragraphs without disturbing either the reader's stomach or his ear. "Dialect was differentiated with a fine gift for mimicry," Rourke noted at the end of her discussion.[29] But there is a difference between declaring the existence of dialect in a sentence dominated by the passive voice and letting the reader confront it directly in quotations. In *American Humor* as a whole, Rourke did not shun dialect altogether, but its incidental place in the book is far out of proportion to its frequency in native humor itself. The result—a function simply of the fact that Rourke's language so outweighs the language of her subject matter—is that the reader never glimpses for more than a moment the raw exuberant style of much American comic material.

Rourke did incorporate two brief fragments of frontier dialect into the paragraph following her quotation from *Flush Times*, but those examples, which are juxtaposed with another in overblown literary language, produce atypically mild images. Milton Rickels, surveying the Sut Lovingood tales, found them dominated by references to "flayed and butchered animals" and other unpleasant figures of speech.[30] Yet Rourke, choosing to illustrate Harris's knack for pithy caricature (" 'He drawed in the puckerin' string ov that legil face of his'n' ") avoided his other, more visible aptitude for grotesque comparisons (a man has a mouth "es red es a split beef"; a woman is as "ugly es a skin'd hoss").[31] Rourke has presented the vivid side of Harris, without indicating what the vividness is usually about. Similarly, the terms in which she generalized about the characters in all of the newspaper sketches tell only half the story: "Their adventures—of the rascally Simon Suggs, the worthless Sut Lovingood, the garrulous Major Jones, the characters in *Georgia*

*Scenes* and *Flush Times on the Mississippi* [her erroneous title]
—had to do with vast practical jokes. . . . Grotesquerie and irreverence and upset made their center." [32] So much is true: but
the grotesquerie is waking up "Old Skissim's Middle Boy" by
tying him down with rope and iron weights, putting red pepper,
insects, and a rat down his clothing, and lighting fire crackers
attached to his body; the irreverence, however warranted, is
sending lizards up Parson John Bullen's pant-leg during a ser-
mon; the upset is driving a bull into hives of live bees to disrupt
"Sicily Burns's Wedding." Rourke's abstract labels, unsupported
by examples, interpolate distance between her subject matter
and her audience; as in her description of the boatman, her style
softens the material.

Frequently, it is Rourke's figurative language that performs
this function. "These stories," she said of the newspaper humor,
"were as coarse-grained as poplar wood and equally light as
timber." The simile is imaginative and charming, for which
Rourke can be commended. But what does poplar wood, with its
pleasant associations to benign nature, have to do with the character of rough frontier tales? It is one thing to call such writing
"coarse" and quite another to blunt the epithet by comparing it
to "coarse-grained" trees. Similarly, Rourke's phrase "a careless
net of stories" supplies the poetry that she required, as if she
were afraid that the stories themselves might not. [33] Rourke's
images mediate between frontier crudeness and acceptability.
To note this stylistic technique is not to suggest that she never
faced the violent or cruel side of the backwoodsman, though it
seems fair to say that nowhere in *American Humor* did she acknowledge his sexuality. [34] Her chapter containing the discussion of the newspaper humorists mentions the prevalence of
gouging and relates the anecdote of the disgruntled steamboat
captain who pulled a house into the river. Sut Lovingood's dia-
tribe against a Yankee "hatched in a crack" appears, as does a
Georgia cracker who raises his rifle at a traveler. Yet her focus
on fantasy, abetted by her prose, lets the reader glide past such

references. Walter Blair commented in *Native American Humor* that "one could not write of the staccato gambolings of frontiersmen in a tranquil style."[35] But Constance Rourke's style, if not quite tranquil, was at least smooth and soothing. Concluding her discussion of the genre, Rourke wrote of Southwestern newspaper sketches that they added "a smutch of gross and homely color to the half-formed American portrait." The language of painting is comforting, for it makes one forget that the color is often the color of blood.

DeVoto or Meine or Blair might have argued that to remove dialect, earthiness, and realism from frontier tales was to excise the sources of their humor, which may account for the disappointment some people express upon finishing *American Humor*: that there are no jokes in it. If Rourke's attempts to sand away the rough edges entailed certain losses, however, they won her more important gains: the boatman and *Sut Lovingood* could be as much evidences of an adequate culture as Audubon or *Moby Dick*.

Additionally, one may speculate that Rourke was more at ease discussing fantasy than violence, and, particularly, sex. In private life, she was not a prude: according to Margaret Marshall, she once regaled a dinner party with a recital of the sexual vocabulary of the frontier.[36] In her letters to her mother, where one might have expected her to be guarded, she spoke openly about a friend's "love affair." But she also evinced a strong sense of propriety, reassuring Mrs. Rourke that she was staying at a women's hotel or that she would be chaperoned when she spent the night at Charles Sheeler's. Her awareness that sex might not be compatible with respectability spilled over into her writing. At work on *Trumpets of Jubilee*, she encountered Victoria Woodhull's newspaper, which she found "amazing" in its sexual outspokenness, but she spared her reader any examples in her book. The alleged adultery between Henry Ward Beecher and Elizabeth Tilton proved trickier. "The Beecher scandal will indeed be a problem to handle," she acknowledged to her mother. "It cannot possibly be blinked," she added, implicitly recognizing that part of her audience might want her to do so.[37] Thus, *Trumpets of Jubilee* dodged Rourke's personal conviction that "there is no question that Beecher was guilty" by asserting both that Beecher had most of the evidence at the trial on his side and that he never responded adequately to Theodore Tilton's charges. The most "lurid" (and dubious) accusations she suppressed, having concluded that she would not use such details "directly," though she might equally well have presented them as rumors surrounding the case. Her equivocation partly stemmed from her publishers' worry that they could still be sued over the matter, yet it is impossible to imagine DeVoto taking such pains to exercise "discretion."[38] Of the letters of Beecher, Tilton, and Mrs. Tilton, she wrote, "They were all highly literary, crowded with metaphorical fine language. . . . They were all enormously vague"; but the same statements could apply to passages in her own work.[39] Her style in *American Humor* served her need to gloss over material that seemed improper and outside the bounds of good taste. Because she no doubt satisfied similar inclinations in readers who deplored "masculine" humor, we may even see her, to use Ann Douglas's phrase, as an agent of the "feminization" of American culture about which Harold Stearns complained.

Yet Rourke had more pressing missions. Though she might displease a few like DeVoto who enjoyed a bawdy story or an account of a physically discomfiting prank, she could appeal to the widest possible audience, letting nothing stand in the way of a rapport with all of the "folks." That desire for broad diffusion of a common—and acceptable—heritage was Rourke's most compelling reason for mitigating the rougher aspects of frontier life. It also underlay the form and language of virtually everything else she wrote. Style, an instrument of mythmaking, was simultaneously an instrument of what Rourke called "possession." For tradition, to be "usable," had to arise out of feelings that the entire community instinctively shared. "A small boy in northern France," Rourke explained, "may grow up with many objects about him which reveal native traditions in the arts, offering him a vocabulary which he can learn to use, without a wrench, without study, almost without thought."[40] When she argued that, by contrast, Americans "do not have that strong and natural association with evidences of the past which is still a commonplace in other countries," Rourke implicitly accepted Brooks's argument in *The Wine of the Puritans* that "we are civilized in proportion to the amount we are able to presuppose." The American "does not feel this and that to be true," Brooks had complained, "because tradition has proved them so. He is independent of tradition; he has to think it all out for himself." Brooks concluded that Americans needed to understand their traditions emotionally: "one should think until one has established a true basis for feeling, and . . . then one should feel."[41] For Rourke as well, the past became "usable" when it was "possessed" as emotional experience.

Rourke's description of "possession" reflects the impact of her experience with progressive education: the process conformed to a progressive teacher's model of learning. "Instinctive possession," Rourke wrote, was a matter of "saturation," of "getting a sense of [tradition] into [the] minds and eyes and at the ends of [the] fingers, without any immediate purpose."[42] In other words, one learned about native culture in the same spontaneous, individually tailored way one might learn from a follower of Dewey about geography or farm products. To facilitate "possession," Rourke even made a specific educational proposal: she advocated a room in school libraries filled with a variety of primary materials—American paintings, records, sculpture, photographs, books. There students might acquire that firsthand experience that, Rourke knew, was the basis of any real education.

Rourke's understanding of "possession" bore another similarity to progressive educational theory: it displayed the vagueness and mysticism attending some teachers' pronouncements about self-expression. This is Rourke's most serious failing, a result of the same uneasiness about the way one actually arrived at an adequate culture that informed her ambivalence toward the "practical" arts. Her repeated use of the passive voice and of abstract language to describe "possession" is symptomatic of the imprecision attending her idea of how tradition functioned. Reconsider her remarks in her essay "The Decline of the Novel": [Our tradition] is rich enough if it can only *be fully seen*. Out of a living perspective those epics, sagas, allegories, tales in which the imagination offers something for men to live by might *come into* . . . startling force and enlargement. . . ."[43] Brooks furnished a glimpse of Rourke's mysticism in his introduction to *The Roots of American Culture* by noting her view that once the materials of our past were assembled "the tradition would declare itself through them."[44] One may well ask whether the declaration is automatic, and how one progresses from a sense of tradition to a vital art. Alfred Kazin raised just those questions in an article about Rourke after her death, concluding that despite her important contributions, "commemoration, somehow, is never enough." The past in Rourke's work, Kazin remarked, "is an image, a story told, not ready ground on which we can stand."[45] Rourke's failure to provide that ground reflects the intersection of her personality and her ideas: the woman who could write "I am a mystic" could easily imagine the inexorable growth of art from the "possession" of the past. Perhaps her own "inward turn"—her strong private streak, her propensity for fantasy—prevented her from supplying the bold guidance for the artist that Kazin demanded.

Nevertheless, Rourke took certain steps to aid the process of "possession"—in the form of choices about her audience. Such an explicitly democratic view of "usable" traditions dictated priorities that placed the readers of popular magazines ahead of subscribers to scholarly journals. Consequently, Rourke welcomed the opportunity to publish excerpts from *Trumpets of Jubilee* in the *Woman's Home Companion* and began *Troupers of the Gold Coast* as a piece commissioned by that magazine. It could be objected that Rourke took on such assignments, and made all her books accessible, merely because she wanted her writing to sell. Rourke did work repeatedly under financial hardship, particularly during the periods when her mother fell ill. But there were many ways she might have earned money—she might, for example, have combined scholarship with a return to teaching. Rourke herself exposed the inadequacy of a simple financial explanation for her approach in a remark that designates income a secondary motive: "I wrote *Davy Crockett, Audubon,* and *Charles Sheeler* first of all because I thought it worth while to write these books. I also wrote them for necessary income."[46] Following the principles she had learned at Vassar years earlier, she told Alfred Harcourt, "It seems to me that there would be no point in centering upon popular culture, and it would be odd to have a great belief in it, without making an attempt to write for those who in some way belong to it."[47]

Rourke also made a commitment to addressing, in part, those most receptive to "possession": children. In an article entitled "Traditions for Young People," which she adapted from a speech before the American Library Association, she spelled out why she thought writing for children an essential step in creating a "usable past": "Importance attaches to young people, not because youth is a plastic period, but because it is an unconscious period, when many experiences may flow together without special purpose or thought, and wellsprings of the imagination be formed." The same essay linked realistic assessment of our "national history" to the training of youth: "we must somehow contrive to know ourselves. . . . The difficulty is that realism cannot be put on like a garment. It is an objective which must be approached with an enormous amount of skill and patience, and probably can be achieved only when a whole generation or so of young people have become habituated to its disciplines."[48] Writing for children was a way of planning for the future, of insuring the strength and sufficiency of tradition in the next generation. For her contribution, Rourke would undertake *Davy Crockett* and *Audubon* for a "young people's" audience. Harcourt, Brace, and Company contracted for publication of them on that basis, assigning editorial supervision to the children's book editor. That fact by itself helps to explain why Rourke's Daniel Boone restrains his tomahawk and why her boatman in *Crockett* shuns brothels, though one must remember that she had earlier drawn the same innocent boatman in *American Humor*.

*Crockett* and *Audubon*, however, were more than children's books: as Rourke always insisted, they rested on original scholarship and had much to offer adults in need of "possessing" traditions. Stressing the value of *Davy Crockett* in negotiations for the book's movie rights, Rourke argued:

> I discovered the two groups of materials which make
> the book definitive, as they say, those which prove
> that Crockett was more than an illiterate scout, that
> he was something of a backwoods statesman, and
> those which show him turned into a kind of poetry in
> the legendaries. Both groups of material are my own
> and nobody else's. There wasn't an iota on either of
> them except in the sources. There are few of my ac-
> complishments as a writer in which I take more pride.
> I feel that these things prove something about the
> country as well as about Crockett. . . . they required
> an intricate and specialized research and a very great
> amount of time.[49]

Similarly, in a letter to the president of Vassar, she emphasized the scholarly contribution *Audubon* represented: "Perhaps I may explain further that I have recently completed a biography of Audubon, portraying him as both an artist and a frontiersman, which Harcourt will bring out in the fall. . . . I wrote this book because it seemed essentially worth doing, since Audubon has for some reason not been studied as an artist. . . ."[50] As a result, Rourke thought the book appropriate not only for children but also for the interested layman and even the historian. Writing to Howard Haycraft, editor of *Twentieth Century Authors*, about the biographical sketch of her he was planning, she remarked: "May I make an amendment to an article published in the Wi[l]son Bulletin, in 1937, as I remember? I have appreciated the article, but I would rather the statement that I wrote *Audubon* for young people wouldn't be used. The explanation in relation to a young people's audience is rather complex, and I think this statement alone may give an erroneous impression."[51]

The complexities surrounding Rourke's view of her readers were so great, in fact, that both books created dilemmas for her publishers. A letter from Rourke's editor in 1936 noted that *Audubon* "started out primarily as a book for young people."[52] The use of the word "primarily" is telling, especially because the editor went on to explain financial complications resulting from distribution of the book—to adult readers—by the Book-of-the-Month Club. *Davy Crockett* caused even greater difficulties. The first letter from Harcourt about the book came from the desk of the children's book editor, and read in part: "We are all immensely enthusiastic about your plan for the Crockett book, and I am delighted at the prospect of a book of yours on our list for young people. The plan as you outline it suggests a book which will appeal to boys and girls and which will certainly be an important contribution to literature on American backgrounds. We would agree with you that a simple narrative form would be much the best, and would have a direct bearing on the problem of suiting the story to the young readers for whom it is intended."[53] The editor's remarks that the book would both "appeal to boys and girls" and "be an important contribution" foreshadowed later exchanges between Rourke and her publisher about the exact nature of what she had agreed to write. A few months after the children's book editor expressed her initial enthusiasm, Donald Brace indicated that he had reservations about the direction the project was taking. His letter implies that Rourke had shifted her view of her audience since the inception of the book, though she probably had had both children and adults somewhat ambiguously in mind from the start. "The appeal of children's books," Brace wrote:

> is bounded by very definite limitations of treatment
> and subject matter, as of course you realize. In your
> first letter regarding this book, you said: "I like a strict
> and simple effect in narrative, and this should keep
> the book well within the range of young people's ca-
> pacities. The result should be something that would
> interest children from 12 up and perhaps attract some
> older people." That expressed an ideal starting point
> from which to produce a book for young readers, but
> your letter of June 14 has caused us some misgivings
> as to whether you aren't having scholars and antiquari-
> ans in mind, possibly to the disadvantage of the young
> people.[54]

Subsequently Rourke wrote her publisher several times stressing the "adult interest" in the book. Once completed, *Crockett* touched off a debate at Harcourt about the best way to advertise it. Rourke herself resolved the controversy by deciding not to insist on the book's adult value,[55] perceiving as she did the importance of conveying a sense of tradition to children. In the end, Harcourt arrived at a compromise. After considering the possibility of issuing the book on the adult list in the spring and as a book for young people in the fall, her editor informed Rourke, "We were finally all agreed that the book should be brought out definitely as a book for young people, but we shall do a special publicity job on it to bring it to the attention of historians and others who would be particularly interested."[56]

Yet *Davy Crockett* and *Audubon*, as they actually appeared, revealed that Rourke's editors need not have worried. For her understanding of the exigencies of "possession," with respect to both children and adults, demanded not only a "strict and simple narrative form" but a prose style with a wide net, even if it meant submerging her painstaking research. Hence the device of fictionalization that Rourke used to describe the Yankee peddler at the beginning of *American Humor* also characterized the Crockett and Audubon biographies, as the opening paragraph of each attests:

In the early summer of 1673 a small party of white men floated in two canoes down the wide waters of the Mississippi. They had passed the mouth of the Ohio, and soon discovered rising bluffs on the eastern shore of the great river. Presently Indians were seen among the trees, armed and observant. They belonged to a small tribe ruled by the powerful Chickasaws. The travelers spoke to them in the Huron language, which this tribe did not understand, and held aloft a feathered calumet given them by the Illinois Indians to the north for use as a friendly sign on their journey. The white men landed, were welcomed, and joined the tribe in a feast of buffalo meat, bear's oil, and delicious white plums.[57]

A boy named Fougère peered through the shutters of a house in the city of Nantes. A procession was passing, gay but a little wild. Men in long red caps swaggered in crowded clusters. Bareheaded women shouted and laughed. The boy watched eagerly, and since he was already a young republican he cried, *"Vive la république!"* But his voice was doubtful. Already the crowds were growing angry, then savage.

Presently men and women in silks and velvets were
dragged along at the cart's tail, jeered at by the rough
throng. "A bas! A bas!" was the loud cry. "Down with
them, down with them! The guillotine!" [58]

Those passages, like the books as a whole, are distillations of
documents about their subjects. But the scholarship is underplayed in favor of a tone of casual storytelling, as if the writer
were recalling the lives of her friends from memory. The absence of footnotes or references in the text either to primary or
secondary documents enhances the storytelling mode, marking
Rourke as a popular writer outside the constraints of scholarly
convention.

It is in such paragraphs that one sees most clearly the charm
and sensitivity to detail that Walton and Brooks acclaimed.
Again, however, Rourke's evocative language served a purpose
beyond merely pleasing the ear. For fictional style, in addition
to sustaining myth, also produced exactly the resonances necessary for understanding native traditions, in Rourke's words,
"almost without thought." Forming a vivid mental picture of
the Indians or the passing procession, the reader becomes immediately involved in the narrative. He, too, rides in the canoe
or hears the boy's uncertain voice, instead of passively receiving
historical data. As Rourke well knew, the use of image-laden
language was a way of roping one's audience into the past, a
method of bridging the distance between past and present by
playing to a feeling of kinship among all people throughout
history. Novelistic or dramatic style said to the reader: here is a
heritage to which you are personally, emotionally connected.

Rourke adopted the device of fictionalization to varying ex-
tents in all but one of her books. Limited in *American Humor*,
it wholly dominated *Davy Crockett* and *Audubon*, as well as the
earlier *Troupers of the Gold Coast*. Though *Trumpets of Jubilee*
was more scholarly, Rourke hoped her nineteenth-century "portraits" (the term is hers) would convey a sense of the "color"

and "tone" of the lives of the Beechers, Greeley, and Barnum. In her initial letter to Alfred Harcourt inquiring whether he might be interested in the project, she stated that each character would be presented "dramatically," and that the book "should read somewhat like a novel, with an effect of connection between the portraits and progression and even climax, the four or five personal dramas revealing a larger social drama."[59] Intending *Trumpets of Jubilee* to recreate the mood of the past, Rourke tinged the book with a fictional quality. The exception was *Charles Sheeler: Artist in the American Tradition*, which differs radically from Rourke's other writings because it is about a living artist, and rests on direct quotation from Sheeler rather than evocation of an earlier time. Yet even in her draft for "A History of American Culture" the requirements of exposition did not prevent Rourke from introducing elements of fictional style. Her introduction, for example, begins with the story of a group of imaginary travelers in Europe who discuss the fate of art in America. No doubt Rourke intended to create an exact counterpart to *The Wine of the Puritans*, itself an argument cast in fictional form. But at the same time, coming as it does at the beginning, the travelers' conversation functions on a small scale the way the device of fictionalization operates in her other work: it disarms her readers, engages their interest, summons their participation, and permits their identification with characters akin to themselves.

A brief examination of Bernard DeVoto's historical writing may illuminate more about the way Rourke's style was a strategy for fostering "possession," for though he and Rourke differed widely with respect to frontier humor, his accounts of the exploration and settlement of the West mirror her desire to make the past part of America's collective emotional life. In fact, DeVoto used the same stylistic method with much more self-consciousness than Rourke. In *The Year of Decision: 1846* (1943), he was explicit about his audience: he announced that he was writing for the "general reader." The purpose of his book, DeVoto noted in his preface, was "to [allow his reader to] realize the pre-Civil War, Far Western frontier as personal experience."[60] His aim, in other words, was not merely to order and display the facts of our Western pioneering, but to make all Americans feel what it was like to have been a pioneer.

A sentence near the beginning of *The Year of Decision* sets the tone for what follows: "This book tells the story of some people who went west in 1846." The phrase "tells the story" leads the reader instantly to expect the comforts of fiction, and the simple language ("some people who went west") conveys the sense that we are about to read an account of average men and women whose adventures, but for the accident of birth, could have happened to us. The imprecise wording removes any expectation of academic treatment and permits the reader to settle back in his chair: it is hardly the sort of sentence that would be footnoted. In the same paragraph, DeVoto wrote that "1846 best dramatizes personal experience as national experience." He went on to state what he had already implied by his tone: "Most of our characters are ordinary people, the unremarkable commoners of the young democracy." Here the word "characters" indicates DeVoto's attitude toward his subject; later he referred to an historical figure "who will be an actor in our drama."[61] For DeVoto, history had all the entertainment value of the spectacle, in which our emotions are captivated by characters with whom we can identify, in which stories "come to life" before our eyes. At least history could be made so personally involving if properly presented.

To that end, DeVoto built dramatic structure into the book as a whole and into a great many sections individually. He used flashbacks and leaps into the future to heighten the importance of single events, borrowed devices from the stage like the "interlude,"[62] employed rhythmic sentences that engaged the reader's emotions more than his intellect, and addressed his audience directly to simulate a face-to-face encounter.[63] DeVoto's purpose, he announced, was a "literary" one, and, like Rourke, he fulfilled it by means of literary techniques. The adjective is ironic in light of his remark elsewhere that "when you set out to write history, no poetry however beautiful and no sentiments however commendable can be substituted for statements of fact."[64] But literary considerations could take precedence over scholarly ones if they aided the "realization" of our cultural inheritance: better that poetry be more visible than the trappings of academic writing. At the end of *The Course of Empire*, DeVoto asserted, "I wish that books could be written without footnotes. Since they cannot be I have written most of my notes to amplify for students matters which are carried no farther in the text than the interest of the general reader requires. Perhaps a dozen notes, and these the longest ones, are obligatory discussions of matters important to specialists."[65] DeVoto's comment is strikingly similar to Rourke's in her selected bibliography for *Trumpets of Jubilee* that "to end a book with a display of the machinery by which it has been assembled is to stress the toil which has gone into its making, not the pleasure. No formal list can truly represent a lively aggregation of sources. . . ."[66] She furnished her bibliography reluctantly, indicating by the words "machinery" and "lively" her assumption that the conventions of scholarly writing drained the life out of style designed to create an instinctive sense of the past.

Rourke's and DeVoto's assumption that the diffusion of tradition required the adoption of nonacademic style received explicit statement from another participant in the search for a "usable past," Constance Lindsay Skinner. Skinner, a popular historian and friend of Rourke's, was, until her death in 1939, general editor of the "Rivers of America" series published by Farrar and Rinehart. Skinner's plan for the series illuminates a great deal about the premises from which Rourke operated. As Skinner explained, each volume would deal with a single American river, chronicling the life of the people who lived along its banks. Rourke herself was to have inaugurated the series with her study of the Ohio. "The series has two purposes," Skinner wrote, "to kindle imagination and to reveal American Folk to one another."[67] (Her description of Americans as "River Folk," and of "the American story as a Folk Saga" may be a sign of Rourke's direct influence; in any case, Skinner shared in the general interest in primitive culture and myth that Rourke also exemplified.) In view of the "troubles" incurred by the Depression, Skinner asserted that Americans had to discover who they were, to understand their origins and their affinities with one another. This understanding, Skinner's language made plain, was to take place primarily on an emotional level; it involved feeling what the past had been like. Moreover, the task of recreating that feeling belonged not to scholars but to artists. The passage in which Skinner assigned them the task of elucidating native traditions is worth quoting at length, for it exactly summarizes the convictions that led Rourke to adopt a popular writing style:

This is to be a literary and not an historical series. The authors of these books will be novelists and poets. On them, now in America, as in all lands and times, rests the real responsibility of interpretation. If the average American is less informed about his country than any other national, knows and cares less about its past and about its present in all sections but the one where he resides and does business, it is because the books prepared for his instruction were not written by artists. Few artists have displayed to him the colors and textures of the original stuff of American life; or made him a comrade of the folk who came from the crowded civilizations of the old world and entered the vast wilderness of the new by all its shining rivers; or thrust him, as one of them, into the clash of spirit with circumstance. . . . He has not been led to feel himself a neighbor and brother in the foreign groups which developed into separate Little Americas. . . .

The average American has been prevented from a
profound self-knowledge, as a descendant and a citizen,
and deprived as an individual of the thrill and inspiration of a dramatic experience, because the epic material
of America has been formulated by the scholastics instead of by the artists.[68]

Skinner's emphasis—as the words "colors and textures," "thrill
and inspiration," "feel himself a neighbor and brother," and
"thrust him, as one of them" make clear—is on the importance
of conveying the emotional experience of the past, an experience
that must be evoked as drama rather than described as fact and
footnoted. Skinner's language also indicates the unifying function she thought tradition might perform. It could replace the
"separateness" dividing ethnic groups with sentiments of neigh-
borliness and brotherhood. It could "bring the vital past into the
living present, unite them," transcend regionalism, overcome
isolation, provide an awareness of "common origin."[69] This was
precisely the sort of unity Rourke welcomed in her discovery of
a native tradition of mythmaking. Early in her statement, Skinner expressed her hopes for tradition in a metaphor that recalls
Rourke's image of "gathered light": "The first necessity of our
times, as they relate to letters, would seem to be the retelling of
the American story as a Folk Saga; if only to make the parts
luminous by shedding on them the light of the whole."[70]

Skinner's plan for the "Rivers of America" series also reveals
that the adoption of popular style was partly a political choice.
In its attempt to strengthen social bonds, the series rested on an
alternative to a class perspective. For Skinner, "tradition" rather
than class solidarity created "comrades." Similarly, Rourke's
writing is strikingly barren of any signs of antagonism between
rich and poor, labor and capital. A stress on creating a sense of
a common heritage implicitly dismissed class consciousness as a
prerequisite for social change. Skinner both recognized and de-
fended this aspect of the style she and Rourke shared, regarding

the "Rivers of America" series as a counterattack on economic determinism and left-wing politics. As she put it, "Everyone, apparently, has his 'revolution' today—the word makes nice large mouthing, anyway—and American writers and illustrators are entitled to theirs against the 'economic interpreters' with their foolish notion that the belly is the hub of the universe and America's own bright and morning star."[71] Instead of listening to revolutionaries on "soap boxes," Skinner argued, each citizen ought to "meet the folks" and renew his faith in the American way of life. New Dealers were issuing the same summons when they called for nationwide cooperation to end economic distress. The "artistry" of the "Rivers of America" series, and the language of Davy Crockett, were analogous to displaying the NRA "blue eagle"—and just as remote from waving the red flag.

Skinner's explicitly antirevolutionary stance suggests an additional attraction of popular writing style: it promised important benefits for the isolated intellectual. Among the "folks," Skinner made clear, were artists and writers themselves. As she described the "Rivers of America" series, "its authors, illustrators, editor, and publishers are also 'folks,' absorbed in issuing the story they have discovered which has been, thus far, a lost version of a great saga."[72] Skinner's confusion of the word "folk" in an anthropological sense with the colloquial phrase "just folks" indicates that popular writing style did more than foster social cohesion generally. Unlike radical politics, founded on repudiating the American system, popular style allowed writers to reach out to the dominant culture. It helped to resolve on a personal level the tension between "high-brow" and "low-brow" that Skinner, and Rourke, sought to dispel in American society at large.

In Rourke's case the conflict between the roles of average citizen and writer or intellectual was less pronounced than for a figure who remained within academia or became closely identified with New York literary circles. Her resignation from Vassar in 1915 and her decision to "root herself" in Grand Rapids were declarations of allegiance to the common man. Yet Rourke retained strong ties to other intellectuals (Brooks, Mumford, Benedict, Sheeler) and to academic teachers of history and folklore. She often sought opportunities for lecturing at colleges and universities. Her long stretches of work in New York and her summers at the MacDowell Colony are evidence of the curious position she occupied between two worlds—she was estranged from academic and self-conscious literary life yet involved with it. Popular style was a way of counteracting whatever pull the "high-brow" world still exerted upon Rourke; it announced that despite her connections with New York artists, she was siding with Michigan lumberjacks. Rourke even used Brooks's terminology in a letter to Alfred Harcourt about her "History of American Culture": "This sounds highbrow and formal—you can't imagine how informal and intelligible it promises to be."[73] That promise—to disguise her painstaking scholarship and to appeal to a wide audience—diminished Rourke's role as intellectual and deprived her of recognition she deserved. Repeatedly denied fellowships from the Guggenheim and Carnegie foundations, she speculated that she may have been turned down in one instance because her style hid her real achievements. "It's hard for me to think that my work can be challenged on the ground of scholarship," she wrote, "because I have had so much recognition on that score, but I know that the scholarship in both *Crockett* and *Audubon* can be invisible to those who do not know the field."[74] It is difficult to know what attention Rourke had in mind, for she was virtually neglected by academic historians: to take one indication, none of her books was ever reviewed in the *American Historical Review*. The failure of academics to award all of Rourke's writing scholarly value has persisted up to the present time, and demonstrates, as Brooks might have said, that the division between "high-brow" and "low-brow" still exists. For example, in a generally laudatory biographical sketch, Kenneth Lynn has recently written: "*Davy*

[169]

*Crockett* (1934) and *Audubon* (1936) show signs of haste and are deservedly forgotten."[75] Yet damaging though it was to Rourke's reputation as a scholar, her popular style had an important positive result. It placed her at what she saw as the center of American life, freeing her from the intellectual's risk of isolation. There were limits to the closeness Rourke welcomed—her friendships, after all, thrived on distance, and her position as critic demanded detachment—but within those boundaries she was more comfortable "getting along with everyone" than identifying herself as cut off from the "folks." Indeed, it may be that popular style enabled Rourke to satisfy through writing yearnings for intimacy that she felt unable to express in personal relationships.

Rourke's style, like that of any novelist or poet, was not accidental. Her use of the language of fiction, which one might misunderstand as merely picturesque, needs to be considered as functional. Like her definition of culture and her understanding of myth, her approach to writing was a way of correcting Brooks's description of a divided America. It enabled her to create new myths and monitor the acceptability of old ones, to diffuse traditions and to participate in them. Constructing a bond of feeling that encompassed writer, subject, and audience, she could achieve unity on an emotional level not only throughout society generally but in particular between herself and the common man.

# 6

## CRITICISM

Rourke's understanding of tradition, myth, and the requirements of style defined a role for the socially responsible critic. In most of her work, she merely implied the dimensions of that role, preferring to forego theory for practice. Yet her explicit statements about the purpose of criticism grew more frequent and took on new shadings in the political climate of the 1930s. To the convictions that had guided her since the beginning of her career, Rourke added her responses to Marxism and fascism—a combination that provides a final perspective on the nature of her search for a "usable past."

Again Van Wyck Brooks's early essays illuminate the context in which Rourke's ideas belong. As he surveyed American culture, Brooks placed much of the blame for its deficiencies on a group of critics who had praised works suited to materialism and "sterile for the living mind."[1] He designated those figures members of a "genteel tradition," borrowing an epithet from George Santayana's famous lecture "The Genteel Tradition in American Philosophy" (1911). Although primarily concerned with late nineteenth-century anglophiles like Stedman, Brooks and others also castigated for identical reasons the New Humanist disciples of Babbitt and More, who Santayana said belonged to "the genteel tradition at bay." Thanks in large part to Brooks, the term "genteel tradition" persists as a catchall for a variety of critical sins, consigning diverse figures to a single, inaccurate stereotype. As Richard Ruland has pointed out, for example, to label as genteel both Stedman's "Band" and the New Humanists is to obliterate the distinction between the earlier group's defense of the status quo and the latter's vehement, reactionary dissent.[2] Though the phrase is full of perils, however, the concept of a "genteel tradition" formed the point of departure for Brooks's—and Rourke's—own concepts of the critic's function.

Brooks and other rebels against gentility commonly attributed certain principles to their critical antagonists. First, the genteel critic had believed himself a "custodian of culture," charged with upholding standards in art and society. In their effort to see that literature preserved conventional moral values, older critics especially had confused morality with "cheerfulness." They assumed, in Brooks's words, that art was to "turn aside the problems of life from the current of emotional experience, . . ." a requirement the thwarted Mark Twain could meet only by becoming a humorist.[3] In contrast, William Dean Howells, when he argued that literature should treat "the more smiling aspects of life," fulfilled genteel expectations. Additionally, gentility seemed to contradict democratic ideals, for the genteel critic saw himself as an aristocrat obligated to elevate the taste of the masses.

As Brooks and his followers in the period before World War I knew all too well, Matthew Arnold's formulation of the need for an adequate culture had licensed some of the worst features of the "genteel tradition." For when Arnold outlined the new role for the artist that the modern predicament demanded, he also reassessed the place of the critic: he was to insure that "culture" was, in Arnold's famous phrase, "the best that has been thought and said in the world." It was here that Brooks and Arnold, sharing a commitment to "adequacy," came to a parting of the ways. Arnold's emphasis on standards, Brooks thought, had made it easy for Americans to evade the responsibility of creating their own literature, allowing them instead "to share vicariously in the heritage of civilization" while pursuing materialistic ends. In Brooks's words, Arnold's doctrine "upholstered their [Americans'] lives with everything that is best in history, with all mankind's most sumptuous effects quite sanitarily purged of their ugly and awkward organic relationships. . . . It made the creative life synonymous in their minds with finished things, things that repeat their message over and over and 'stay put.' In short, it conventionalized for them the spiritual experience of humanity, pigeon-holing it, as it were, and leaving them fancy-free to live 'for practical purposes.' "[4] Moreover, Brooks believed, Arnold's elitist conception of criticism had enthroned the genteel critic in the university. Entrenched in academia, the "professorial mind" could fulfill its obligations to educate the people while remaining aloof from them. In a phrase that implies remoteness from experience, Brooks wrote that academic critics had "placed a sort of Talmudic seal upon the American tradition."[5]

Brooks's friend Randolph Bourne nourished his dissatisfaction with Arnold. Bourne's essay in the *Atlantic Monthly* for October 1914, on the Arnoldian view of culture, which Brooks later reprinted in *The History of a Literary Radical* (1920), deplored the way the Englishman's definition of culture had put Americans in a position of "cultural humility." "This tyranny of the 'best,' " wrote Bourne, "objectifies all our taste. It is a 'best' that is always outside of our native reactions to the freshnesses and sincerities of life, a 'best' to which our spontaneities must be disciplined. By fixing our eyes humbly on the ages that are past, and on foreign countries, we effectually protect ourselves from that inner taste which is the only sincere 'culture.' " Arnold's idea that "somehow culture could be imbibed," Bourne concluded, had prompted genteel critics to look upon the "treasures of Europe" as the only source of salvation, at the expense of native traditions.[6]

When Constance Rourke became a critic herself, she perpetuated Brooks's and Bourne's reaction against gentility. For example, in one of her first contributions to the *New Republic*, a review in 1921 of Mrs. Thomas Bailey Aldrich's *Crowding Memories*, she complained, "Boston suddenly appears for what it largely was, an imitative society trying to keep up the most genteel of social and literary traditions, but at bottom really provincial and self-inhibitive." Citing Santayana's characterization of mid-nineteenth-century New England as a "kind of Indian summer of the mind" (a phrase that Brooks adopted), Rourke added: "The picture of the succeeding period suggests that pale afterlight which falls briefly upon the stripped landscape of November. The faint brightness has about it something factitious and transient. There is no reason why it should remain. When a critic wrote of Aldrich that he seemed aloof from experience, he thought he was being advised to treat of topics of the day."[7] Rourke made a similar comment in "The Roots of American Culture," characterizing Lyly as "the perfect pattern of gentility or sheer dalliance with words."[8] The same view marked her description of the unknown painter Voltaire Combe as a refugee from gentility, a native artist whose career "dispels certain ideas as to the pervasiveness of the genteel tradition."[9]

Rourke also shared Brooks's prejudice against genteel academics who made a virtue of isolation from experience. She had outlined a discussion of the nature of academic criticism for the introduction to "A History of American Culture." "In undertakings which have to do with immediacy, with life," Rourke noted, "we are accustomed to collect a good many disparagements under the heading 'academic.' " In terms that link her to Brooks, she deplored a "school of academic thought which recognizes that we have a past but believes we must wait until it has been excavated . . . then we can piece it together and interpret it." To Rourke, that approach constituted a "refinement," a "withdrawal" from an urgent issue; it assumed that culture was a "matter of study not a matter of experience or use" and instructed the critic to "wait, wait, as if this were only a battle of the books." University professors had also enshrined the concept of art as "luxury," directing what Rourke called "*odium academicum*" at native literary and folk culture. In particular, noting the way American subjects had been slighted in course offerings, Rourke denounced the tendency for colleges to treat American literature as a subsidiary of English literature.[10]

As one might predict from her other efforts to rescue American culture from Brooks's condemnation, however, Rourke was less willing than Brooks was, in his early writings, to reject his and her own critical predecessors. Rather, she perceived an existing current of vitality within academic criticism that supplied a basis for the future. Just as Voltaire Combe had "escaped the pervasiveness" of the "genteel tradition," so had some American scholars. Asserting that it was "not difficult to prove that a living creative academic tradition has wound its way through our culture," she cited such figures as Noah Webster, Lester Ward, "Henry Adams's friend Samuel Langly," Robert Lovett, and Robert Herrick as "free lance experimenters in ideas who have been in and out" of university life.[11] For Rourke, the healthy strain in American academia culminated in Parrington, whom she acknowledged as the critic she "should most like to emulate, not as to his ideas, which I have (of course) not been able to accept in toto, but in his engaging humility." By humility, Rourke meant Parrington's willingness to forsake final, cleanly drawn formulations of the American heritage in favor of a "rough working drawing" that took into account "the synthesis of forces, the concrete lively perception of phrases of human expressiveness in the arts, in customs, social choices, likings, distrusts, failures, consistent drops into the abyss when these have occurred." Parrington's "courage," as Rourke saw it, lay in his commitment to "take the plunge toward this understanding, this acceptance of ourselves and our past more fully. . . . " Unafraid of making mistakes, Parrington admitted that certain of his judgments were "downright guesses." His approach was, for Rourke, the best sort of "living" criticism. If such "experimentation" and "adventure" resulted in critical controversy, so much the better, Rourke concluded, because debate signified that the questions involved were sufficiently engaging and important.[12]

Rourke found the example of Parrington and other lively academics heartening in view of the special services that she thought academic criticism, once extricated from the "genteel tradition," might provide. For these scholars, schooled in research techniques and with access to university libraries, could turn those resources to the study of folklore and native art. Moreover, the academic critic could offer a unique perspective with respect to Europe; his broad training gave him "a sense of the whole" that would enable him to determine the extent to which American cultural movements were independent of European ones. He could apply his knowledge about matters of form to the study of folk art, practicing, along with nonacademics, "a new kind of aesthetic criticism dealing not with the final work of art but with the potentialities of materials." Finally, academic critics, by drawing "within college halls and the schoolroom the sense of immediacy as to our culture which exists outside," could substitute for the dry study of literature the excitement of discovering "streams of popular expression."[13] To that end, Rourke urged the creation of courses about America stressing "social orientations" rather than simply literature. She also applauded the incorporation of the arts into the curricula of small colleges like Black Mountain, Antioch, and Bennington, and praised the beginnings of a regional approach to folklore as an academic subject at Duke and the University of Oklahoma. In fact, despite her awareness of a tendency among academics toward intellectualization and the repression of creativity, Rourke observed that the "gap between the academic and the creative life is undoubtedly closing" and spoke of a "whole conspicuous movement toward acceptance of creative forces even in our most conservative institutions."[14] When Tre-

maine McDowell, in 1948, called for the development of inter-
disciplinary programs in American Studies, he pushed Rourke's
ideas to their logical conclusion: her view that a synthetic approach to the American "pattern" could provide a link between
university education and the exigencies of modern life became
a mainstay of early American Studies rhetoric.

Rourke's vision of an active role for academic critics derived
in part from her years at Vassar. "Social orientations," a willingness to make tentative "guesses," and a criticism free of final
judgments were exactly what Laura Wylie and Gertrude Buck
had advocated in their classrooms. Moreover, they themselves
spent their personal as well as their professional lives strengthening the bond between academia and the wider community.
At Wylie's death in 1932, a Poughkeepsie newspaper hailed her
as "not a remote academic type but a woman who bridged the
gap between campus and town with myriad activities."[15] A local leader of the woman suffrage movement between 1900 and
1916, she was president of the Women's City Club of Poughkeepsie. (Her colleague Lucy M. Salmon was second vice-pres-
ident.) When she died, she left $110,000 "to perpetuate the
friendly relations between city and college realized by her associate, the late Professor Gertrude Buck, in the founding of the
Community Theatre."[16] Contrary to the common stereotype of
turn-of-the-century Vassar as "genteel," Wylie and Buck were
living counterexamples to the estranged intellectuals or the
passive representatives of gentility Brooks had depicted; they
personally denied any separation between "high-brow" and
"low-brow." Hence Rourke's early exposure to academia, albeit
in the peripheral setting of a woman's college, contradicted
what she read in Brooks's essays and convinced her that a precedent already existed for the American critic opposed to the "genteel tradition."

Yet Rourke's animus toward gentility should not obscure the
degree to which her stance accorded with genteel principles.
The literary theory she studied and taught at Vassar depended

on earlier formulations—and specifically on the writings of Matthew Arnold. For "social criticism," though it democratized the critical process, sanctioning whatever gave new meaning to the life of the ordinary reader, still required the intervention of an "intellectual middleman," or, in Arnold's phrase, an "intellectual deliverer," to insure that a writer's ideas reached his audience. In *The Social Criticism of Literature*, Buck had called Arnold's conception of the critic's role "fundamental," and had approvingly paraphrased his views: "From poet to critic, from critic to readers, from readers to new poets, passes the divine afflatus, in a self-perpetuating cycle. And thus society periodically catches up with its leaders, only to cast forward in the stream of its own progress new leaders whom it must overtake."[17] In other words, "social criticism," however relativistic with respect to conventional morality and aesthetics, incorporated Arnold's understanding of the critic's ethical position. Moreover, Buck's impossibly vague phrase "the divine afflatus" masks the degree to which she—and Rourke—also retained some of Arnold's concern with "the best." Not all writing was "divine afflatus." Only those works that would broaden a reader's social consciousness could qualify. Buck's substitution of "social" requirements for narrow moral strictures like the need for "cheerfulness" made her no less committed to charging the critic with the task of maintaining standards. In a move that brought her close to the "genteel tradition," for example, Buck exempted from critical consideration writing that was "palpably insincere" or "notably crude," and distinguished the "legitimately popular" from the "wholly commercial."[18]

Rourke was an even better Arnoldian, though she focused much of her own demand for standards on phenomena that were outside Buck's purview. She assigned the critic the specific obligation of warding off nostalgia and antiquarianism in the treatment of the past. For example, she deplored the "thin sentimentalism" of a collection of tales about the West.[19] "Folksongs have been set like rosettes on the surface of plays and novels," she complained in "A Note on Folklore," "and quaint old American furniture has been so precisely and ardently described in the course of a narrative that one can fairly see the antique-dealer at the door."[20] At the outset of *American Humor*, Rourke warned that studying humor out of an "antiquarian interest" led to the pitfall of "pedantry."[21] At the same time, she stood guard against the opposite danger: the shallow oversimplification that might result in a vulgarization of the American arts. As she remarked in one review, her demand for approaches that would create a consciousness of tradition did not mean that she sought a "rough-and-ready popularization."[22]

Rourke was particularly concerned about the encroachments of technology upon culture. In "The Decline of the Novel," she observed:

Even as mere entertainment the novel has lost ground, not of course because all readers have grown studious but because entertainment of a similar kind can be had in easier, gayer, more social forms, at the movies and over the radio with diminished cost. The 'hammock novel' now rarely receives even the flattery of scorn. If it exists at all this is because habit is strong for the elderly and middle-aged. The young seem rarely to linger in hammocks for literate purposes, and when they do it is not for a leisurely pace in reading. The novels they choose are less and less like novels: they are made up of telegrams, radiograms, swift climaxes.

Noting the rising popularity of the detective story, she added, "With another twirl or two on the part of the inventors, with expanded television, one can imagine that the detective story as well as other novels of entertainment will be translated into pictorial and audible terms, available in what used to be the library, or if one likes, in the forest primeval—or what used to be the forest primeval."[23] Rourke's commitment to an art reflective of popular social values allowed her to welcome, rather than lament, changes in the novel. Moreover, she understood that the spread of mass media held the potential to enhance as well as to undermine culture. For example, she asserted that "collective consciousness in this country has been heightened on some levels created within recent years by mechanical devices which might seem to destroy consciousness," concluding that in a sense radio had returned the nation to the "emotional unity of the folk."[24] Similarly, in the *Nation* for August 15, 1934, she recommended that those interested in preserving and popularizing native American ballads grapple "on a large scale with the snares of broadcasting."[25] Nevertheless, the existence of "snares" made it imperative that the critic, rather than the engineer, assume responsibility for making certain that technological achievements fostered art that was "best" for society.

In short, Rourke's understanding of the critic's role combined a critique of the "genteel tradition" with an acceptance of many of its premises.[26] She valued standards along with democratic ideals, morality along with relativism. Recognition of Rourke's debt to the "genteel tradition" provides more than a sense of her place in American critical circles. Her dualistic view of criticism had significant implications for the politics of the 1930s. Determined to judge a work against the "social" standard of human fulfillment, she could not adopt a perspective that wholly rejected gentility—that of the Marxists. Advocates of "proletarian culture," like V. F. Calverton and Granville Hicks, repudiated the view that art could be ideologically neutral and urged the evaluation of literature according to another criterion: did a given piece of writing serve the cause of revolution? Those Marxist critics endowed an interest in culture with an explicitly political function, a demand in which Rourke saw the distortion of aesthetic values.

She planned to array her objections to Marxist criticism in her introduction to "A History of American Culture." Rourke granted, first of all, that "the major charges of the Marxian critics against our principal literary figures of the past may be readily admitted." But she questioned the usefulness of those charges. Summarizing Hicks's statements in *The Great Tradition*, Rourke agreed with him that Melville, setting stories in the South Seas, had failed to confront the social consequences of industrialization. Nor, according to Hicks, did Hawthorne supply any more directly pertinent vision, whereas Thoreau's excessive individualism marked him as equally deficient. Similarly, Rourke reported, Hicks judged Dickinson, Howells, and James inadequate because they tried to escape the major issues facing American civilization; James, for example, Hicks dubbed a "fugitive." "The writers to whom Granville Hicks gives an accolade," Rourke observed, "are those who dealt specifically with economic questions[:] Henry George, Henry Demarest Lloyd, Edward Bellamy." Those authors, Rourke contended, were reformers whose schemes Marx himself had repudiated. Thus to Rourke it appeared that "it becomes increasingly difficult to understand of what 'the great tradition' consists: a consideration of poverty, of social and economic issues, the uses of realism in relation to societies. . . ." Such subjects for literature were hardly confined to America; in fact, Rourke commented that elsewhere they were often more highly developed. "It is only when Hicks reaches contemporary writers of the Marxist position," she continued, "that he finds 'the great tradition' becoming explicit. Similar distinctions are emphasized by other Marxian critics dealing historically with our culture. As a final extreme we are told that we must anticipate a plan to classify our poets, novelists, and critics as 'Party writers and non-Party writers.'" In addition to rigid categorization, Rourke judged Marxists guilty of distorting the facts: "Individualism, the Marxists say [and Rourke penciled "Calverton" in the margin], flourished in all its extremes on the American frontier." That thesis was diametrically opposed to Rourke's own, which described pioneer communities at least partly as centers of collective striving and democracy. How, then, could the frontier have been the wellspring of American capitalism? Moreover, Rourke found the Marxist approach rooted in a constrained view of literary form; demanding realism, the Marxist critic also demanded novels. The statement that the novel is " 'the major literary form today' " (which she quoted from William Phillips's and Philip Rahv's contribution to Hicks's *Proletarian Literature in the United States*) is one to which Rourke, foreseeing and partially welcoming the decline of the novel, could hardly have assented. "Even the drama," she remarked, "has remained secondary in these discussions [of appropriate form]. . . . With its special concentrations poetry may reveal some of the great type economic situations or become declamatory, a call to action or a mass lament, yet the uses of poetry in this respect have not been greatly stressed by Marxian critics." Nor had they widened their view of acceptable varieties of art to take in music and nonrealistic graphic or plastic arts. More important, according to Rourke, Marxist critics fell victim to a narrow application of dogmatic principles that denied the true character of literature. As Rourke phrased this inflexibility: "The Marxists have given us an organon of criticism which is both hortatory and didactic, diagrammatic and static, not progressing beyond attitudes already defined except by the imposition of the economic formula. All writers must proceed in the same way in the use of this formula [here the quotation is again from Phillips and Rahv]: 'The class struggle must serve as a premise, not as a discovery.' " That perspective led in Rourke's estimation not only to a "neglect of aesthetics" but to a disregard for "those human areas through which aesthetics in any broad sense must be approached." "What is absent from these critical speculation[s]," Rourke concluded, "is a conception of literature as whole, rich, and many-sided, as wayward, creating dynamic changes, subject to no explicit law. The concept underlying this criticism is that the arts can take off like flyers lifting from a narrow runway into space, tossing aside the ballast of the past, throwing overboard complexities of motive, disregarding the human wealth of creative forces, concerned with a limited group of themes, aiming at the simple goal of realism in the treatment of those themes."[27]

The deficiencies of the Marxist viewpoint notwithstanding, Rourke credited several writers engaged in exploring the proletarian subject with important breakthroughs in literary form. She counted such works as *Waiting for Lefty*, *The Grapes of Wrath*, and *Pins and Needles* significant for the way they exhibited "a sudden freedom which might more truly be called revolutionary than the modes prescribed by the critics." But those efforts succeeded because they followed a "sequence out of the past," whereas the Marxists were "intent upon a complete break with tradition." As Rourke put it, "Marxist criticism had almost consistently thrown aside the past, but these new pieces have somehow contrived in spite of prescribed limitations to build upon a tradition or have unconsciously slipped into its long chain." Here Rourke was working once again from her assumption that literature divorced from tradition could only be sterile. The proponents of the view that writers must pay attention to the working class had, as Rourke saw it, cut themselves off from the one source that promised to nurture the growth of "proletarian literature": a native heritage of writing about the common man. Melville, Rourke noted as one example, "concentrated a cosmic symbolism in the figures of the common folk. . . ." Instead of relegating Melville to the category of irrelevant writer of travelogues, Rourke argued, the critic should recognize that he offered "something to be cherished and to build upon." "Such native figures," she added, "were often emblematic of the racy energy and lively imaginative force which have belonged to us on just those human levels with which one would suppose the Marxists to be most concerned: levels of the 'folk.' " But, to Rourke's dismay, Calverton, Hicks, and other likeminded critics had failed to recognize the value of a folk tradition, and were instead preoccupied with insisting that art directly address contemporary social issues.[28]

As in the case of her disavowal of gentility, it is important to recognize that Rourke and her adversaries squared off on common ground. If the Marxists assumed that an interest in culture could perform a political function, so, ever since her Vassar days, had Rourke. But Calverton's vision was hardly what Laura Wylie had in mind when she spoke of the "revolutionary" potential of poetry. As a type of Progressive-era reform, "social criticism" entailed a commitment only to the growth of the individual in a democratic context. This, and not the redistribution of power or the transformation of the state, was always Rourke's paramount political concern. Thus, Rourke's ideal critic was not an agitator but an educator: the gatherer of light for the artist, the interpreter of national myths, the instructor in human fulfillment. When Rourke herself adopted that role, by writing about America's popular figures, national traits, and artistic achievements in a style accessible to the ordinary reader, she assumed what Lawrence Cremin has described as the characteristic Progressive stance: that of the "socially responsible reformist pedagogue."[29] Translating the assumptions beneath progressive education into directives for his own pursuits, the explorer of native traditions could help society advance by freeing each person for self-expression. In that way he fulfilled his obligation, in Gertrude Buck's phrase, to "further the activity of literature as an agent of social progress."[30]

Rourke's article "Traditions for Young People," which appeared in 1937 against the backdrop of Marxist criticism, illustrates more than the way she drew on progressive educational theories for a model of "possession." It also reveals the political premises that in the last years of her life came more and more to color her search for a "usable past." When Rourke proposed a room of primary materials for schoolchildren, she was not simply thinking of a resource for learning. Like a good progressive teacher, at the conclusion of her article she made the school a reflection of the larger society, calling her room a "symbol of those balances and coordinations which we still lack." Her final remarks go beyond aesthetic and educational issues to social ones; they give the study of tradition the power to improve the quality of American life: "If we could open our past to young people in genuine abundance, with its poetry and homeliness, its occasional strange sparseness, its cruelties and dark failures, we might have a great literature and music and art upon us before we know it. We might even be able to devise equable ways of living."[31]

As a phrase like "before we know it" indicates, Rourke was as vague and mystical in suggesting the possible social benefits of a "usable past" as she was in describing the artistic ones. In contrast to proposals for collective action articulated by her socialist contemporaries, Rourke's view of the way one proceeded from an awareness of tradition to a better society was highly unprogrammatic, as if "equable ways of living" might simply sneak up on each American imbued with a sense of "possession." Her model of social change, like her vision of the way tradition safeguarded art, depended not on legislation or lobbies or protests but on each person's ability to alter his own consciousness. When Kazin complained that Rourke's work furnished no "ready ground on which we can stand," his main concern was aesthetic, but the same could be said for the usefulness of Rourke's concept of tradition as an instrument of reform.

Nevertheless, in the late 1930s and early '40s, Rourke increasingly expressed her assumptions about culture and politics in the form of concrete political actions, for the rise of fascism in Europe lent the goal of cultural unity—for which Rourke had long labored—added meaning and urgency. The fascist threat heightened (though it also modified) the need for tradition, for myth, for a style that would reach a popular audience, for a vital criticism—all those aspects of the search for a "usable past" that Rourke's writing typified. Hence Rourke's efforts, and those of many other intellectuals on behalf of imperilled democracy, focus and summarize the major themes of her writing.

Stephen Vincent Benét, whom Rourke knew, revealed in an address entitled "We Stand United" the meaning "cultural unity" could have beyond signifying a common heritage; to Benét, in 1940, unity meant the absence of party or class conflict:

> In the troubled years to come, we must have unity and a united nation—not the blind unity of the slave state, but the deliberate unity of free men. . . .
> We cannot afford the creeping paralysis that destroys the effective will of democracy—the paralysis carried by hate and rancor, between class and class, person and person, party and party, as plague is carried through the streets of a town. . . .
> Let each one of us say: "I am an American. I intend to stay an American. I will do my best to wipe from my heart hate, rancor and political prejudice.[32]

The April 1941 program of the Fight for Freedom Committee, an internationalist organization committed to war against Hitler, echoed Benét's plea for a united America: "We can win this supreme test of democracy at home even as we fight the foreign enemy abroad. We can win on both fronts, if we remember in every waking moment of our lives that we are one people, and that we have one common purpose. Whether we are white or black—Catholic, Protestant, or Jew—rich or poor—from the North or South or East or West—we are one."[33] These and other appeals for unity rested on a transformed idea of the "folk," who were now not primitive mythmakers but rather a dedicated "people" who had supported and sustained a democratic government. Thus Walter Johnson, writing about the work of the Committee to Defend America by Aiding the Allies, could describe William A. White, the committee's chairman, as "something of a folk hero to America."[34]

As in Rourke's earlier work, antifascist writers saw the "folk" as bearers of traditions—but now the traditions were politicized. Lewis Mumford warned the readers of his tract *Men Must Act* that "those who do not believe in our American past" are "already in the fascist camp." Mumford's subsequent use of the phrase "usable past" indicates how the term had evolved to encompass an express political purpose: "I appeal only to those who, though they are deeply imbued with the American tradition, still shrink from undertaking the active task of every generation: that of re-examining our usable past, revaluing it, and re-translating it into fresh purposes and worthy deeds. The presence of fascism in the world has given us a special incentive to discover whatever is, by contrast, most excellent in our own heritage."[35] Reversing his previous denunciation of pioneering, Mumford included in that heritage steady devotion to freedom, "braced by the long experience of the frontier, with its free land and its sturdy opportunities for the self-reliant man." Mumford wrote that "the dislike of servility and authoritarianism is deeply engrained in the American character." Urging a position of nonintercourse with fascist nations, he declared that "this policy is based upon our national tradition of self-reliance: it does not involve us in blanket commitments or entangling alliances in Europe. . . ."[36] Other antifascist writers culled similar messages from the American past. In particular, Benét, Robert Sherwood, and Carl Sandburg returned to the figure of Lincoln to establish historical precedent for a crusade to achieve unity and freedom.[37] Rourke herself, commending *Men Must Act*, described Mumford's program for economic measures against the Axis powers as "built upon fundamentals in our character and tradition."[38]

An emphasis on the way a heritage of freedom linked one American to another served several crucial purposes. First, it reassured the nation that it was equipped to stave off a fascist conquest. For some, the Depression had exposed a flawed, corrupt system; when belief in that system seemed required for its survival, a fresh look at the past could help restore necessary faith. Bernard DeVoto recognized the way history could be used to bolster the impending war effort in his remarks on the surge of interest in Lincoln: "At a time when American democracy has reached a crisis which many think it cannot survive, the American people have invoked the man who, by general consent, represents the highest reach of the American character and who, in that earlier crisis, best embodied the strength of our democracy."[39] The moral of studying the historical record, as Alfred Jones has put it, was that "democracy could provide both the leadership and the resources to meet the gravest challenge."[40]

Moreover, apart from revealing America's capacity to fight "the foreign enemy abroad," the discovery of democratic traditions furnished comforting evidence of the strength of the home front. Such proof was necessary because with the rise of fascism, in Alfred Kazin's words, "it looked as if Americans had been thrown back on their own resources as never before."[41] No longer did one even ask whether America showed signs of "cultural lag." With the overturn of Europe's civilized values, America seemed the only "repository of Western culture,"[42] the promise of the future. Now the question was whether its traditions were adequate to fulfill that promise. The answer came forth, as Kazin has demonstrated, as a resounding "yes": "There was suddenly a whole world of marvels on the continent to possess—a world of rivers and scenes, of folklore and regional culture, of a heroic tradition to reclaim and of forgotten heroes to follow . . . , an inheritance to rejoice in and to find strength in."[43]

Rourke had directed her energies toward discovering that "world" for many years; given the need to mobilize the nation, she turned those discoveries into fortification for democracy. Specifically, in 1940, she worked with Mumford on plans for an

[188]

exhibition "on the meaning of America as a political and cultural entity."[44] Visitors were to pass through a series of rooms, each of which would convey an antifascist message. For instance, in the "Avenue of American Character and History," the viewer would see a "large raised map," illuminated by colored lights. Mumford's scenario read: "Without words, the map retells the story of the many nations which gave America its people, the motion of the lines of light and the great brilliance of America, suggesting the progression of darkness to light, from oppression to freedom." The "Room of Achievement," built around sketches of various historical figures, was to offer the visitor this message: "*Let us follow the lead of all these great men. Let us point to the problems of America and overcome them in our American tradition.*"[45] Rourke found the "whole concept" of Mumford's plan "magnificent."[46]

The exhibition, as Mumford wrote Rourke, was "conceived as a drama," aiming at maximum involvement of the audience. The "style" of the show can thus be seen as an extension of Rourke's recourse to the device of fictionalization, with the added urgent purpose of arousing the spectator to political action as well as fostering his "possession" of American history. Rourke had pitched her writing to a wide audience from *Trumpets of Jubilee* onward. But in 1938, given the importance of creating a sense of national spirit to combat German nationalism, "even so solidly respectable a historian as Allan Nevins launched an appeal, in *The Gateway to History*, for a more colorful history, a history richer in human interest and literary skill."[47] The exhibition complied with Nevins's demands.

Mumford and Rourke designed their show for the Museum of Modern Art, though opposition from trustees forced its eventual cancellation.[48] Their adoption of the form of an artistic event for a political crusade reveals the extent to which Mumford and Rourke, like the advocates of "proletarian literature," perceived the exploration of culture as a type of political activity: art could help keep democracy alive.

Rourke operated from the same premise in her plans for "A History of American Culture." Her notes refer to culture as "essentially a mode of communication," a "common language" that can tell us "what we are." That need, Rourke asserted, had never been "greater than at present, in the midst of the conflict, the regressions, the descent into the pit of the present time." Cultural explorations might meet the "demands of the present for a recognition of the prime forces that have been at work among us," helping to "articulate unmistakably, in language all will understand, our underlying ideas, emotions, the traditions which have been sustained. . . ."[49] Though here she made no explicit reference to democracy, the phrase "the pit of the present time" is in keeping with language she employed elsewhere (as in her review of Mumford's *Men Must Act*) to describe the rise of fascism. She amplified her position in a draft of her autobiography for *Twentieth Century Authors*. Her remarks shed light on her conception of the responsibilities of the critic as well as on the equation she made between politics and art:

When we first looked backward—those of us who enjoy such tasks—some years ago we were rather lighthearted about it, regarding the past as a phase of entertainment; at worst we jeered at our forbears in the debunking era. But now the matter has grown serious. Can the American past offer what men live by, in the way of ideals, ambitions, methods, ways of living—a foundation for the present? We need the sense of foundations in the midst of the tempest, obviously not by way of past glory, not as a vague "heritage," but as clarifying the democratic way of life and furthering knowledge of the methods of democracy. Democracy, whose principles are simple, has been infinitely complex in its workings, and these reach far beyond the economic and political sphere.

Our social history may reveal many of the tensions, results, progressions, setbacks of democracy. The arts of the past can have much to say as to our unities and disunities, continuities and discontinuities, failures, hopes, and miraculous accomplishments. If a democracy is a way of life as well as a political system, then its culture will offer basic clues as to its character and future.[50]

For her own part, Rourke had never regarded the past as "entertainment." From the beginning of her career, she had viewed democracy, in Dewey's words, as "primarily a mode of associated living, of conjoint communicated experience" requiring the knowledge of popular traditions;[51] in fact, his definition could have served as her watchword as she set out to describe the culture Americans shared. But her sense of "seriousness," as she put it, had grown with the times. Elsewhere in the draft of the same autobiographical statement, Rourke acknowledged both her long-standing assumptions and their new relevance: "The word 'ancestries' does not cover my interest. 'Continuities' is the better word. Though nearly all my writing has had to do with the past, I regard it as strictly contemporaneous. I never quite 'lose' myself, as the phrase is, in the past: it is what the past has to say to the difficult and precarious, strange and tragic present that seems important."[52] Rourke's apology to Donald Brace for slowness in completing the manuscript for "A History of American Culture" best summarizes her identification of cultural criticism with political action. Reviewing her activity in the Committee to Defend America by Aiding the Allies, she added, "I thought I ought to mention it since I'm supposed to be working on American culture, which it seems to me I really have."[53] That statement was essentially a refinement of Rourke's prior understanding that teaching and literary interpretation could be agents of social change.

Rourke's belief that an exploration of tradition could perform a political function links her closely to the intellectuals Christopher Lasch has designated "new radicals." In a now well-known argument, Lasch asserted that figures like Addams, Dewey, and Bourne evinced a tendency to value self-expression as the key to social betterment, a view Rourke also adopted. By relying on education (broadly conceived) to release the possibilities for individual fulfillment, such intellectuals, Lasch maintained, confused culture and politics. They assumed that a cultural concern could be "an instrument of social change in its own right" and that, conversely, political efforts could improve "the quality of American culture as a whole."[54] Rourke's apology to Brace reflects her participation in the latter view; her affinity with the "new radicals" appears primarily, however, in the hopes she attached to education and criticism. The difficulty with designating Rourke part of the "new radicalism" is that the phrase seems so inappropriate a description of an effort to depict and safeguard the mainstream of American society. If Rourke shared a common starting point with Addams or Dewey, she ended up by pursuing her interest in culture on behalf of a liberal government and a war to protect the American way of life—hardly radical activities. As Constance Lindsay Skinner well knew, the discovery of a heritage common to all Americans could serve deliberately antiradical purposes. To Rourke's credit, she never slid over into anything like blind chauvinism. But the wartime necessity of delineating a tradition of dedication to freedom— a tradition transcending class, racial, ethnic, and religious divisions—subverted potentially productive conflict and promoted a version of American history in which there was no room for slaves and slaveowners, workers and bosses, and radicals, either old or new.

Still, Rourke and others who investigated American culture in order to defend democracy shared with the "new radicals" the need to carve out an important social role for the intellectual. If settlement work satisfied, in Addams's phrase, a "subjective necessity" to be a useful member of the community, the delegation of political obligations to the critic likewise saved him from a position on the sidelines of American society. Rourke's description in *American Humor* of the writer's connection to popular traditions had performed this rescue operation on paper; her attention to the need for an explicator of native myths had similarly spelled an end to isolation. But the threat of fascism gave the intellectual at once more power and more palpable responsibilities, responsibilities that could take care of the "deep creative need" Rourke detected in some of the critics of her generation.[55] The critic was, in 1940, more than a guardian of standards, more than an educator: he was an indispensable, active participant in an attempt to preserve the American way of life. One could go no further in repudiating a division between "high-brow" and "low-brow."

Yet Rourke's involved, democratic stance chipped away at the critic's position as judge, as outsider. Arnold, after all, had insisted that criticism "show disinterestedness"—that it refuse "to lend itself to any of those ulterior, political, practical considerations about ideas. . . ."[56] Otherwise art might be compromised by the popular or the expedient—by what Eliot disparaged as "mass values."[57] When she appended the need for democratic orientation to Arnold's definition of "adequacy," Rourke risked the possibility that the democratization of culture would bring with it a lowering of standards, a risk that neither Arnold nor Eliot would have run. In her concern with criticism for the "people," she moved away from the elevated position of genteel critics toward the Marxists' subservience of art to politics.

To some, in fact, she was no better than the Marxists. William Phillips, Philip Rahv, and other writers for *Partisan Review* in the years just before World War II—who, in Richard Pells's words, "often seemed to regard Philistinism [Arnold's term] as a greater danger to America than fascism"[58]—found in any conflation of culture and politics the abdication of moral responsibility. As Pells summarized the *Partisan Review* writers' conception of their role, "they would speak for literary standards and intellectual ideals in a time of commercial vulgarity, shoddy thinking, and political manipulation."[59] Any other stance exposed the critic to the danger of becoming "the official voice of society," a charge that Phillips specifically leveled against Brooks.[60]

The judgment of the *Partisan Review* critics (who, as Pells demonstrated, themselves moved over to a postwar position of acquiescence toward the state) is a measure of the distance Rourke had come from Arnold and the "genteel tradition." But the *Partisan Review* attack ignored the possibility that a critic like Rourke, partaking of both Arnoldian and Marxist assumptions, could occupy a middle ground. Rourke's view of the critic's role reflected an old dilemma: that of reconciling the detached pose of the intellectual with the desire for participation in social life. Years earlier, Brooks had formulated the problem as one of joining "high-brow" and "low-brow." Throughout the 1930s, Rourke had responded with a vision of a unified society, imposing that unity through an alternative definition of culture, demonstrating it through a description of native mythmaking, creating it in her adoption of popular writing style. At the end of the decade, as fascism spread, her critical position balanced moral, artistic, and political considerations, representing a further mediation between the complete detachment of culture from daily life and the sacrifice of art to politics.

Those strategies reflect the strength and sensitivity of Rourke's mind, and make her as well a model of the modern American intellectual. "She sought what so many modern Americans have lost," as Alfred Kazin eulogized her, "what so many Europeans have established as the first principle of a human existence— the sense of locality, the simple happiness of *belonging* to a particular culture. . . . To understand this is to understand how fundamentally simple and yet rare was her curiosity, how deeply she had grasped the inner truth and the pain of the modern American alienation. 'Belief makes the mind abundant,' Yeats said; Constance Rourke knew something about the lack of belief and continuity, the damaging void in the modern American spirit."[61] But Rourke's accomplishments lay in her striving, not in the actual attainment of cultural unity. That remained, in her work, merely a willed construct. Only the outbreak of war, less than a year after Rourke's death, produced a temporarily unified America, searching not for a "usable past" but merely for an imaginable future.

# NOTES

### INTRODUCTION

1. Lewis Mumford, *The Golden Day*, pp. 143–44.
2. Ibid., p. 19.
3. Ibid., p. 144.
4. Williams to Sheeler, July 17, 1938, Constance Rourke MSS.

### CHAPTER 1

1. The remark belongs to Nelle Curry, quoted back to her by Helen Balph. Balph to Curry, Sept. 8, 1945, Margaret Marshall MSS.
2. *Grand Rapids Herald*, Dec. 25, 1944, and Margaret Marshall's notes for a book about Rourke, Marshall MSS.
3. Nelle Curry, "The Constance Rourkes," unpublished essay, p. 11; Balph to Curry, Sept. 27, 1945, Marshall MSS.
4. See Kenneth S. Lynn, "Rourke, Constance Mayfield," 3:199. My account of Mrs. Rourke's life comes from letters and notes in the papers of Margaret Marshall, the literary critic and close friend of Rourke's who once began a biography of her, and from the reminiscences of Linda Butler and Nelle Curry.
5. Margaret Marshall, notes on the Rourkes, Marshall MSS.
6. *Grand Rapids Press*, June 5, 1923, and Balph to Curry, Sept. 27, 1945, Marshall MSS.
7. Balph to Curry, Sept. 27, 1945, Marshall MSS.
8. Z. Z. Lydens, ed., *The Story of Grand Rapids*, p. 435.
9. Lawrence Cremin, *The Transformation of the School*, p. 118.
10. Ibid., p. ix.
11. Christopher Lasch, *The New Radicalism in America*, p. xiv.
12. Balph to Curry, Sept. 8, 1945, Marshall MSS.
13. Curry, "The Constance Rourkes," p. 7.

14. Constance Rourke (CR) to Constance Davis Rourke (CDR), 1896, Rourke MSS.
15. Curry, "The Constance Rourkes," p. 14.
16. Ibid., p. 16.
17. It is possible that the correspondence was lost when Vassar began collecting students' letters home. Rourke referred at one point to some letters that Miss Underhill, a college librarian, would be glad to have. CR to CDR, July 1, 1920, Rourke MSS. On the other hand, the Rourkes destroyed letters about sensitive matters. See note 56.
18. CR to CDR, Mar. 14, 1910, Rourke MSS.
19. See, for example, James Monroe Taylor and Elizabeth Hazelton Haight, *Vassar* and Agnes Rogers, *Vassar Women.*
20. Rogers, *Vassar Women*, p. 91.
21. Gertrude Buck, *The Social Criticism of Literature*, p. 48.
22. Constance Rourke, "Vassar Classrooms," p. 72.
23. Buck, *Social Criticism*, p. 39.
24. Ibid., p. 40.
25. Cremin, *The Transformation of the School*, pp. 118, 121, 123.
26. Buck, *Social Criticism*, p. 60.
27. Rourke, "Vassar Classrooms," p. 72.
28. Constance Rourke, "Inducements for Elementary School Teachers," p. 91.
29. Rourke, "Vassar Classrooms," p. 74.
30. CR to CDR, Oct. 13, 1924, Rourke MSS.
31. Lasch, *The New Radicalism*, pp. 3–37.
32. Peter Gabriel Filene, *Him/Her/Self*, pp. 31–32 and passim; Rogers, *Vassar Women*, p. 115.
33. Constance Rourke, "Report Submitted to the William Borden Memorial Fund Committee," p. 438.
34. *Poughkeepsie Daily Eagle*, June 13, 1907; Vassar College Catalog, 1907–1908.
35. Rourke, "Borden Report," p. 438.
36. Ibid., pp. 439–40.
37. CR to CDR, Dec. 2, 1909; Dec. 10, 1909, Rourke MSS.
38. Rourke, "Borden Report," p. 440.
39. Constance Rourke, *Charles Sheeler*, p. 27.
40. CR to CDR, ca. Nov. 2, 1909, Rourke MSS.

41. CR to CDR, Dec. 1909, Rourke MSS.
42. Ibid.
43. CR to CDR, Dec. 13, 1909, Rourke MSS.
44. CR to CDR, ca. Dec. 1909, Rourke MSS.
45. CR to CDR, Dec. 21, 1909, Rourke MSS.
46. Ibid.
47. CR to CDR, Mar. 3, 1910; Mar. 4, 1910, Rourke MSS.
48. CR to CDR, Mar. 19, 1910, Rourke MSS.
49. CR to CDR, Mar. 27, 1911, Rourke MSS.
50. Laura J. Wylie to CR, Nov. 22, 1918, Rourke MSS.
51. CR to CDR, Nov. 25, 1911, Rourke MSS.
52. Amy Reed, "Homage to Constance Rourke," p. 12.
53. CR to CDR, Mar. 9, 1913, Rourke MSS.
54. CR to CDR, ca. Feb. 26, 1912, Rourke MSS.
55. CR to CDR, Mar. 27, 1913, Rourke MSS.
56. A letter Rourke wrote to her mother in 1924 reads: "Please destroy this part of my letter dealing with prescriptions and ailments, and also don't think of it further." CR to CDR, July 6, 1924, Rourke MSS.
57. Curry, "The Constance Rourkes," p. 6; Linda Butler, "Constance Rourke," unpublished essay, p. 1; Marshall to Samuel Bellman, May 23, 1973, Marshall MSS.
58. CR to CDR, Aug. 27, 1915, Rourke MSS.
59. Ibid.
60. Ibid.
61. CR to CDR, 1915, Rourke MSS.
62. Balph to Curry, Sept. 27, 1945, Marshall MSS.
63. Wylie to CR, Jan. 3, 1918, Rourke MSS.
64. CR to CDR, June 6, 1920; ca. July 7, 1920; Sept. 9, 1920, Rourke MSS.
65. CR to CDR, June 10, 1920; June 2, 1920, Rourke MSS.
66. CR to CDR, June 5, 1920, Rourke MSS.; Van Wyck Brooks to Rourke, July 1, 1921, and July 17, 1921, Rourke MSS.
67. CR to CDR, May 25, 1920; Sept. 26, 1920, Rourke MSS.
68. CR to CDR, Sept. 7, 1920, Rourke MSS.
69. CR to CDR, Nov. 24, 1926, Rourke MSS.
70. CR to CDR, Sept. 30, 1924, Rourke MSS.
71. CR to CDR, Oct. 29, 1924, Rourke MSS.

72. CR to CDR, Oct. 27, 1924, Rourke MSS.
73. CR to CDR, June 9, 1928, Rourke MSS.
74. Balph to Curry, Sept. 8, 1945, Marshall MSS.
75. CR to CDR, Oct. 30, 1924, Rourke MSS.
76. CR to CDR, June 17, 1924, Rourke MSS.
77. CR to CDR, Nov. 12, 1924, Rourke MSS.
78. CR to CDR, June 17, 1924, Rourke MSS.
79. CR to CDR, Dec. 3, 1926, Rourke MSS.
80. CR to CDR, Oct. 28, 1936, Rourke MSS.
81. Constance Rourke, *Troupers of the Gold Coast*, pp. 245–46. See also Kenneth S. Lynn, *Visions of America*, p. 165.
82. CR to CDR, Jan. 21, 1912, Rourke MSS., and Rourke, *Troupers*, pp. 237, 241.
83. See Charlotte Perkins Gilman, *The Living of Charlotte Perkins Gilman*, pp. 1–24.
84. Curry, "The Constance Rourkes," p. 8.
85. Balph to Curry, Sept. 8, 1945, Marshall MSS.
86. Balph to Curry, Sept. 27, 1945, Marshall MSS.
87. Reed, "Homage," p. 12.
88. Curry, "The Constance Rourkes," p. 7.
89. Marshall, notes on the Rourkes, Marshall MSS.
90. CR to CDR, Sept. 16, 1924, Rourke MSS.
91. CR to CDR, Aug. 1, 1924, Rourke MSS.
92. CR to CDR, Oct. 18, 1924, Rourke MSS.
93. Curry, "The Constance Rourkes," p. 24.
94. The writer was Serrell Hillman. Cited in Butler, "Constance Rourke," pp. 67–68.
95. CR to CDR, June 30, 1938, Rourke MSS.
96. Marshall, notes on the Rourkes, Marshall MSS.
97. Constance Rourke, Carnegie Foundation application, 1939, Rourke MSS.

CHAPTER 2

1. Constance Rourke, "The Decline of the Novel," pp. 14–15, Rourke MSS., and Butler, "Constance Rourke," p. 34.

2. Cited in Howard Mumford Jones, *The Theory of American Literature*, pp. 121, 150.
3. Barrett Wendell, *A Literary History of America*, p. 136.
4. John Macy, *The Spirit of American Literature*, pp. 15, 8, vi.
5. Van Wyck Brooks, "America's Coming-of-Age," in *Van Wyck Brooks: The Early Years*, edited by Claire Sprague, p. 83. Unless otherwise noted, all citations to Brooks refer to the Sprague collection.
6. Van Wyck Brooks, "The Wine of the Puritans," p. 18.
7. Ibid., p. 4.
8. Ibid., p. 7.
9. Ibid., p. 19.
10. Ibid., p. 22.
11. Van Wyck Brooks, "Letters and Leadership," in *Three Essays on America*, pp. 140, 128.
12. Brooks, "Wine," p. 37.
13. Brooks, "Letters and Leadership," p. 134.
14. Ibid., p. 124.
15. Ibid., p. 126.
16. Ibid., p. 121.
17. Ibid., p. 137.
18. Van Wyck Brooks, "The Literary Life in America," in *Three Essays on America*, p. 202.
19. Harold Stearns, ed., *Civilization in the United States*, p. vii.
20. Richard H. Pells, *Radical Visions and American Dreams*, pp. 7–8.
21. Mumford, *The Golden Day*, p. 52.
22. Brooks, "America's Coming-of-Age," p. 158.
23. Ibid., p. 111.
24. Van Wyck Brooks, "On Creating a Usable Past," p. 220.
25. Brooks, "Letters and Leadership," p. 122.
26. Brooks, "On Creating a Usable Past," p. 223.
27. James Hoopes, *Van Wyck Brooks*, p. 127.
28. Cited in Richard Ruland, *The Rediscovery of American Literature*, p. 155.
29. Mumford to John Chamberlain, Aug. 6, 1942, in *The Van Wyck Brooks-Lewis Mumford Letters*, pp. 218–19.
30. Van Wyck Brooks to CR, July 1, 1921, Rourke MSS.

31. Constance Rourke, *American Humor*, p. 236. Hereafter cited as *AH*.
32. Constance Rourke, "A History of American Culture," Rourke MSS. Hereafter cited as "HAC."
33. Richard Dorson, *American Folklore and the Historian*, pp. 24–25.
34. Constance Rourke, *The Roots of American Culture*, pp. vi–viii.
35. Rourke, *AH*, p. 30.
36. Ibid., p. 67.
37. Ibid., p. 91.
38. Ibid., p. 5.
39. Ibid., p. 76.
40. Ibid., p. 260.
41. Ibid., pp. 99–100.
42. Ibid., pp. 167, 184, 178, 190, 260–61.
43. Ibid., p. 8.
44. Ibid., pp. 186, 191, 197.
45. Ibid., p. 133.
46. Brooks, "Wine," pp. 3, 8.
47. Rourke, *AH*, p. 138.
48. Ibid., p. 8.
49. Ibid., p. 203.
50. Brooks, "America's Coming-of-Age," p. 132.
51. Rourke, *AH*, pp. 38, 72.
52. Ibid., p. 101.
53. Ibid., p. 142.
54. Van Wyck Brooks, *Days of the Phoenix*, p. 104. Both Brooks and Mumford sometimes underplayed the impact of Rourke's writing, though it is clear her influence was considerable. Mumford disputed John Chamberlain's suggestion in a review of *The Roots of American Culture* that Rourke was responsible for Brooks's change of heart: "If one didn't check oneself on dates one might easily take Brooks' affirmative attitude toward American culture as the result in part of this [*Trumpets of Jubilee*] and later books by Constance Rourke. I have no doubt that he was affected by her, as was I: we all maintained a fairly close relationship by correspondence. But the fact is it was not Miss Rourke but Emerson, that effected the great change in Brooks. . . ." Mumford to Chamberlain, Aug. 6, 1942, in *The Van Wyck Brooks-Lewis*

*Mumford Letters*, p. 218. See also Mumford's reference to Chamberlain in his own review of *The Roots of American Culture* (*Saturday Review of Literature*, Aug. 15, 1945, p. 3). Thanking Mumford for his reply to Chamberlain, Brooks phrased his denial of Rourke's influence a bit more strongly: "Of course Constance Rourke did not influence either of us, though she was a fine companion on the way." Brooks traced his "reorientation" not to Emerson but to his "breakdown." Brooks to Mumford, Aug. 9, 1942, in *The Van Wyck Brooks-Lewis Mumford Letters*, p. 219.

55. Rourke, "HAC," Rourke MSS.

CHAPTER 3

1. CR to Lewis Mumford, Apr. 10, 1940, Rourke MSS.
2. Marvin Harris, *The Rise of Anthropological Theory*, p. 292.
3. Ibid., p. 172. Harris argues that Tylor's use of the phrase "substantially uniform" undercuts the common formulation of his position as "unilinear evolutionism." He believes that Tylor and Lewis Morgan have been systematically misunderstood, and that their evolutionary stages were not "fixed sequences, every step of which had to be gone through by all cultures." Ibid., p. 171. If Harris is correct, Rourke was nevertheless in the company of many trained anthropologists in her error.
4. In his introduction to *The Roots of American Culture*, Van Wyck Brooks credited the phrase "transit of civilization" to John Fiske, an important American popularizer of Spencer and follower of Tylor. Fiske's name also appears in the title essay in that collection, but in her notes Rourke ascribed the phrase only to Eggleston. This discrepancy may indicate that Brooks altered Rourke's manuscript in editing it.
5. Rourke, "HAC," Rourke MSS.
6. See Henry Nash Smith, *Virgin Land*, pp. 271–76.
7. Dixon Ryan Fox, *Ideas in Motion*, p. 33.
8. Ibid., p. 6.
9. Ibid., pp. 25, 27.
10. Ibid., p. 11.
11. Constance Rourke, "The Roots of American Culture," in *The*

*Roots of American Culture*, pp. 45–46. The title essay is hereafter cited as "Roots."

12. Edward Eggleston, *The Transit of Civilization from England to America in the Seventeenth Century*, pp. 231–32.
13. Rourke, "HAC," Rourke MSS.
14. William Fielding Ogburn, *Social Change with Respect to Culture and Original Nature*, p. 201.
15. Pells, *Radical Visions*, pp. 24–25.
16. William Fielding Ogburn, "Culture" (1937), in *On Culture and Social Change*, p. 5.
17. Rourke, "HAC," Rourke MSS.
18. Ibid.
19. Rourke, "Roots," p. 55.
20. Rourke, "HAC," Rourke MSS.
21. Rourke, "Roots," p. 55.
22. Harris, *Anthropological Theory*, p. 250.
23. Interview with Margaret Marshall, Dec. 9, 1972.
24. Rourke, "Roots," pp. 49–50.
25. Ibid., p. 50.
26. Harris, *Anthropological Theory*, p. 408; Pells, *Radical Visions*, p. 114.
27. Rourke, "HAC," Rourke MSS.
28. Ibid.
29. Rourke, *AH*, p. 315.
30. Mumford, *The Golden Day*, pp. 37, 38. Cited in Warren Susman, "The Useless Past," p. 13.
31. Susman, "The Useless Past," p. 17.
32. Rourke, "HAC," Rourke MSS.
33. Ibid.
34. Bernard DeVoto to CR, [1932], Rourke MSS.
35. DeVoto to CR, Sept. 11, 1932, Rourke MSS.
36. Rourke, "HAC," Rourke MSS.
37. DeVoto to CR, [1932], Rourke MSS., and Rourke, *AH*, p. 211.
38. Rourke, "Roots," p. 51.
39. Ibid., p. 24.
40. F. M. Barnard, ed., *J. G. Herder on Social and Political Culture*, p. 27.
41. Rourke, "HAC," Rourke MSS.

42. Rourke, "Roots," p. 23. See also Sir Isaiah Berlin, "The Philosophical Ideas of Giambattista Vico," pp. 186–87, 198–205.
43. Rourke, "The Decline of the Novel," p. 13, Rourke MSS.
44. Rourke, *AH*, pp. 287–88.
45. Ibid., p. 159.
46. Cremin, *The Transformation of the School*, p. 125.
47. Rourke, "Roots," pp. 27–34.
48. Ibid., pp. 8–9.
49. Ibid., p. 59.
50. Rourke, "HAC," Rourke MSS.
51. T. S. Eliot, *Notes towards the Definition of Culture*, p. 17.
52. Ibid., pp. 21, 110.
53. Roger Kojecky, *T. S. Eliot's Social Criticism*, p. 208.
54. Eliot, *Notes*, p. 32.
55. Rourke, "HAC," Rourke MSS.
56. Rourke, "Roots," p. 34.
57. Rourke, "HAC," Rourke MSS.
58. Rourke, "Roots," p. 33.
59. Rourke, *Charles Sheeler*, p. 71.
60. Rourke, "HAC," Rourke MSS.
61. Ibid.
62. Ibid.
63. Ibid.
64. Rourke, "Roots," pp. 55–56.
65. Bernard DeVoto, *The Literary Fallacy*, p. 43.
66. Rourke, "HAC," Rourke MSS; Rourke, "The Decline of the Novel," p. 8, Rourke MSS.
67. Rourke, "HAC," Rourke MSS.
68. Ibid.
69. Rourke, *AH*, pp. 159, 161.
70. Constance Rourke, "A Note on Folklore," in *The Roots of American Culture*, pp. 238–50.
71. Dorson, *American Folklore and the Historian*, pp. 24–26.
72. John A. Kouwenhoven, *The Arts in Modern American Civilization* (original title *Made in America*), pp. 112–13, 123–24, 133, 148.
73. John A. Kouwenhoven, "American Studies: Words or Things?" p. 26.

74. Rourke, "HAC," Rourke MSS.
75. Ibid. The ellipses are Rourke's.
76. Ibid.
77. Rourke, *AH*, p. 178.
78. Rourke, "HAC," Rourke MSS.
79. Rourke, *AH*, pp. 65, 155.
80. Ibid., pp. 157, 203.
81. Ibid., p. 271.
82. Ibid., p. 259.
83. Vernon L. Parrington, *Main Currents in American Thought*, 2:170–71.
84. Constance Rourke, *Davy Crockett*, pp. 26–27. Rourke's language is taken from *Sketches and Eccentricities of Colonel David Crockett of West Tennessee*, p. 147.
85. David Crockett, *A Narrative of the Life of David Crockett of the State of Tennessee*, p. 64.
86. Rourke, *Davy Crockett*, pp. 29, 83.
87. Ibid., p. 83.
88. Ibid., pp. 93–94.
89. Ibid., p. 111.
90. Ibid., pp. 139, 141.
91. Crockett, *Narrative*, p. xvi.
92. Richard Dorson, *Davy Crockett: American Comic Legend*, p. 30.
93. Constance Rourke, *Audubon*, pp. 321–22.
94. Rourke, *Charles Sheeler*, pp. 198–99.
95. Rourke, "HAC," Rourke MSS.
96. Ibid.
97. Ibid.
98. Rourke, *AH*, pp. 16, 29. See also John Clive and Bernard Bailyn, "England's Cultural Provinces: Scotland and America," p. 209.
99. Hoopes, *Van Wyck Brooks*, p. 104.

CHAPTER 4

1. Constance Rourke, "Old American Theatricals," p. 1, Rourke MSS.

2. Rourke, *AH*, pp. 64, 131, 141, 99, 77.
3. CR to Max Eastman, July 16, 1936, Marshall MSS.
4. CR to DeVoto, Mar. 3, 1932, Rourke MSS.
5. DeVoto to CR, Dec. 17, 1931, Rourke MSS.
6. CR to DeVoto, Mar. 3, 1932, Rourke MSS.
7. Rourke, *AH*, p. 25.
8. Ibid., p. 131.
9. CR to DeVoto, Mar. 3, 1932, and Sept. 25, 1931, Rourke MSS.
10. Rourke, "Roots," p. 58.
11. Rourke, "HAC," Rourke MSS.
12. Ibid.
13. Constance Rourke, *Trumpets of Jubilee*, p. 426.
14. Stanley Kunitz and Howard Haycraft, eds., *Twentieth Century Authors*, pp. 1206–07; Constance Rourke, draft of Kunitz-Haycraft statement, Rourke MSS.
15. Rourke, *Troupers*, p. 65.
16. Ibid., p. 67.
17. Ibid., p. 241.
18. Ibid., pp. 7, 249.
19. Lynn, "Rourke, Constance Mayfield," 3:199.
20. Stanley Hyman, *The Armed Vision*, p. 130.
21. Ibid.
22. Crockett, *Narrative*, p. xix.
23. Rourke, *Davy Crockett*, pp. 178–79.
24. Crockett, *Narrative*, p. xix.
25. Rourke, draft of Kunitz-Haycraft statement, Rourke MSS.
26. Richard Chase, *Quest for Myth*, p. 34.
27. Gene Bluestein, *The Voice of the Folk*, p. 5.
28. Hyman, *The Armed Vision*, p. 134.
29. Part of Rourke's library was destroyed in transit. Her friend Margaret Marshall thought it "ridiculous" to contend that Rourke had not read Frazer's *The Golden Bough* or Jessie Weston's *From Ritual to Romance*. Interview with Margaret Marshall, Dec. 9, 1972.
30. Jane Ellen Harrison, *Ancient Art and Ritual*, p. 74.
31. Rourke, *AH*, pp. 135–36. See also pp. 36–37, 54.
32. Harrison, *Ancient Art*, p. 49.

33. Rourke, *AH*, p. 88.
34. Ibid., pp. 95–96.
35. Harrison, *Ancient Art*, p. 72.
36. Constance Rourke, "American Art: A Possible Future," in *The Roots of American Culture*, p. 276.
37. Rourke, "Old American Theatricals," p. 1, Rourke MSS.
38. Rourke, *AH*, pp. 12–13.
39. Margaret Mead, *Ruth Benedict*, p. 48.
40. See Richard Ellmann and Charles Feidelson, Jr., eds., *The Modern Tradition*, pp. 619–20.
41. William Troy, *Selected Essays*, p. 42.
42. Ibid., p. 40.
43. Philip Rahv, "The Myth and the Powerhouse" (1953), in John B. Vickery, ed., *Myth and Literature*, p. 109.
44. Bronislaw Malinowski, "Myth in Primitive Psychology" (1926), in *Magic, Science and Religion, and Other Essays*, p. 99.
45. Rourke, "HAC," Rourke MSS.
46. Ibid.
47. Rourke, *AH*, p. 135.
48. Rourke, "HAC," Rourke MSS. The ellipses are Rourke's.
49. Rourke, *AH*, pp. 219–20.
50. Ibid., p. 99.
51. Ibid., p. 297.
52. DeVoto to CR, [1932], Rourke MSS. In her reply, Rourke accused DeVoto of being himself "a victim to the urge for simplification" in making Southwestern humor stand for American humor as a whole. CR to DeVoto, Mar. 3, 1932, Rourke MSS.
53. Rourke, *AH*, p. 302.
54. T. S. Eliot, "Tradition and the Individual Talent" (1919), in *Selected Essays*, p. 7.
55. Rourke, "HAC," Rourke MSS.
56. Rourke, *Charles Sheeler*, p. 58.
57. CR to DeVoto, Mar. 3, 1932, Rourke MSS.
58. Rourke, *AH*, p. 100.
59. Ibid., p. 190.
60. Ibid., p. 191.
61. Rourke, "HAC," Rourke MSS.
62. Ibid.

63. Ibid.
64. Rourke, *Charles Sheeler*, p. 188.
65. Rourke, "HAC," Rourke MSS.
66. Constance Rourke, "The Shakers," in *The Roots of American Culture*, p. 196.
67. Warren Susman, ed., *Culture and Commitment, 1929–1945*, p. 19.
68. Pells, *Radical Visions*, p. 315.
69. See, in addition to the books discussed here, John William Ward, *Andrew Jackson: Symbol for an Age* (New York: Oxford University Press, 1953) and William R. Taylor, *Cavalier and Yankee* (New York: George Braziller, 1961).
70. F. O. Matthiessen, *American Renaissance*, p. xix; Leo Marx, *The Machine in the Garden*, pp. 132–33.
71. Rourke, *Charles Sheeler*, p. 69.
72. Rourke, *AH*, pp. 283, 202.
73. Matthiessen, *American Renaissance*, p. 637.
74. Ibid., pp. 626–29.
75. R.W.B. Lewis, *The American Adam*, pp. 3–4.
76. Ibid., p. 129.
77. Rourke, *AH*, p. 30.
78. Smith, *Virgin Land*, pp. 4, 153.
79. Ibid., pp. 199, 194, 227.
80. Bruce Kuklick, "Myth and Symbol in American Studies," p. 437.
81. Marx, *Machine*, p. 319.
82. Kuklick, "Myth and Symbol," p. 437.
83. Rourke, *Trumpets of Jubilee*, p. 432. The phrase suggests Mumford's metaphor in *The Golden Day*.

CHAPTER 5

1. Eda Lou Walton, "The Roots of American Literature," p. 456.
2. Rourke, *The Roots of American Culture*, p. v.
3. Rourke, *Troupers*, p. 146, and Butler, "Constance Rourke," p. 11.
4. Rourke, *AH*, p. 3.
5. Walter Blair, *Native American Humor*, p. 17.

6. Rourke, *Audubon*, p. 121.
7. Ibid., p. 104.
8. Ibid., p. 319.
9. Rourke, *AH*, pp. 11, 45, 74, 77, 115, 138, 269.
10. Rourke, *Audubon*, p. 60.
11. Maria R. Audubon, *Audubon and His Journals*, p. 243.
12. Bernard DeVoto, *Mark Twain's America*, pp. 58–60.
13. Rourke, *Davy Crockett*, p. 31.
14. Rourke, *AH*, pp. 40–41.
15. Ibid., p. 42.
16. Blair, *Native American Humor*, p. 316.
17. Ibid., p. 347.
18. Ibid., p. 69.
19. Ibid., pp. 296, 555.
20. George Washington Harris, *Sut Lovingood's Yarns*, p. 21.
21. Edmund Wilson, *Patriotic Gore*, p. 509.
22. Harris, *Sut Lovingood*, p. 201.
23. Cited in Wilson, *Patriotic Gore*, p. 511.
24. Harris, *Sut Lovingood*, p. 118.
25. Ibid., p. 279.
26. Ibid., pp. 207, 211.
27. Wilson, *Patriotic Gore*, p. 512.
28. DeVoto, *Mark Twain's America*, p. 153.
29. Rourke, *AH*, pp. 68, 70.
30. Milton Rickels, "The Imagery of George Washington Harris," p. 159.
31. Ibid., pp. 157–58.
32. Rourke, *AH*, p. 69.
33. Ibid.
34. Her passing remark that Mark Twain's "obscenity was also of the pioneer piece" is too oblique to qualify. Rourke, *AH*, p. 218.
35. Blair, *Native American Humor*, p. 69.
36. Interview with Margaret Marshall, Dec. 9, 1972.
37. CR to CDR, Apr. 28, 1938, Rourke MSS.
38. CR to CDR, July 28, 1924, Rourke MSS.
39. Rourke, *Trumpets of Jubilee*, p. 219.
40. Constance Rourke, "Traditions for Young People," p. 562.

41. Brooks, "Wine," pp. 13–15.
42. Rourke, "Traditions," p. 563.
43. Rourke, "The Decline of the Novel," p. 15, Rourke MSS. Italics mine.
44. Rourke, *The Roots of American Culture*, p. viii.
45. Alfred Kazin, "The Irreducible Element," p. 260.
46. Constance Rourke, fellowship application, Rourke MSS.
47. CR to Alfred Harcourt, Mar. 27, 1939, Harcourt Archives.
48. Rourke, "Traditions," pp. 563–64.
49. CR to Donald Brace, Dec. 12, 1939, Rourke MSS.
50. CR to H. N. MacCracken, Apr. 6, 1936, Rourke MSS.
51. CR to Howard Haycraft, June 13, 1940, Rourke MSS.
52. Elizabeth Bevier Hamilton to CR, Aug. 19, 1936, Rourke MSS.
53. Elizabeth R. Bevier to CR, Apr. 20, 1931, Rourke MSS.
54. Donald Brace to CR, July 17, 1931, Rourke MSS.
55. Bevier to CR, Feb. 9, 1933, Rourke MSS.; CR to Brace, Feb. 9, 1933, Rourke MSS.
56. Hamilton to CR, Dec. 26, 1933, Rourke MSS.
57. Rourke, *Davy Crockett*, p. 3.
58. Rourke, *Audubon*, p. 3.
59. CR to Harcourt, July 31, 1922, Rourke MSS.
60. Bernard DeVoto, *The Year of Decision: 1846*, p. xxv.
61. Ibid., pp. 4, 38.
62. Ibid., p. 215.
63. Ibid., p. xxv.
64. Bernard DeVoto, *Forays and Rebuttals*, p. 165.
65. Bernard DeVoto, *The Course of Empire*, p. 634.
66. Rourke, *Trumpets of Jubilee*, p. 435.
67. Constance Lindsay Skinner, "Rivers and American Folk," p. 446.
68. Ibid., pp. 439–40.
69. Ibid., pp. 437–45.
70. Ibid., p. 437.
71. Ibid., p. 447.
72. Ibid., p. 446.
73. CR to Alfred [Harcourt], Mar. 27, 1939, Rourke MSS.
74. CR to Alfred [Harcourt], Mar. 22, 1939, Rourke MSS.
75. Lynn, "Rourke, Constance Mayfield," 3:200.

CHAPTER 6

1. Brooks, "On Creating a Usable Past," p. 220.
2. Ruland, *The Rediscovery of American Literature*, p. 12.
3. Brooks, "Letters and Leadership," p. 138 and *The Ordeal of Mark Twain*, p. 106.
4. Brooks, "Letters and Leadership," p. 135.
5. Brooks, "On Creating a Usable Past," p. 219.
6. Randolph Bourne, *The History of a Literary Radical*, pp. 33, 39.
7. Constance Rourke, "The Brahmin Caste," p. 176.
8. Rourke, "Roots," p. 28.
9. Constance Rourke, "Voltaire Combe," in *The Roots of American Culture*, p. 260.
10. Rourke, "HAC," Rourke MSS.
11. Ibid.
12. Ibid.
13. Ibid.
14. Ibid., and Rourke, "A Note on Folklore," pp. 248–49.
15. *Poughkeepsie Sunday Courier*, Apr. 3, 1932.
16. Ibid.
17. Buck, *Social Criticism*, p. 40.
18. Ibid., pp. 58, 56.
19. Constance Rourke, "Tall Tales of the Northwest," p. 19.
20. Rourke, "A Note on Folklore," p. 238.
21. Rourke, *AH*, p. ix.
22. Constance Rourke, "Studies in American Culture," p. 328.
23. Rourke, "The Decline of the Novel," p. 2, Rourke MSS.
24. Rourke, "HAC," Rourke MSS.
25. Constance Rourke, "The Noble Sport of Ballad Hunting," p. 193.
26. Despite his rebellious pronouncements, Brooks occupied a similarly complex relationship to "genteel" critics. See John Henry Raleigh, *Matthew Arnold and American Culture*, and James Hoopes, *Van Wyck Brooks*.
27. Rourke, "HAC," Rourke MSS.
28. Ibid.
29. Cremin, *The Transformation of the School*, p. 89.
30. Buck, *Social Criticism*, p. 60.

31. Rourke, "Traditions," p. 364.
32. Stephen Vincent Benét, *We Stand United and Other Radio Scripts*, pp. 6–8.
33. Cited in Walter Johnson, *The Battle Against Isolation*, p. 224.
34. Ibid., p. ix.
35. Lewis Mumford, *Men Must Act*, p. 50.
36. Ibid., pp. 46, 126.
37. See Alfred H. Jones, "Roosevelt and Lincoln," passim.
38. Constance Rourke, "In Time of Hesitation," p. 207.
39. Bernard DeVoto, "Father Abraham," p. 333.
40. Jones, "Roosevelt and Lincoln," p. 159.
41. Alfred Kazin, *On Native Grounds*, p. 393.
42. Ibid., p. 380.
43. Ibid., pp. 393–94.
44. Mumford to CR, Aug. 30, 1940, Rourke MSS.
45. Lewis Mumford, exhibition scenario, Rourke MSS.
46. CR to Mumford, Sept. 4, 1940, Rourke MSS.
47. Kazin, *On Native Grounds*, p. 400.
48. Lewis Mumford to the author, Nov. 7, 1973.
49. Rourke, "HAC," Rourke MSS.
50. Rourke, draft of Kunitz-Haycraft statement, Rourke MSS.
51. Cited in Cremin, *The Transformation of the School*, p. 122.
52. Rourke, draft of Kunitz-Haycraft statement, Rourke MSS.
53. CR to Brace, Jan. 12, 1938, Harcourt Archives.
54. Lasch, *The New Radicalism*, pp. xiv, 89–90, and passim.
55. Rourke, "HAC," Rourke MSS.
56. Matthew Arnold, "The Function of Criticism at the Present Time" (1864), in *Four Essays on Life and Letters*, p. 15.
57. See Kojecky, *T. S. Eliot's Social Criticism*, pp. 148, 157.
58. Pells, *Radical Visions*, p. 336.
59. Ibid., pp. 336–37.
60. William Phillips, "The Intellectuals' Tradition," p. 490.
61. Kazin, "The Irreducible Element," p. 259.

# BIBLIOGRAPHY

MANUSCRIPT COLLECTIONS

*Carbondale, Illinois*
Constance Rourke Manuscripts, 1896–1941. Privately held papers.
Uncataloged.

*New Haven, Connecticut*
Beinecke Rare Book and Manuscript Library, Yale University. Margaret Marshall Manuscripts. Uncataloged.

WORKS BY CONSTANCE ROURKE

"The Music of Poetry as Distinguished from the Music of Prose."
*Vassar Miscellany*, Feb. 1907, pp. 109–11.
"Report Submitted to the William Borden Memorial Fund Committee." *Vassar Miscellany*, Oct. 1909, pp. 438–41.
"Changes at Vassar." *Vassar Miscellany*, Nov. 1914, pp. 37–42.
"The Rationale of Punctuation." *Educational Review*, Oct. 1915, pp. 246–58.
*The Fiftieth Anniversary of the Opening of Vassar College.* Poughkeepsie: Vassar College, 1916.
"An English Raconteur." Review of *Arthur's Sixpenny Pieces, Robert Blatchford, Cottage Pie, Clara, Simple Simon, Kitchener Chaps,* and *Thereabouts* by Neil Lyons. *New Republic*, June 8, 1918, pp. 180–82.
"Inducements for Elementary School Teachers." *Vassar Quarterly*, Feb. 1919, pp. 89–95.
"Caradoc Evans." Review of *My People and Capel Sion* by Caradoc Evans. *New Republic*, Feb. 1, 1919, pp. 30–32.
"The Ethical Novel." Review of *The Modern Novel* by Wilson Fol-

# Bibliography

lett. *New Republic*, May 17, 1919, pp. 94–97.

"The Antique World of Bliss." Review of *Far Away and Long Ago* by W. H. Hudson. *New Republic*, May 24, 1919, pp. 125–26.

"Vaudeville." *New Republic*, Aug. 27, 1919, pp. 115–16.

"Dorothy M. Richardson." Review of *Pilgrimage, Pointed Roofs, Backwater, Honeycomb*, and *The Tunnel* by Dorothy M. Richardson. *New Republic*, Nov. 26, 1919, Fall Literary Review, pp. 14–15.

"Virginia Woolf." Review of *The Voyage Out* and *Night and Day* by Virginia Woolf. *New Republic*, May 5, 1920, pp. 320–22.

"Paul Bunyon." *New Republic*, July 7, 1920, pp. 176–79.

"Transitions." Review of *Peace in Friendship Village* and *Miss Lulu Bett* by Zona Gale. *New Republic*, Aug. 11, 1920, pp. 315–16.

"Under the Microscope." Review of *Jane Austen* by O. W. Firkens. *Freeman*, Aug. 18, 1920, pp. 549–50.

"Scholars and Gentlewomen." Review of *The Learned Lady in England, 1650–1760* by Myra Reynolds. *Freeman*, Sept. 29, 1920, pp. 68–69.

"The American Short Story." Review of *The Great American Short Stories*, edited by William Dean Howells. *Freeman*, Oct. 6, 1920, p. 91.

"Contemporary French Writers." Review of *Twentieth Century French Writers* by Mary Duclaux. *Freeman*, Oct. 20, 1920, pp. 140–41.

"Mr. Robinson's 'Lancelot.'" Review of *Lancelot* by E. A. Robinson. *Freeman*, Oct. 27, 1920, p. 164.

"A Tale of the Folk." Review of *Ditte: Girl Alive* by Martin A. Nexö. *Freeman*, Nov. 10, 1920, p. 213.

"Contemporary Poets." Review of *Studies of Contemporary Poets* by Mary C. Sturgeon. *Freeman*, Dec. 15, 1920, pp. 331–32.

"The Brahmin Caste." Review of *Crowding Memories* by Mrs. Thomas Bailey Aldrich. *New Republic*, Jan. 5, 1921, pp. 175–76.

"Novels with a Purpose." Review of *The Romantic* by Mary Sinclair. *Freeman*, Jan. 12, 1921, p. 429.

"On the Road to Castaly." Review of *Development* by W. Bryher. *New Republic*, Jan. 26, 1921, p. 270.

"Portrait of a Home Town." *New Republic*, Feb. 23, 1921, pp. 369–71.

"Concerning Satire." Review of *Satire* by Gilbert Cannan and *Satire in the Victorian Novel* by F. T. Russell. *Freeman*, Mar. 2, 1921, pp. 596–97.

"The Adams Mind." Review of *A Cycle of Adams Letters: 1861–65*, edited by W. C. Ford and *Letters to a Niece* and *Prayer to the Virgin of Chartres* by Henry Adams. *Freeman*, Mar. 23, 1921, pp. 43–44.

"A Middle-Class Emperor." Review of *Memoirs of the Empress Eugenie* by Comte Fleury. *Freeman*, Apr. 27, 1921, p. 164.

"Enchantment." Review of *The Boy Who Knew What the Birds Said, The Boy Apprenticed to an Enchanter, The Girl Who Sat by the Ashes, The Children of Odin*, and *The Children's Homer* by Padraic Colum. *New Republic*, May 4, 1921, pp. 300–301.

"When Feminism Was in Flower." Review of *Diaries of Court Ladies of Old Japan*, translated by K. Doi. *Freeman*, June 15, 1921, pp. 333–34.

"The Disintegration of a Poet." *Freeman*, July 27, 1921, pp. 468–69.

"Private Life for Children." *New Republic*, Aug. 10, 1921, pp. 294–96.

"The Porch." *Dial*, Oct. 1921, pp. 418–22.

"The Springs of Poetry." Review of *Poetic Origins and the Ballad* by Louise Pound. *Freeman*, Oct. 12, 1921, pp. 116–17.

"Portrait of a Young Woman." *Dial*, Nov. 1921, pp. 149–51.

"The Genius of the Novel." *New Republic*, Jan. 4, 1922, pp. 149–51.

"Some Vassar Letters: 1865–70." *Vassar Quarterly*, May 1922, pp. 153–63.

"The Flying Horse." Review of *Gold by Gold* by Herbert S. Gorman. *New Republic*, Aug. 26, 1925, p. 26.

"The Making of an Epic." Review of *Paul Bunyon* by James Stevens and *Paul Bunyon* by Esther Shephard. *Saturday Review of Literature*, Aug. 29, 1925, p. 81.

*Trumpets of Jubilee*. New York: Harcourt, Brace & Company, 1927.

*Troupers of the Gold Coast*, or *The Rise of Lotta Crabtree*. New York: Harcourt, Brace & Company, 1928.

"The Vanishing Evangelical." Review of *In the Service of the King* by Aimee Semple McPherson. *New York Herald Tribune Books*, Apr. 8, 1928, p. 5.

# Bibliography

"Poetry of the North." Review of *The Search Relentless* by Constance Lindsay Skinner. *New York Herald Tribune Books*, Sept. 16, 1928, p. 7.

"Portrait of a Reformer." Review of *Susan B. Anthony: The Woman Who Changed the Mind of a Nation* by Rheta Childe Dorr. *New York Herald Tribune Books*, Oct. 21, 1928, p. 3.

"Tall Tales of the Northwest." Review of *Homer in the Sage-Brush* by James Stevens. *New York Herald Tribune Books*, Nov. 25, 1928, p. 19.

"Not All Ladies." Review of *Forgotten Ladies* by Richardson Wright. *New York Herald Tribune Books*, Dec. 9, 1928, p. 20.

"An Anatomy of Zeal." Review of *The Stammering Century* by Gilbert Seldes. *New York Herald Tribune Books*, Dec. 9, 1928, p. 5.

"This is Legend." Review of *Eilly Orum, Queen of the Comstock* by Swift Paine. *New York Herald Tribune Books*, Apr. 21, 1929, p. 20.

*American Humor: A Study of the National Character.* 1931. Reprint. New York: Harcourt Brace Jovanovich, 1959.

"Our Comic Heritage." *Saturday Review of Literature*, Mar. 21, 1931, pp. 678–79.

"Rafinesque." Review of *Green River: A Poem for Rafinesque* by James Whaler. *New York Herald Tribune Books*, Apr. 26, 1931, p. 14.

"For Friends." Review of *A Girl of the Eighties* by Martha Pike Conant. *New York Herald Tribune Books*, Aug. 16, 1931, p. 10.

"Folk Songs of America." Review of *American Songs for Children*, collected by Winthrop B. Palmer. *New York Herald Tribune Books*, Aug. 23, 1931, p. 6.

"A Myth Comes Into Its Own." Review of *John Henry* by Roark Bradford. *New York Herald Tribune Books*, Sept. 6, 1931, p. 1.

"Drawn from a Rich Abundance." Review of *Jane Matthew* by Eda Lou Walton. *New York Herald Tribune Books*, Oct. 11, 1931, p. 7.

"An American Grand Style." Review of *Portrait of an American* by Robert P. Tristram Coffin. *New York Herald Tribune Books*, Oct. 25, 1931, p. 1.

"Romanticism of the Border." Review of *The Rediscovery of the Frontier* by Percy H. Boynton. *New York Herald Tribune Books*, Nov. 1, 1931, p. 16.

"Keene, Laura." *Dictionary of American Biography*. 1932, 1933. Reprint. New York: Charles Scribner's Sons, 1960, 1961. Vol. 5, pt. 2, 283–84.

"Bret Harte." Review of *Bret Harte: Argonaut and Exile* by George R. Stewart, Jr. and *Selected Works of Bret Harte. New Republic*, Mar. 2, 1932, pp. 77–78.

"Emily Dickinson's Own Story." Review of *Letters of Emily Dickinson*, edited by Mabel Loomis Todd. *New Republic*, Apr. 20, 1932, pp. 279–80.

"Letters to the Editor." *American Literature*, May 1932, pp. 207–10.

"In the Time of Daniel Boone." Review of *Debby Barnes, Trader* by Constance Lindsay Skinner. *New York Herald Tribune Books*, June 16, 1932, p. 6.

"In Defense of Mark Twain's Genius." Review of *Mark Twain's America* by Bernard DeVoto. *New York Herald Tribune Books*, Sept. 11, 1932, p. 3.

"Rich Seeding Ground." Review of *Sketches in Criticism* by Van Wyck Brooks. *New York Herald Tribune Books*, Oct. 23, 1932, p. 4.

"One Reality in a World of Shadows." Review of *Biography and the Human Heart* by Gamaliel Bradford. *New York Herald Tribune Books*, Dec. 4, 1932, p. 2.

"The Unfolding Earth." Review of *Earth Horizon: An Autobiography* by Mary Austin. *New Republic*, Dec. 21, 1932, pp. 166–67.

"On the Texas-Mexican Border." Review of *Tone the Bell Easy*, edited by J. Frank Dobie. *New York Herald Tribune Books*, Jan. 1, 1933, p. 5.

"Cross Country." Review of *Folksay IV*, edited by B. A. Botkin. *New Republic*, Feb. 1, 1933, p. 331.

"The Early American Mind in the Making." Review of *American Folk Art: The Art of the Common Man in America*, text by Holger Cahill. *New York Herald Tribune Books*, Mar. 12, 1933, p. 3.

"The King of the Mississippi Keelboatmen." Review of *Mike Fink* by Walter Blair and Franklin J. Meine. *New York Herald Tribune Books*, Apr. 2, 1933, p. 4.

"The Seacoast of Bohemia." Review of *Garrets and Pretenders* by Albert Parry. *New York Herald Tribune Books*, Apr. 23, 1933, p. 10.

Review of *Josh Billings: Yankee Humorist* by Cyril Clemens. *American Literature*, May 1933, pp. 199–200.

# Bibliography

"The Gaudy Life of San Francisco's Underworld." Review of *The Barbary Coast* by Herbert Asbury. *New York Herald Tribune Books*, Aug. 6, 1933, p. 5.

"Singing on the Kentucky Mountainsides." Review of *The Traipsin' Woman* by Jean Thomas. *New York Herald Tribune Books*, Aug. 13, 1933, p. 2.

"Fur Trading and the Destiny of Nations." Review of *Beaver, Kings and Cabins* by Constance Lindsay Skinner. *New York Herald Tribune Books*, Sept. 17, 1933, p. 7.

"The Significance of Sections." *New Republic*, Sept. 20, 1933, pp. 148–51.

"Marvels, a History, and a Character." Review of *The Journey of the Flame* by Antonio de Fierro Blanco. *Nation*, Nov. 8, 1933, p. 543.

*Davy Crockett*. New York: Harcourt, Brace & Company, 1934.

"Stowe, Harriet Beecher." *Encyclopedia of the Social Sciences.* 1934. Reprint. New York: Macmillan, 1950. 14:414.

"Vassar Classrooms: 'English J' and 'Romanticism.' " In *Miss Wylie of Vassar*, edited by Elizabeth Woodbridge Morris, pp. 72–76. New Haven: Yale University Press, 1934.

"The Land and Its People in a Living Alliance." Review of *Culture in the South*, edited by W. T. Couch. *New York Herald Tribune Books*, Feb. 4, 1934, p. 4.

"Comic Undertones of American History." Review of *A History of American Graphic Humor* by William Murrell. *New York Herald Tribune Books*, Mar. 18, 1934, p. 8.

"Eastward of Lake Michigan." Review of *Belly Fulla Straw* by D. C. DeJong. *New York Herald Tribune Books*, Apr. 1, 1934, p. 7.

"The National Folk Festival." *New Republic*, May 30, 1934, pp. 72–73.

"Words and Music." Review of *Stephen Foster: America's Troubadour* by J. T. Howard. *New Republic*, July 4, 1934, pp. 217–18.

"Story of a Dictator." Review of *Pico, Bandit and Dictator* by Antonio de Fierro Blanco. *Nation*, Aug. 8, 1934, pp. 166–67.

"The Noble Sport of Ballad Hunting." *Nation*, Aug. 15, 1934, pp. 192–93.

"Our Wealth of Song and Legend." *New York Herald Tribune Books*, Nov. 11, 1934, p. 1.

"In America's Hearty, Sentimental Years." Review of *The Senti-*

*mental Years: 1836–1860* by E. Douglas Branch. *New York Herald Tribune Books,* Nov. 18, 1934, p. 9.

"The First National Folk Festival." *Vassar Quarterly,* Feb. 1935, pp. 9–13.

"Examining the Roots of American Humor." *American Scholar,* Spring 1935, pp. 249–54.

"The Significance of Sections." Review of *The United States, 1830–1850* by F. J. Turner. *Nation,* Apr. 17, 1935, p. 458.

"Settling of the Southeast." Review of *Trade and Travel Around the Southern Appalachians* by Randle Bond Truett. *New York Herald Tribune Books,* June 16, 1935, p. 13.

"American Art: A Possible Future." *Magazine of Art,* July 1935, pp. 390–405.

"Continuities in Music." Review of *The Puritans and Music in England and New England* by Percy A. Scholes, and *National Music* by Ralph Vaughan Williams. *Nation,* July 3, 1935, pp. 23–24.

"Glory Days." Review of *Kit Carson Days: 1809–1868* by Edwin L. Sabin. *New York Herald Tribune Books,* Sept. 8, 1935, p. 12.

*Audubon.* New York: Harcourt, Brace & Company, 1936.

"Yankee Crusader." Review of *Theodore Parker* by Henry Steele Commager. *Yale Review,* June 1936, pp. 833–34.

"Artists on Relief." *New Republic,* July 15, 1936, pp. 286–88.

"A Way of Living." Review of *A Small House in the Sun* by Samuel Chamberlain. *New York Herald Tribune Books,* Sept. 13, 1936, p. 20.

"American Prints of Variety and Power." Review of *America Today: A Book of One Hundred Prints* published under the auspices of the American Artists' Congress. *New York Herald Tribune Books,* Dec. 27, 1936, p. 6.

*Index of American Design.* Catalog for exhibition at Fogg Museum, Jan. 27–Feb. 10, 1937. Federal Art Project, Works Progress Administration, 1937.

"Index of American Design." *Magazine of Art,* Apr. 1937, pp. 207–11.

"Authentic American Communal." Review of *Shaker Furniture* by Edward D. Andrews and Faith Andrews. *New York Herald Tribune Books,* May 16, 1937, p. 17.

"The Mystery of Audubon." Review of *I Who Should Command All*

# Bibliography

by Alice Jaynes Tyler. *New York Herald Tribune Books*, July 25, 1937, p. 13.

"How Primitive Races Look at the Whites." Review of *The Savage Hits Back* by Julius Lips. *New York Herald Tribune Books*, Sept. 26, 1937, p. 5.

"Traditions for Young People." *Nation*, Nov. 20, 1937, pp. 562–64.

"Native Crafts." Review of *Handicrafts of the Southern Highlands* by Allen H. Eaton, and *The Arts Workshop of Rural America* by Marjorie Patten. *New York Herald Tribune Books*, Dec. 5, 1937, p. 37.

*Charles Sheeler: Artist in the American Tradition*. New York: Harcourt, Brace & Company, 1938.

"A Survey of Regionalism." Review of *American Regionalism: A Cultural Historical Approach to National Integration* by Howard W. Odum and Harry Estill Moore. *Nation*, Oct. 1, 1938, pp. 330–31.

"Ballads as History." Review of *Minstrels of the Mine Patch* by George Korson. *Nation*, Dec. 10, 1938, pp. 630–32.

"From Nast to Disney." Review of *A History of American Graphic Humor, 1865–1938* by William Murrell. *New York Herald Tribune Books*, Dec. 25, 1938, p. 3.

"From Plains to Salt Water." Review of *Cowboy Songs and Other Frontier Ballads* by John A. Lomax and Alan Lomax, *Songs of American Sailormen* by Joanna Colcord, and *Whale Ships and Whaling* by Albert Cook Church. *Nation*, Jan. 21, 1939, p. 96.

"In Time of Hesitation." Review of *Men Must Act* by Lewis Mumford. *Nation*, Feb. 18, 1939, pp. 206–7.

"Our Earliest Cities." Review of *Cities in the Wilderness* by Carl Bridenbaugh. *Nation*, May 6, 1939, pp. 535–36.

"Studies in American Culture." Review of *Liberal Kentucky, 1780–1828* by N. H. Sonne, *Jedidiah Morse, A Champion of New England Orthodoxy* by James King Morse, and *The Early Days of Christian Socialism in America* by James Dombrowski. *Nation*, Sept. 23, 1939, pp. 327–28.

"Storehouse of Balladry." Review of *Ballads and Songs of Southern Michigan*, edited by Emelyn E. Gardner and Geraldine J. Chickering. *New York Herald Tribune Books*, Sept. 24, 1939, p. 10.

"Voltaire Combe." *Nation*, Oct. 7, 1939, pp. 379–81.

"An Artist By Way of Philadelphia and Tahiti." Review of *An American Artist's Story* by George Biddle. *New York Herald Tribune Books*, Oct. 8, 1939, p. 7.

"Have We an American Art?" Review of *Gist of Art* by John Sloan, *An American Artist's Story* by George Biddle, *And He Sat Among the Ashes* by William Slack, *Modern American Painting* by Peyton Boswell, *A Treasury of Art Masterpieces* by Thomas Craven, *Have We an American Art?* by E. A. Jewell, *America's Old Masters* by James Thomas Flexner, and *The Artist of the Revolution* by Charles C. Sellers. *Nation*, Nov. 11, 1939, pp. 527–29.

"Prints with Life, Fun, Character." Review of *A Treasury of American Prints* by Thomas Craven. *New York Herald Tribune Books*, Nov. 19, 1939, p. 10.

"Letters to the Editors." *Nation*, Nov. 25, 1939, p. 592.

"Good Morning." Review of *Art Young: His Life and Times* by Art Young. *Nation*, Feb. 10, 1940, pp. 214–16.

"American Painting as American." Review of *The Birth of the American Tradition in Art* by Oskar Hagen. *Nation*, Mar. 9, 1940, p. 342.

"Art in Our Town." *Nation*, Mar. 30, 1940, pp. 424–25.

"Study of a Culture." Review of *Modern French Painters* by R. H. Wilenski. *Nation*, July 20, 1940, pp. 54–55.

"Audubon." Review of *Audubon's America*, edited by Donald C. Peattie. *Nation*, Dec. 7, 1940, pp. 565–68.

*The Roots of American Culture*, edited by Van Wyck Brooks. New York: Harcourt, Brace & World, 1942.

"What Is American Design?" In *Art for the Millions: Essays from the 1930s by Artists and Administrators of the WPA Federal Art Project*, edited by Francis V. O'Connor, pp. 165–66. Greenwich, Conn.: New York Graphic Society, 1973.

BOOKS AND ARTICLES

Arnold, Matthew. *Civilization in the United States*. Boston: Cupples and Hurd, 1888.

———. *Essays, Letters, and Reviews*. Edited by Fraser Neiman. Cambridge, Mass.: Harvard University Press, 1960.

# Bibliography

————. *Four Essays on Life and Letters*. Edited by E. K. Brown. New York: Appleton-Century-Crofts, 1947.

Audubon, Maria R. *Audubon and His Journals*. 1897. Reprint. New York: Dover Publications, 1960.

Barnard, F. M. *J. G. Herder on Social and Political Culture*. London: Cambridge University Press, 1969.

Becker, Carl. *Everyman His Own Historian*. 1931. Reprint. El Paso: Texas Western College Press, 1960.

Benedict, Ruth. *Patterns of Culture*. 1934. Reprint. Boston: Houghton Mifflin Company, Sentry Edition, 1961.

Benét, Stephen Vincent. *We Stand United and Other Radio Scripts*. New York: Farrar & Rinehart, 1945.

Berlin, Sir Isaiah. "The Philosophical Ideas of Giambattista Vico." In *Art and Ideas in Eighteenth-Century Italy*, pp. 156–233. Rome: Edizioni di Storia e Letteratura, 1960.

Berman, Milton. *John Fiske: The Evolution of a Popularizer*. Cambridge, Mass.: Harvard University Press, 1961.

Blair, Walter. *Native American Humor*. New York: American Book Company, 1937.

Bluestein, Gene. *The Voice of the Folk: Folklore and American Literary Theory*. Amherst: University of Massachusetts Press, 1972.

Bourne, Randolph. *The History of a Literary Radical*. Edited by Van Wyck Brooks. New York: B. W. Huebsch, 1920.

Brooks, Van Wyck. *Days of the Phoenix: The Nineteen-Twenties I Remember*. New York: Dutton, 1957.

————. *The Ordeal of Mark Twain*. New York: Dutton, 1920.

————. *Three Essays on America*. "America's Coming-of-Age," 1915; "Letters and Leadership," 1918; "The Literary Life in America," 1927. Reprint. New York: Dutton, 1934.

————. *Van Wyck Brooks: The Early Years: A Selection from His Works, 1908–1921*. Edited by Claire Sprague. New York: Harper Torchbooks, 1968.

Buck, Gertrude. *The Social Criticism of Literature*. New Haven: Yale University Press, 1916.

Canby, Henry Seidel. *Classic Americans: A Study of Eminent American Writers from Irving to Whitman*. New York: Harcourt, Brace & Company, 1931.

Carmer, Carl. *The Hudson*. New York: Farrar & Rinehart, 1939.

Caskey, Marie. "Rourke, Constance Mayfield." In *Dictionary of American Biography: Supplement Three: 1941–45*, pp. 672–73. New York: Charles Scribner's Sons, 1973.

Chamberlain, John. Review of *The Roots of American Culture* by Constance Rourke. *New York Times*, Aug. 6, 1942, p. 17.

Chase, Richard. *Quest for Myth*. Baton Rouge: Louisiana State University Press, 1945.

Clive, John, and Bailyn, Bernard. "England's Cultural Provinces: Scotland and America." *William and Mary Quarterly* 3d ser., 11 (1954): 200–213.

Commager, Henry Steele. *The American Mind: An Interpretation of American Thought and Character since the 1880's*. 1950. Reprint. New Haven: Yale University Press, 1964.

———. "The Old Frontier." Review of *Davy Crockett* by Constance Rourke. *Yale Review*, June 1934, pp. 844–48.

Cowley, Malcolm. *After the Genteel Tradition: American Writers 1910–1930*. 1936. Reprint. Carbondale: Southern Illinois University Press, 1967.

Cremin, Lawrence. *The Transformation of the School*. 1961. Reprint. New York: Vintage, 1964.

Crockett, David. *A Narrative of the Life of David Crockett of the State of Tennessee*. 1834. Edited by James A. Shackford and Stanley Folmsbee. Knoxville: University of Tennessee Press, 1973.

Davis, Clyde Brion. *The Arkansas*. New York: Farrar & Rinehart, 1940.

DeVoto, Bernard. *The Course of Empire*. Boston: Houghton Mifflin Company, 1952.

———. "Father Abraham." *Harper's*, Feb. 1940, pp. 333–36.

———. *Forays and Rebuttals*. Boston: Little, Brown, and Company, 1936.

———. *The Literary Fallacy*. Boston: Little, Brown, and Company, 1944.

———. *Mark Twain's America*. Boston: Little, Brown, and Company, 1932.

———. *The Year of Decision: 1846*. Boston: Houghton Mifflin Company, 1942. Reprinted in a Sentry Edition, no date.

# Bibliography

Dorson, Richard M. *America in Legend*. New York: Pantheon, 1973.
————. *American Folklore*. Chicago: University of Chicago Press, 1959.
————. *American Folklore and the Historian*. Chicago: University of Chicago Press, 1971.
————. *Davy Crockett: American Comic Legend*. New York: Rockland Editions, 1939.
————. *Jonathan Draws the Long Bow*. Cambridge, Mass.: Harvard University Press, 1946.
Douglas, Ann. *The Feminization of American Culture*. New York: Avon Books, 1977.
Downie, R. Angus. *Frazer and the Golden Bough*. London: Victor Gollanz, 1970.
Duffey, Bernard. *The Chicago Renaissance in American Letters: A Critical History*. 1954. Reprint. East Lansing: Michigan State University Press, 1956.
Eggleston, Edward. *The Transit of Civilization from England to America in the Seventeenth Century*. New York: D. Appleton and Company, 1901.
Eliot, T. S. *Notes towards the Definition of Culture*. London, 1948. Reprint. New York: Harcourt, Brace & Company, 1949.
————. *Selected Essays*. New ed., 1950. Reprint. New York: Harcourt, Brace & World, 1964.
Ellmann, Richard, and Feidelson, Charles, Jr., eds. *The Modern Tradition: Backgrounds of Modern Literature*. New York: Oxford University Press, 1965.
Filene, Peter Gabriel. *Him/Her/Self: Sex Roles in Modern America*. New York: Harcourt Brace Jovanovich, 1974, 1975.
Ford, Alice. *Audubon, By Himself*. Garden City, N. Y.: The Natural History Press, 1969.
Fox, Dixon Ryan. *Ideas in Motion*. New York: D. Appleton-Century Company, 1935.
Frank, Waldo. *The Re-Discovery of America*. New York: Charles Scribner's Sons, 1929.
Frankfort, Roberta. *Collegiate Women: Domesticity and Career in Turn-of-the-Century America*. New York: New York University Press, 1977.

[226]

Gilman, Charlotte Perkins. *The Living of Charlotte Perkins Gilman.* 1935. Reprint. New York: Harper Colophon Books, 1975.

Harris, George Washington. *Sut Lovingood's Yarns.* Edited by M. Thomas Inge. New Haven: College and University Press, 1966.

Harris, Marvin. *The Rise of Anthropological Theory: A History of Theories of Culture.* New York: Thomas Y. Crowell Company, 1968.

Harrison, Jane Ellen. *Ancient Art and Ritual.* New York: Henry Holt and Company, 1913.

Hexter, J. H. *Doing History.* Bloomington: Indiana University Press, 1971.

Hoffman, Daniel G. *Paul Bunyan: Last of the Frontier Demigods.* Philadelphia: Temple University Publications, 1952.

————. *Form and Fable in American Fiction.* New York: Oxford University Press, 1961.

Hoopes, James. *Van Wyck Brooks: In Search of American Culture.* Amherst: University of Massachusetts Press, 1977.

Hyman, Stanley Edgar. *The Armed Vision: A Study in the Methods of Modern Literary Criticism.* Revised ed. New York: Vintage Books, 1955.

Johnson, Walter. *The Battle against Isolation.* Chicago: University of Chicago Press, 1944.

Jones, Alfred. "Roosevelt and Lincoln: The Political Uses of a Literary Image." Ph.D. dissertation, Yale University, 1967.

Jones, Howard Mumford. *The Theory of American Literature.* 1948. Reprint. Ithaca: Cornell University Press, 1965.

Kazin, Alfred. "The Irreducible Element." Review of *The Roots of American Culture* by Constance Rourke. *New Republic,* Aug. 31, 1942, pp. 259–60.

————. "Letters to the Editors." *Nation,* Nov. 14, 1942, p. 523.

————. *On Native Grounds.* 1942. Reprint. Garden City, N.Y.: Doubleday Anchor Books, 1956.

————. *Starting Out in the Thirties.* Boston: Little, Brown, and Company, 1962.

Kojecky, Roger. *T. S. Eliot's Social Criticism.* 1971. Reprint. New York: Farrar, Straus, and Giroux, 1972.

Kouwenhoven, John A. "American Studies: Words or Things?" In

# Bibliography

*American Studies in Transition*, edited by Marshall W. Fishwick, pp. 15–35. Boston: Houghton Mifflin Company, 1964.

———. *The Arts in Modern American Civilization*. Originally published as *Made in America*. 1948. Reprint. New York: Norton, 1967.

Kuklick, Bruce. "Myth and Symbol in American Studies." *American Quarterly* 24 (1972): 435–50.

Kunitz, Stanley, and Haycraft, Howard. *Twentieth Century Authors: A Biographical Dictionary of Modern Literature*. New York: H. W. Wilson, 1942.

Lasch, Christopher. *The New Radicalism in America: The Intellectual as a Social Type*. New York: Vintage, 1965.

Lawrence, D. H. "America, Listen to Your Own." *New Republic*, Dec. 15, 1920, pp. 65–70.

Levine, George. Review of *Interpretations and Forecasts, 1922–72* by Lewis Mumford. *New York Times*, Apr. 22, 1973, p. 21.

Lewis, Lloyd. *Myths after Lincoln*. New York: Harcourt, Brace & Company, 1929.

Lewis, R.W.B. *The American Adam*. Chicago: University of Chicago Press, 1955.

Lowie, Robert H. *The History of Ethnological Theory*. New York: Holt, Rinehart and Winston, 1937.

Lucy, Sean. *T. S. Eliot and the Idea of Tradition*. London: Cohen & West, 1960.

Lydens, Z .Z., ed. *The Story of Grand Rapids*. Grand Rapids: Kregel Publications, 1966.

Lynn, Kenneth. "F. O. Matthiessen." *American Scholar*, Winter 1976/77, pp. 86–92.

———. "Rourke, Constance Mayfield." In *Notable American Women, 1607–1950: A Biographical Dictionary*, 3:199. Cambridge, Mass.: Harvard University Press, 1971.

———. *Visions of America*. Westport, Conn.: Greenwood Press, 1973.

Macy, John. *The Spirit of American Literature*. 1908. Reprint. Garden City, N.Y.: Doubleday, Page & Company, 1913.

Malinowski, Bronislaw. *Magic, Science and Religion, and Other Essays*. Garden City, N.Y.: Doubleday Anchor Books, 1954.

Marshall, Margaret. "The Artist in America." Review of *Charles Sheeler* by Constance Rourke. *Nation*, Sept. 17, 1938, pp. 270–71.
———. "Constance Rourke: Artist and Citizen." *Nation*, June 21, 1941, pp. 726–28.
———. "Constance Rourke in the Critics' Den." *Nation*, Oct. 24, 1942, pp. 418–20.
Marx, Leo. *The Machine in the Garden*. 1964. Reprint. New York: Oxford University Press, 1968.
Matthiessen, F. O. *The Achievement of T. S. Eliot*. 1935. 3d ed. Reprint. New York: Oxford University Press, 1958.
———. *American Renaissance: Art and Expression in the Age of Emerson and Whitman*. 1941. Reprint. New York: Oxford University Press, 1968.
———. *The Responsibilities of the Critic*. Edited by John Rackliffe. New York: Oxford University Press, 1952.
May, Henry F. *The End of American Innocence*. 1959. Reprint. Chicago: Quadrangle Books, 1964.
Mead, Margaret. *Ruth Benedict*. New York: Columbia University Press, 1974.
Meine, Franklin J. *The Crockett Almanacks*. Chicago: The Caxton Club, 1955.
———. *Tall Tales of the Southwest*. New York: Knopf, 1930.
Meredith, Robert, ed. *American Studies: Essays on Theory and Method*. Columbus: Charles E. Merrill Publishing Company, 1968.
Millett, Fred B. *Contemporary American Authors*. New York: Harcourt, Brace & Company, 1940.
Morgan, Lewis Henry. *Ancient Society, or Researches in the Lines of Human Progress from Savagery through Barbarism to Civilization*. 1877. Edited by Eleanor Burke Leacock. Cleveland: Meridian Books, 1963.
Mumford, Lewis. "The Cultural Bases of America." Review of *The Roots of American Culture* by Constance Rourke. *Saturday Review of Literature*, Aug. 15, 1942, pp. 3–4.
———. *The Golden Day: A Study in American Literature and Culture*. 1926. 3d ed. 1957. Reprint. New York: Dover Publications, 1968.

# Bibliography

————. *Interpretations and Forecasts, 1922–72*. New York: Harcourt Brace Jovanovich, 1973.

————. *Men Must Act*. New York: Harcourt, Brace & Company, 1940.

Murray, Henry, ed. *Myth and Myth-Making*. Boston: Beacon Press, 1968.

Ogburn, William Fielding. *Social Change with Respect to Culture and Original Nature*. New York: B. W. Huebsch, 1922.

————. *William F. Ogburn on Culture and Social Change*. Edited by Otis Dudley Duncan. Chicago: University of Chicago Press, 1964.

Parrington, Vernon L. *Main Currents in American Thought*. New York: Harcourt, Brace & World, Vols. 1 and 2, 1927; Vol. 3, 1930.

Pells, Richard H. *Radical Visions and American Dreams*. New York: Harper and Row, 1973.

Phillips, William. "The Intellectuals' Tradition." *Partisan Review*, Nov.–Dec. 1941, pp. 481–90.

Rahv, Philip. "The Progress of Cultural Bolshevism (Cont'd.)." *Partisan Review*, Summer 1944, pp. 361–63.

Raleigh, John Henry. *Matthew Arnold and American Culture*. Berkeley: University of California Press, 1957.

Reed, Amy. "Homage to Constance Rourke." *Vassar Alumnae Magazine*, Oct. 1941, pp. 12–13.

Rickels, Milton. "The Imagery of George Washington Harris." In *The Frontier Humorists*, edited by M. Thomas Inge, pp. 155–69. Hamden, Conn.: Archon Books, 1975.

Rogers, Agnes. *Vassar Women*. Poughkeepsie: Vassar College, 1940.

Ruland, Richard. *The Rediscovery of American Literature*. Cambridge, Mass.: Harvard University Press, 1967.

Sandburg, Carl. *Home Front Memo*. New York: Harcourt, Brace & Company, 1940.

Santayana, George. *Character and Opinion in the United States*. 1924. Reprint. New York: Norton, 1967.

————. *The Genteel Tradition: Nine Essays by George Santayana*. Edited by Douglas L. Wilson. Cambridge, Mass.: Harvard University Press, 1967.

Schapiro, Meyer. "Rebellion in Art." In *America in Crisis*, edited by Daniel Aaron, pp. 203–42. New York: Knopf, 1952.

Shackford, James A. *David Crockett: The Man and the Legend*.

Chapel Hill: University of North Carolina Press, 1956.
"The Situation in American Writing." *Partisan Review*, Part 1, Summer 1939, pp. 25–51; Part 2, Fall 1939, pp. 103–23.
*Sketches and Eccentricities of Colonel David Crockett of West Tennessee.* New York: J. & J. Harper, 1835.
Skinner, Constance Lindsay. "Rivers and American Folk." In *The Hudson* by Carl Carmer, pp. 437–46. New York: Farrar & Rinehart, 1939.
Smith, Henry Nash. *Virgin Land.* Cambridge, Mass.: Harvard University Press, 1950.
"A Special Issue on Myth." *Chimera: A Literary Quarterly*, Spring 1946.
Stearns, Harold, ed. *Civilization in the United States.* New York: Harcourt, Brace & Company, 1922.
Stegner, Wallace. *The Uneasy Chair.* Garden City, N.Y.: Doubleday, 1974.
Stott, William. *Documentary Expression and Thirties America.* New York: Oxford University Press, 1973.
Susman, Warren, ed. *Culture and Commitment, 1929–45.* New York: George Braziller, 1973.
———. "History and the American Intellectual: Uses of a Usable Past." *American Quarterly* 16 (1964): 243–63.
———. "The Thirties." In *The Development of an American Culture*, edited by Stanley Coben and Lorman Ratner, pp. 179–218. Englewood Cliffs, N.J.: Prentice-Hall, 1970.
———. "The Useless Past: American Intellectuals and the Frontier Thesis, 1910–1930." *Bucknell Review* 11 (1963): 1–20.
Tate, Cecil F. *The Search for a Method in American Studies.* Minneapolis: University of Minnesota Press, 1973.
Taylor, James Monroe, and Haight, Elizabeth Hazelton. *Vassar.* New York: Oxford University Press, 1915.
Tomsich, John. *A Genteel Endeavor: American Culture and Politics in the Gilded Age.* Stanford: Stanford University Press, 1971.
Trachtenberg, Alan. *Critics of Culture.* New York: Wiley, 1976.
Trilling, Lionel. *Matthew Arnold.* 1939. Reprint. New York: Columbia University Press, 1949.
Troy, William. *Selected Essays.* Edited by Stanley E. Hyman. New Brunswick: Rutgers University Press, 1967.

# Bibliography

Tylor, Edward B. *Primitive Culture: Researches into the Development of Mythology, Philosophy, Religion, Art, and Custom.* 2 vols. London: John Murray, 1871.

Van Doren, Mark. "A Coonskin Classic." Review of *Davy Crockett* by Constance Rourke. *Nation*, Feb. 28, 1934, pp. 252–53.

———. "The Age of Animals." Review of *Audubon* by Constance Rourke. *Nation*, Oct. 31, 1936, p. 525.

*The Van Wyck Brooks–Lewis Mumford Letters: The Record of a Literary Friendship, 1921–1963.* Edited by Robert E. Spiller. New York: Dutton, 1970.

Vickery, John B. *The Literary Impact of the Golden Bough.* Princeton: Princeton University Press, 1973.

———, ed. *Myth and Literature.* Lincoln: University of Nebraska Press, 1966.

Vico, Giambattista. *The New Science.* 1725. 3d ed. 1744. Translated, abridged, and revised by Thomas Goddard Bergin and Max Harold Fisch. Garden City, N.Y.: Doubleday Anchor Books, 1961.

Walton, Eda Lou. "The Roots of American Literature." Review of *American Humor* by Constance Rourke. *Nation*, Apr. 22, 1931, p. 456.

Wellek, René. "Van Wyck Brooks and a National Literature." *American Prefaces* 7 (1942): 292–306.

Wendell, Barrett. *A Literary History of America.* New York: Charles Scribner's Sons, 1900.

Williams, Stanley R. "Explorers of the Natural World." Review of *Audubon* by Constance Rourke. *Yale Review*, Dec. 1936, pp. 399–401.

———. "Our Early Literature." Review of *The Roots of American Culture* by Constance Rourke. *Yale Review*, Dec. 1942, pp. 375–77.

Wilson, Edmund. *Patriotic Gore.* New York: Oxford University Press, 1966.

# INDEX

# Index

# Index

Society, American, 45, 47, 48
South, 55, 79
*Southern Literary Messenger*, 147
Southwest, 51, 94
Spencer, Herbert, 62, 64
*Spirit of American Literature, The*, 44
*Spirit of the Times*, 52, 147
Stearns, Harold, 48, 70, 154
Stedman, E. C., 44, 171
Stedman's "Band," 172
Stein, Gertrude, 97
Stowe, Harriet Beecher, 50
Strachey, Lytton, 97
Style: Rourke's popular, 50, 53, 136, 166, 167, 169–70; Rourke's fictional, 54–55, 135–41, 143–44, 151, 152, 162–63, 170
Suffrage movement, 177
Suffragist meetings, 16
Surrealism, 50, 96, 97, 124
Susman, Warren, 70, 125
*Sut Lovingood*, 129, 148, 150, 153
*Swiss Family Robinson, The*, 11
Symbolism, 96–97, 99, 124

*Tall Tales of the Southwest*, 146, 149
Tennessee, 51, 91, 108, 138, 147
Tennyson, Alfred, 67
*Texas Exploits*, 108
Thackeray, William Makepeace, 84
Theater, American, 52, 53, 55, 103, 105
Third International Art Congress, 15
Thompson, William T., 145
Thoreau, Henry David, 48, 52, 55, 57, 128, 129, 181
Thorpe, T. B., 145, 147; "Big Bear of Arkansas," 52, 147

Tilton, Elizabeth, 153, 154
Tilton, Theodore, 154
"Tradition and the Individual Talent," 120
Traditions, American, 42, 53, 59, 60, 124–25, 127, 154–55, 156, 157, 160, 162, 166, 167, 171, 184, 187; in American literature, 43, 48–49; T. S. Eliot's view of, 120; and art, 121; diffusion of, 165, 170. *See also* Culture, American
"Traditions for Young People," 157, 184; quoted, 157, 185
*Transit of Civilization from England to America in the Seventeenth Century, The*, 64
"Trapping a Sheriff," 148
*Troupers of the Gold Coast*, 30, 35, 105–6, 136, 156–57, 162; quoted, 31, 106, 135–36
Troy, William, 115; quoted, 115–16
*Trumpets of Jubilee*, 27, 29, 51, 105, 134, 153, 154, 156, 162, 163, 165, 189
Turner, Frederick Jackson, 71, 72, 80, 91, 94, 131; quoted, 71; "The Significance of the Frontier in American History," 71
Twain, Mark, 47, 52, 53, 73, 74, 103, 104, 119, 128, 172; *The Connecticut Yankee*, 104
*Twentieth Century Authors*, 105, 108, 159; quoted, 190–91
*Twenty Years at Hull House*, 13
Tyler, Royall, 51; *The Contrast*, 51, 104
Tylor, Edward B., 62, 63, 64, 93; *Primitive Culture*, 62; cultural change model of, 63, 66

Vandenberg, Sen. Arthur, 39

## Index